Amazing Web Sites

IN FULL COLOR

VISUAL **3D** SERIES

by: maranGraphics' Development Group

Corporate Sales

Contact maranGraphics
Phone: (905) 890-3300
      (800) 469-6616
Fax: (905) 890-9434

Canadian Trade Sales

Contact Prentice Hall Canada
Phone: (416) 293-3621
      (800) 567-3800
Fax: (416) 299-2529

Visit our Web site at:
http://www.maran.com

Amazing Web Sites

Copyright©   1996 by maranGraphics Inc.
5755 Coopers Avenue
Mississauga, Ontario, Canada
L4Z 1R9

Canadian Cataloguing in Publication Data

Main entry under title:

Amazing web sites

(Visual 3-D series)
Includes index.
ISBN 1-896283-23-3

1. Computer network resources - Directories.   2. World Wide Web (Information retrieval system) - Directories.
I. maranGraphics' Development Group.   II. Series.

TK5105.888.A53 1996   025.04   C96-931620-8

Trademark Acknowledgments

maranGraphics Inc. has attempted to include trademark information for products, services and companies referred to in this guide. Although maranGraphics Inc. has made reasonable efforts in gathering this information, it cannot guarantee its accuracy.

All other brand names and product names used in this book are trademarks, registered trademarks, or trade names of their respective holders. maranGraphics Inc. is not associated with any product or vendor mentioned in this book.

©1996
maranGraphics, Inc.

The animated characters are the copyright of maranGraphics, Inc.

Bookmark file available
from our Web site:
http://www.maran.com

Amazing Web Sites

IN FULL COLOR

VISUAL 3D SERIES

maranGraphics™

*Every maranGraphics book represents
the extraordinary vision and commitment of a unique family:
the Maran family of Toronto, Canada.*

Back Row (from left to right): Sherry Maran, Rob Maran, Richard Maran, Maxine Maran, Jill Maran.
Front Row (from left to right): Judy Maran, Ruth Maran.

Richard Maran is the company founder and its inspirational leader. He developed maranGraphics' proprietary communication technology called "visual grammar." This book is built on that technology—empowering readers with the easiest and quickest way to learn about computers.

Ruth Maran is the Author and Architect—a role Richard established that now bears Ruth's distinctive touch. She creates the words and visual structure that are the basis for the books.

Judy Maran is the Project Manager. She works with Ruth, Richard, and the highly talented maranGraphics illustrators, designers, and editors to transform Ruth's material into its final form.

Rob Maran is the Technical and Production Specialist. He makes sure the state-of-the-art technology used to create these books always performs as it should.

Sherry Maran manages the Reception, Order Desk, and any number of areas that require immediate attention and a helping hand.

Jill Maran is a jack-of-all-trades and dynamo who fills in anywhere she's needed anytime she's back from university.

Maxine Maran is the Business Manager and family sage. She maintains order in the business and family—and keeps everything running smoothly.

Oh, and three other family members are seated on the sofa. These graphic disk characters help make it fun and easy to learn about computers. They're part of the extended maranGraphics family.

Credits

Author:
maranGraphics
Development Group

Copy Development & Site Selection:
Neil Mohan

Researchers:
Ian Mckay   Peter Dube
John Williams   Jinnean Barnard
Simon Parker

**Copy Development & Architect
for Chapters 1–3:**
Ruth Maran

Project Manager:
Judy Maran

Editors:
Brad Hilderley   Alison MacAlpine
Susan Beytas   Karen Derrah
Kelleigh Wing   Diana MacPherson

**Layout, Illustrations
& Cover Design:**
Tamara Poliquin

Illustrators:
Chris K.C. Leung
Russell Marini
Andrew Trowbridge
Julie Lane
Noel Clannon

Indexer:
Kelleigh Wing

Screen Shot Permissions:
Jill Maran

Post Production:
Robert Maran

Acknowledgments

Thanks to the dedicated staff of maranGraphics, including Susan Beytas, Noel Clannon, Karen Derrah, Francisco Ferreira, Brad Hilderley, Julie Lane, Chris K.C. Leung, Alison MacAlpine, Jill Maran, Judy Maran, Maxine Maran, Robert Maran, Sherry Maran, Russ Marini, Tamara Poliquin, Andrew Trowbridge, Christie Van Duin, Paul Whitehead and Kelleigh Wing.

Finally, to Richard Maran who originated the easy-to-use graphic format of this guide. Thank you for your inspiration and guidance.

Screen Shot Permissions

Screen Shot Permissions *continued*

Introduction to Object-Oriented Programming Using C++ screen used by permission.
Israel Line screen used by permission.

J
JARS is a TradeMark of Web Creations of Blue Spring, MO. All Material located at http://www.jars.com is copyrighted Web Creations, and or the respective owners. All rights reserved.
JavaWorld. From JavaWorld magazine, http://www.javaworld.com Copyright 1996 Web Publishing Inc., and IDG Communications Company.
Jazclass. Copyright 1996 Michael Furstner. All Rights Reserved.
Jeremiah Kitchens. Steven Thompson, eathomp@erols.com, fax: 202-319-7958.
JewelryNet. Copyright 1995-1996 Solowing Concepts. Some contents are paid advertisement provided by our advertisers, and may be copyrighted by our advertisers.
Jolly Joker Free For All Treasure Hunt screen used by permission.
Juggling Information Service. Information and images from the Juggling Information Service are copyrighted and used with permission. Barry Bakalor, jis@juggling.org.
Jump screen used by permission.

K
Kabuki for Everyone. Copyright © Kabuki for Everyone and Matthew Johnson 1995, 1996.
Kali Software. All Kali software and web pages are copyright 1995, 1996 Kali, Inc. The Kali name and logo are trademarks of Kali, Inc.
Kansas City Star. Copyright © The Kansas City Star.
Kellogg's Cereal City. TM ® Kellogg Company © 1996 Kellogg Company.
Khaleej Times Online. Copyright Galadari Printing and Publishing LLC.
Kirshenbaum bond & partners. Copyright 1995, 1996 kirshenbaum bond & partners.
Korea Window. Copyright 1995-1996 Korean Overseas Information Service.

L
L'Hotel Chat screen used with permission.
La Mode de Marin screen used with permission.
Landings. Copyright 1996, DRIVE, Inc. All rights reserved.
Laurel & Hardy screen used by permission.
LensCrafters screen used by permission. Web creation by Poppe.Tyson.
Lewis Galoob Toys. Galoob Toys Web Site © 1996 Lewis Galoob Toys, Inc. All Rights Reserved.
Liqueurs Online. Credit to the Web Gang.
LlamaWeb. Copyright Dale Graham.
Lusty Love Shack screen used by permission.

M
Macintosh Educator's Site screen used by permission.
Mall of America screen used by permission.
Matchpoint screen used by permission.
Maytag screen used by permission.
Medical Education Information Center. All information contained within the Medical Education Information Center (MEDIC TM) is the property of The University of Texas-Houston Health Science Center. Reproduction, redistribution, or modification of the MEDIC TM information for commercial purposes is prohibited without the express written permission of The University of Texas-Houston Health Science Center.
Mercantile Stores Company, Inc screen used by permission.
Mercedes-Benz screen used by permission.
Microbial Underground. Copyright Mark Pallen 1995. All opinions stated here are the author's alone and do not represent any academic institution or department. No liability is accepted for the use of the accompanying information in the treatment of individual patients.
Microsoft Internet Explorer. Screen shot of Internet Explorer Web site reprinted by permission of Microsoft Corporation.
Minnesota screen used by permission of State of Minnesota.
Minor Leagues, Major Dreams screen used by permission.
Monkeys Typing Shakespeare used with permission.
Monte Cristo Antique Mall. Copyright Monte Cristo Antiques and Collectibles 1995. All rights reserved.
Mountain Bike Resources Online screen used with permission.

Movie Critic, a patented, artificial intelligent piece of software, was developed by Songline Studios, Inc., a major content provider on the World Wide Web. Songline Studios is an affiliate of O'Reilly and Associates, and has received a minority investment from America Online.
MovieWeb screen used by permission.
Mr. Showbiz screen used by permission.
MuscleNet Ventures. Copyright 1996 MuscleNet Ventures 1996.

N
NASA screen shot used by permission.
National Baseball Hall of Fame and Museum used by permission.
National Corvette Museum. Copyright 1995 Kentucky Info Web Incorporated. All rights reserved.
National Genealogical Society screen used by permission.
National Library of Medicine screen used by permission.
National Museum of the American Indian screen used by permission.
National Talk Show Guest Registry. Copyright © The Research Department and The National Talk Show Guest Registry.
National Weather Service. The Inclusion of the U.S. National Weather Service web site does not constitute an endorsement, either expressed or implied, of this maranGraphics publication or any other product herein.
Natural History Museum. Reproduced by permission of the Trustees of The Natural History Museum.
Nature. Copyright © Macmillan Magazines Ltd.
NBC Sports screen used by permission.
NCSA Software screen used by permission.
NetTax '96. Rick Sovitzky.
New Balance Cyberpark screen used by permission.
NHL Hockey Trivia. Any reproduction of any photos or any hockey questions is strictly forbidden. © Liam Maguire ™.
Nolo Press. Copyright © Nolo Press 1996.
Notable Citizens of Planet Earth screen used by permission.
Novell. The contents of Novell World Wide are protected by the copyright laws of the United States. No portion may be reproduced in any form, or by any means, without the prior written consent of Novell, Inc.

O
On Beauty and Love. © 1995, 1996 Gary Boone.
OnHoops screen used by permission.
Online Career Center used by permission.
Online DailyNews screen used by permission.
Online Vacation Mall screen shot used with permission. Copyright 1996, Mark Net World.
Organization of American States. The copyright of the information in the OAS Web server is held by the Organization of American States (OAS) which reserves all rights. The OAS makes its documentation available without warranty of any kind and accepts no responsibility for its accuracy or for any consequence of its use.
OS/2 e-Zine! screen used by permission.
OS/2 Warp FAQ List screen used by permission. Some OS/2 Warp pages appear courtesy Timothy Sipples, IBM Corp. Questions may be directed to tsipple@vnet.ibm.com
Outbreak screen used by permission.

P
PA NewsCenter. PA NewsCenter home page reproduced with the kind permission of PA Data Design, The Bishop's Manor, Howden, North Humberside DN14 7BL, England.
ParaScope Copyright © 1996 ParaScope Inc.
Pariscope © Filipacchi Medias, 151 rue Anatole-France, 92534 Levallois-Perret, France.
Pasta Home Page used by permission.
PBS ONLINE ® is a trademark of the Public Broadcasting Service.
PC Demos Explained screen used by permission.
PC Flowers and Gifts screen used with permission.
Pella Windows and Doors. © 1995-96 Pella Corporation.
Persistence of Vision Ray Tracer screen used by permission. Copyright Eric Weber.
Pet Shoppe screen used by permission.
Peterson's Education Center. From Peterson's Education Center (SM)

TABLE OF CONTENTS

CHAPTER 4 WEB SITES

A Web Sites

B Web Sites

C Web Sites

D Web Sites

TABLE OF CONTENTS

CHAPTER 4 WEB SITES *continued*

I

Web Sites

J

Web Sites

L

Web Sites

M

Web Sites

TABLE OF CONTENTS

CHAPTER 4 WEB SITES *continued*

INTRODUCTION TO THE INTERNET

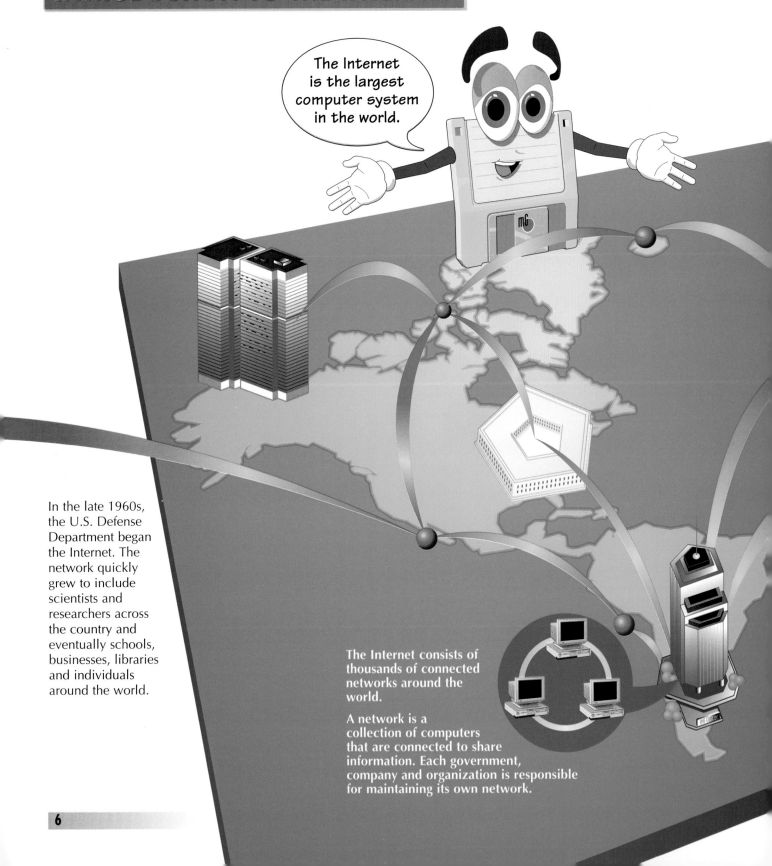

The Internet is the largest computer system in the world.

In the late 1960s, the U.S. Defense Department began the Internet. The network quickly grew to include scientists and researchers across the country and eventually schools, businesses, libraries and individuals around the world.

The Internet consists of thousands of connected networks around the world.

A network is a collection of computers that are connected to share information. Each government, company and organization is responsible for maintaining its own network.

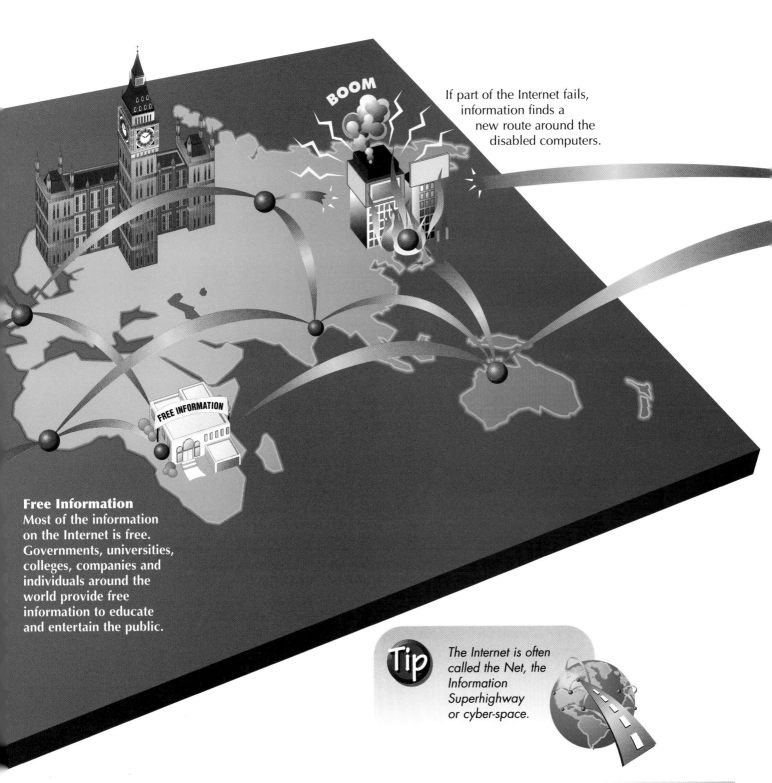

BOOM

If part of the Internet fails,
information finds a
new route around the
disabled computers.

FREE INFORMATION

Free Information
Most of the information
on the Internet is free.
Governments, universities,
colleges, companies and
individuals around the
world provide free
information to educate
and entertain the public.

Tip

*The Internet is often
called the Net, the
Information
Superhighway
or cyber-space.*

WHAT THE INTERNET OFFERS

ELECTRONIC MAIL

Exchanging electronic mail (e-mail) is the most popular feature on the Internet. You can exchange electronic mail with people around the world, including friends, colleagues, family members, customers and even people you meet on the Internet.

Electronic mail is fast, easy, inexpensive and saves paper.

INFORMATION

The Internet gives you access to information on any subject imaginable. You can review newspapers, magazines, government documents, television show transcripts, recipes, job listings, airline schedules and much more.

PROGRAMS

Thousands of programs are available on the Internet. These programs include word processors, spreadsheets, games and much more.

ENTERTAINMENT

Hundreds of simple games are available for free on the Internet, including backgammon, chess, poker, football and much more.

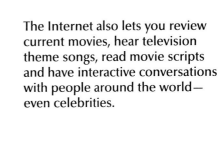

The Internet also lets you review current movies, hear television theme songs, read movie scripts and have interactive conversations with people around the world—even celebrities.

DISCUSSION GROUPS

You can join discussion groups on the Internet to meet people around the world with similar interests. You can ask questions, discuss problems and read interesting stories.

There are thousands of discussion groups on topics such as the environment, food, humor, religion and sports.

ONLINE SHOPPING

You can order goods and services on the Internet without ever leaving your desk. You can buy items such as books, computer programs, flowers, pizza, used cars and much more.

WHO PAYS FOR THE INTERNET?

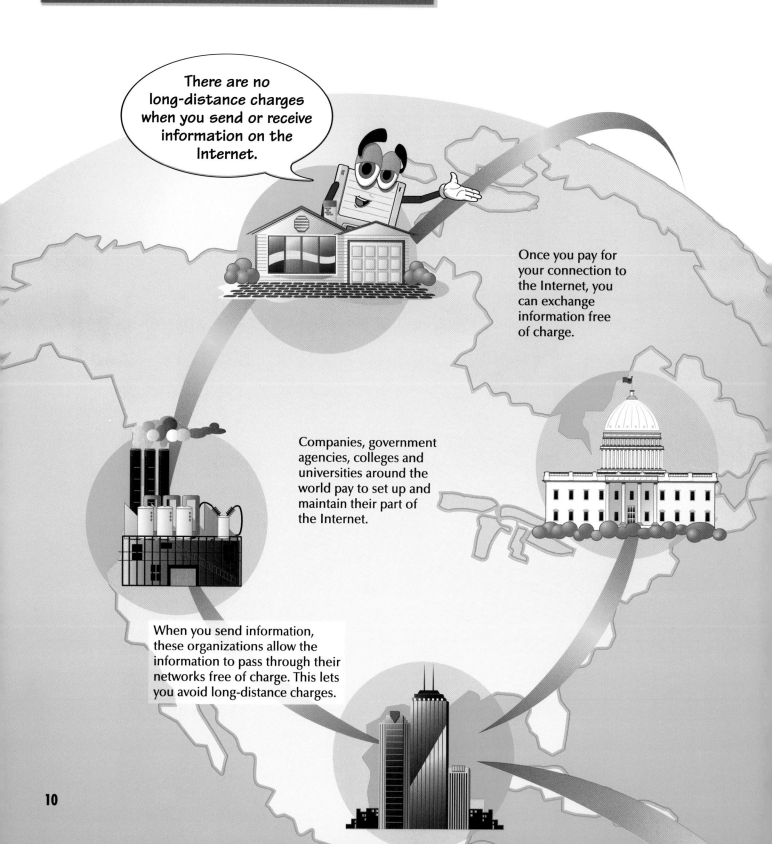

There are no long-distance charges when you send or receive information on the Internet.

Once you pay for your connection to the Internet, you can exchange information free of charge.

Companies, government agencies, colleges and universities around the world pay to set up and maintain their part of the Internet.

When you send information, these organizations allow the information to pass through their networks free of charge. This lets you avoid long-distance charges.

10

WHO OFFERS FREE INFORMATION?

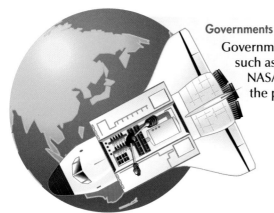

Governments

Governments offer information such as federal budgets and NASA reports to educate the public.

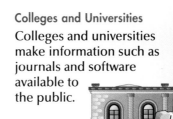

Colleges and Universities

Colleges and universities make information such as journals and software available to the public.

Companies

Companies offer free information to promote a good reputation and to interest you in their products. For example, Ford offers information about its cars and trucks on the Internet.

Individuals

Individuals around the world offer information to give something back to the community. For example, one individual offers more than 1,000 television theme songs that you can access and hear for free on the Internet.

HOW INFORMATION TRANSFERS

All computers on the Internet work together to transfer information back and forth around the world.

Packets

When you send information through the Internet, the information is broken down into smaller pieces, called packets. Each packet travels independently through the Internet and may take a different path to arrive at the intended destination.

When information arrives at its destination, the packets are reassembled.

TCP/IP

Transmission Control Protocol/Internet Protocol (TCP/IP) is a language computers on the Internet use to communicate with each other. TCP/IP divides information you send into packets and sends the packets across the Internet. When information arrives at the intended destination, TCP/IP ensures that all the packets arrived safely.

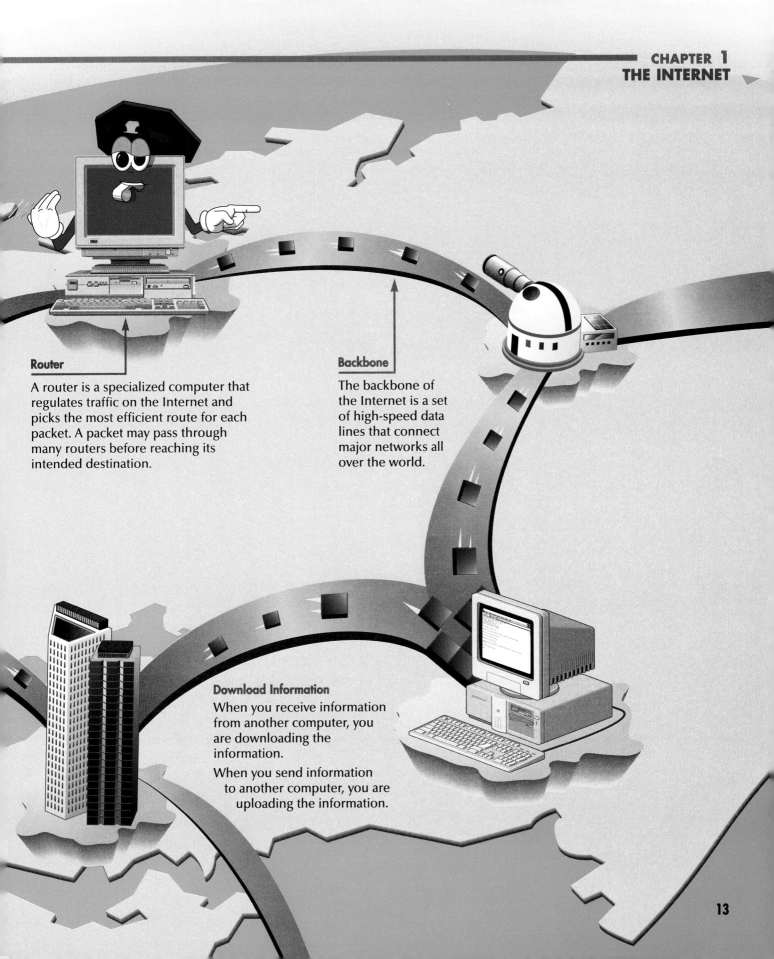

Router

A router is a specialized computer that regulates traffic on the Internet and picks the most efficient route for each packet. A packet may pass through many routers before reaching its intended destination.

Backbone

The backbone of the Internet is a set of high-speed data lines that connect major networks all over the world.

Download Information

When you receive information from another computer, you are downloading the information.

When you send information to another computer, you are uploading the information.

GETTING CONNECTED

COMPUTER

You can use any type of computer, such as an IBM-compatible or Macintosh computer, to connect to the Internet.

> You need specific equipment and programs to connect to the Internet.

IBM compatible   Macintosh

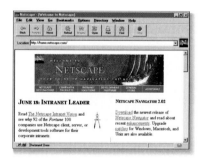

PROGRAMS

You need special programs to use the Internet. Most companies that connect you to the Internet provide the programs you need free of charge.

MODEM

You need a modem to connect to the Internet. Choose a modem with a speed of at least 14,400 bps, although a modem with a speed of 28,800 bps is recommended.

WAYS TO CONNECT

Connection Service

An Internet service provider (ISP) or commercial online service can connect you to the Internet for a fee.

Make sure you choose a connection service with a local telephone number to avoid long-distance charges.

Freenets

A freenet is a free, local service that provides community information and access to the Internet. Most freenets do not let you see graphics, so you can only view text on your screen.

Freenets can be difficult to connect to because they are often busy.

USER NAME AND PASSWORD

You have to enter a user name and password when you want to connect to the Internet. This ensures that you are the only one who can access your Internet account.

Choosing a Password

When choosing a password, do not use words that people can easily associate with you, such as your name or favorite sport. The most effective password connects two words or number sequences with a special character (example: blue@123).

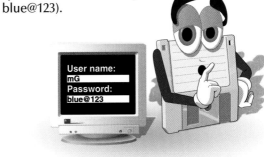

CHAPTER 2
THE WEB

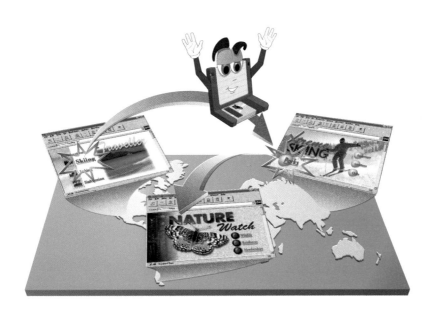

INTRODUCTION TO THE WEB

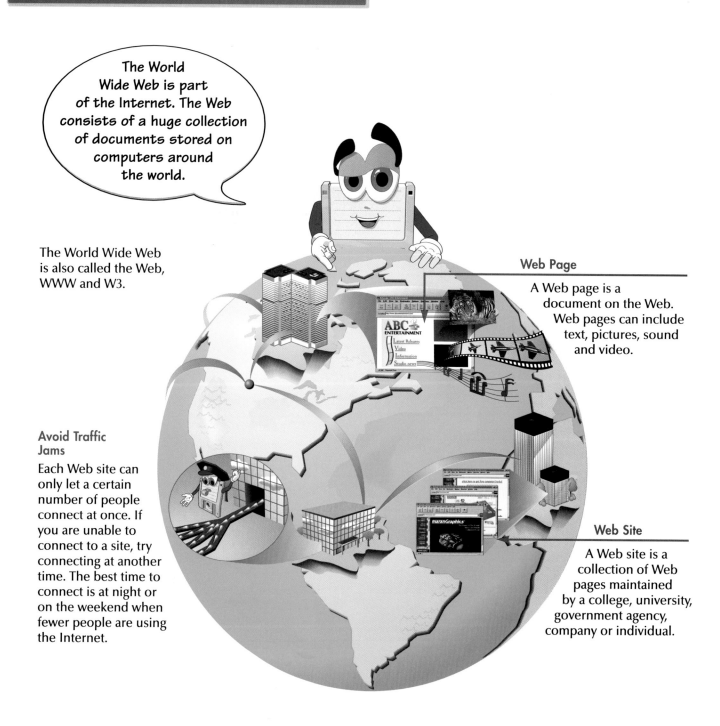

The World Wide Web is part of the Internet. The Web consists of a huge collection of documents stored on computers around the world.

The World Wide Web is also called the Web, WWW and W3.

Avoid Traffic Jams

Each Web site can only let a certain number of people connect at once. If you are unable to connect to a site, try connecting at another time. The best time to connect is at night or on the weekend when fewer people are using the Internet.

Web Page

A Web page is a document on the Web. Web pages can include text, pictures, sound and video.

Web Site

A Web site is a collection of Web pages maintained by a college, university, government agency, company or individual.

URL

Each Web page has a unique address, called the Uniform Resource Locator (URL). You can instantly display any Web page if you know its URL.

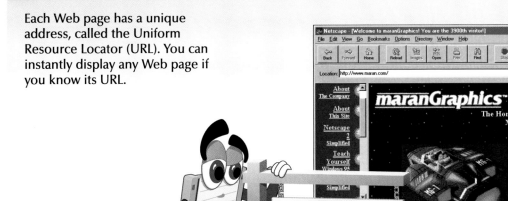

■ All Web page URLs start with http (HyperText Transfer Protocol).

HYPERTEXT

Web pages are hypertext documents. A hypertext document contains highlighted text that connects to other pages on the Web. You can easily jump from one Web page to another by selecting the highlighted text.

Selecting highlighted text can take you to a page located on the same computer or a computer across the city, country or world.

WEB BROWSER

> A Web browser is a program that lets you view and explore information on the Web.

A bookmark file that contains all of the Web sites listed in this book is available at the following site:

URL http://www.maran.com

POPULAR BROWSERS

Netscape Navigator is currently the most popular browser. Other popular browsers include Microsoft Internet Explorer and NCSA Mosaic.

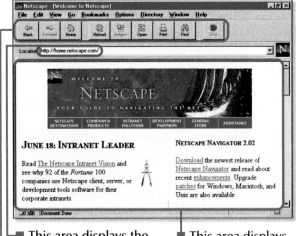

■ This area displays the address of the page you are currently viewing.

■ This area displays a toolbar to help you quickly perform common tasks.

■ This area displays a Web page.

HOME PAGE

The home page is the page that appears each time you start a Web browser.

You can choose any page on the Web as your home page. Make sure you choose a home page that provides a good starting point for exploring the Web.

WEB BROWSER FEATURES

Bookmarks

The bookmarks feature lets you store the addresses of Web pages you frequently visit. Bookmarks save you from having to remember and constantly retype your favorite Web page addresses. The bookmarks feature is also called a hotlist or favorites feature.

History

The History feature keeps track of all the pages you have viewed since you last started the Web browser. This feature lets you instantly return to any of the pages you have viewed.

Turn Off Graphics

Graphics may take a while to appear on the screen. You can save time by turning off the display of graphics. When you turn off the display of graphics, an icon (example:) will appear in place of any graphics.

GRAPHICS ON

GRAPHICS OFF

SHOPPING ON THE WEB

You can buy products and services on the Web without ever leaving your desk.

There are thousands of products you can buy on the Web, such as clothing, flowers, office supplies and computer programs.

The Web also offers a range of services, such as banking and financial or real estate advice.

COMPANIES

Thousands of companies have Web sites where you can get product information and buy products and services online.

You can view a list of companies on the Web at the following site:

URL http://www.directory.net

SHOPPING MALLS

There are shopping malls on the Web where you can view and buy products and services offered by many different companies.

You can view a list of shopping malls on the Web at the following site:

URL http://nsns.com/MouseTracks/HallofMalls.html

SECURITY ON THE WEB

Security is very important when you want to send confidential information such as credit card numbers or bank records over the Internet.

SECURE SITES

You can safely transfer confidential information to a secure site on the Web. The address of a secure site usually starts with https rather than http.

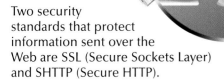

Two security standards that protect information sent over the Web are SSL (Secure Sockets Layer) and SHTTP (Secure HTTP).

RECOGNIZING SECURE SITES

Web browsers usually indicate if a site displayed on the screen is secure.

Netscape displays a broken key icon at the bottom of the screen when you are not at a secure site.

Netscape displays a solid key icon at the bottom of the screen when you are at a secure site.

WEB PAGE FEATURES

FRAMES

Some Web pages divide information into rectangular frames. Each frame can display a different document and has its own unique address.

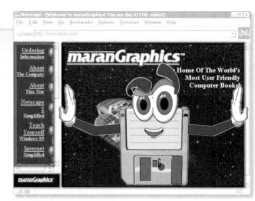

FORMS

Some Web pages include forms that let you enter data. The information you type into a form travels across the Web to the computer that maintains the page.

Shopping sites often have forms that let you fill in your name, address and phone number to order products.

Search sites also have forms that let you enter the topic you want to search for.

TABLES

Some Web pages display information in tables. A table organizes information into an easy-to-follow, attractive format. Tables can include graphics as well as text.

JAVA

Java is a programming language that allows Web pages to display animation and moving text, play music and much more.

Programs written in Java are called Java applets.

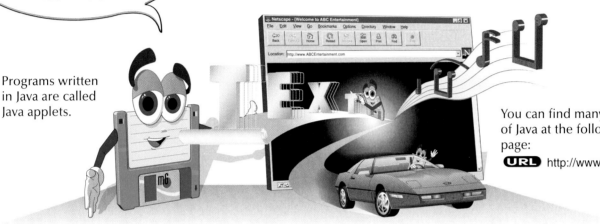

You can find many examples of Java at the following Web page:

URL http://www.gamelan.com

JAVA FEATURES

Animated Characters
Java lets you watch animated characters move on a Web page.

Interaction
Java lets you interact with information on the screen.
You can play games, such as tic-tac-toe. You can also type in data and have a Java applet perform calculations, such as working out mortgage payments.

Moving Text
Java lets you view text that blinks or scrolls across the screen. Information such as stock quotes and weather reports can update before your eyes.

A Web page can contain text, graphics, sound, video and animation.

A Web browser needs special programs, called plug-ins or helpers, to work with certain types of files on the Web. These programs perform tasks that a browser cannot perform on its own. Most plug-ins and helpers are available for free on the Web.

TRANSFER TIME

Some files take a while to transfer to your computer. A Web page usually shows you the size of a file to give you an indication of how long the file will take to transfer.

	File Size		Time
Bytes	Kilobytes (KB)	Megabytes (MB)	(estimated)
10,000,000	10,000	10	1 hour
5,000,000	5,000	5	30 minutes
2,500,000	2,500	2.5	15 minutes

Use this chart as a guide to determine how long a file will take to transfer to your computer.

This chart is based on transferring files with a 28,800 bps modem. A modem with a speed of 14,400 bps or lower will transfer files more slowly than shown in the chart.

GRAPHICS

You can view graphics such as album covers, pictures of celebrities and famous paintings on the Web.

Popular Files

There are common types of graphics files you will find on the Web.

Graphics Interchange Format (.gif)

Joint Photographics Expert Group (.jpeg or .jpg)

Inline Graphics

Most graphics on the Web are inline graphics. Inline graphics can include pictures, photographs, arrows and buttons.

Thumbnail Graphics

A thumbnail graphic is a small version of a larger graphic that transfers quickly to your computer. If you want to see the larger graphic, select the thumbnail graphic.

Imagemaps

An imagemap is a graphic divided into sections, called hotspots. Each hotspot contains a link to another page on the Web. Selecting a hotspot will take you to the linked page.

MULTIMEDIA ON THE WEB

TEXT

You can view documents on the Web such as newspapers, magazines, plays, famous speeches and television show transcripts.

Text transfers quickly to your computer so you do not have to wait long to read text on a Web page.

Popular Files

There are common types of text files you will find on the Web.

Document (.doc)

HyperText Markup Language (.html or .htm)

Text (.txt)

SOUND

You can hear sound on the Web such as T.V. theme songs, movie soundtracks, sound effects and historical speeches.

You need a sound card and speakers to hear sound generated by a computer. A sound card is a device you place inside a computer to play high-quality sound.

Popular Files

There are common types of sound files you will find on the Web.

Audio Player (.au)

RealAudio (.ra or .ram)

Wave (.wav)

VIDEO AND ANIMATION

You can view video and animation on the Web such as movie clips, cartoons and interviews with celebrities.

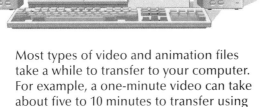

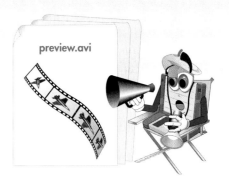

Most types of video and animation files take a while to transfer to your computer. For example, a one-minute video can take about five to 10 minutes to transfer using a 28,800 bps modem.

Popular Files

There are common types of video and animation files you will find on the Web.

Audio Video Interleaved (.avi)

Motion Picture Experts Group (.mpg)

QuickTime (.mov)

3-D WORLDS

You can view three-dimensional worlds and objects on the Web.

3-D worlds are created using a language called Virtual Reality Modeling Language (VRML).

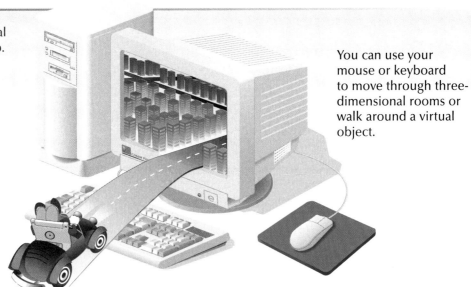

You can use your mouse or keyboard to move through three-dimensional rooms or walk around a virtual object.

SEARCH THE WEB

There are many free services you can use to find information on the Web. These services are called search tools.

A search tool catalogs Web pages to make them easier to find. Some search tools record every word on a Web page, while others only record the name of each page.

You can see a list of various search tools at the following Web sites:

URL http://www.search.com/alpha.html

URL http://home.netscape.com/home/internet-search.html

HOW SEARCH TOOLS FIND WEB PAGES

There are two ways a search tool finds pages on the Web.

Since hundreds of new pages are created each day, it is impossible for a search tool to catalog every new page on the Web.

Spiders
Most search tools have automated robots, called spiders, that travel around the Web looking for new pages.

Submissions
People submit information about pages they have created.

There are two ways a search tool can help you find information on the Web.

Search by Category

You can browse through categories such as arts, science and sports to find information that interests you.

Select a category of interest and a list of subcategories appears.

Continue to select subcategories until you find a page that interests you.

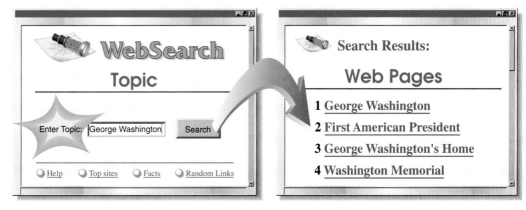

Search by Topic

You can search for a specific topic that interests you.

Type in a topic of interest.

When the search is complete, a list of pages containing the topic you specified appears.

SEARCH THE WEB

Alta Vista

Alta Vista lets you search for a specific topic of interest. You can choose to search Web pages or Usenet, a part of the Internet that contains discussion groups, called newsgroups.

You can access Alta Vista at the following Web site:

URL http://altavista.digital.com

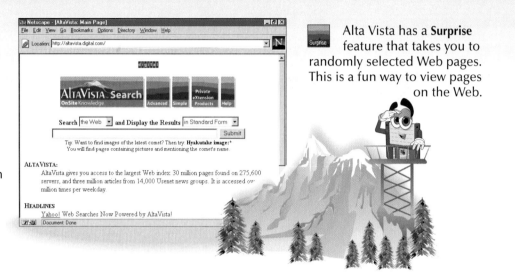

Alta Vista has a **Surprise** feature that takes you to randomly selected Web pages. This is a fun way to view pages on the Web.

Infoseek

Infoseek lets you search for a specific topic of interest or browse through categories, such as education or travel.

You can choose to search Web pages, e-mail addresses or Usenet, a part of the Internet that contains discussion groups, called newsgroups.

You can access Infoseek at the following Web site:

URL http://www.infoseek.com

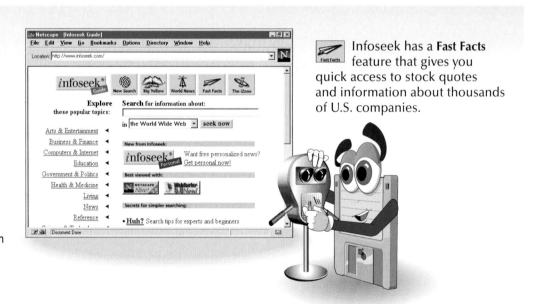

Infoseek has a **Fast Facts** feature that gives you quick access to stock quotes and information about thousands of U.S. companies.

Lycos

Lycos lets you search for a specific topic of interest or browse through categories, such as computers or sports.

You can access Lycos at the following Web site:

URL http://www.lycos.com

POINT Lycos offers a connection to **Point**, a search tool that keeps track of the best pages on the Web. You can browse through categories or type in a topic and Point will display the top-ranked pages matching your request.

Yahoo

Yahoo lets you search for a specific topic of interest or browse through categories, such as arts or science.

You can access Yahoo at the following Web site:

URL http://www.yahoo.com

Yahoo has a **Cool** feature that takes you to Web pages Yahoo considers innovative and interesting.

Yahoo also has a **Headlines** feature that gives you up-to-date news for various categories such as entertainment, politics and sports.

CHAPTER 3

NEWSGROUPS AND CHAT

INTRODUCTION TO NEWSGROUPS

A newsgroup is a discussion group that allows people with common interests to communicate with each other.

There are thousands of newsgroups on every subject imaginable. Each newsgroup discusses a particular topic such as jobs offered, puzzles or medicine.

Usenet, short for Users' Network, refers to all the computers that distribute newsgroup information.

NEWSGROUP NAMES

The name of a newsgroup describes the type of information discussed in the newsgroup. A newsgroup name consists of two or more words, separated by dots (.).

The first word describes the main topic (example: rec for recreation). Each of the following words narrows the topic.

ARTICLES

A newsgroup can contain hundreds or thousands of articles.

Article

An article is a message that an individual posts (sends) to a newsgroup. An article can be a few lines of text or the length of a small book.

I have a week's vacation coming up. Any suggestions for a fun place to spend it?

I had a great time in Hawaii.

I really enjoyed Mexico.

Get on a ship! A cruise is very relaxing!

Thread

A thread is an article and all replies to the article. A thread may include an initial question and the responses from other readers.

NEWSREADER

A newsreader is a program that lets you read and post articles to newsgroups.

Netscape Navigator comes with a built-in newsreader, called Netscape News. Other popular newsreaders include News Xpress and Free Agent.

NETSCAPE NEWS

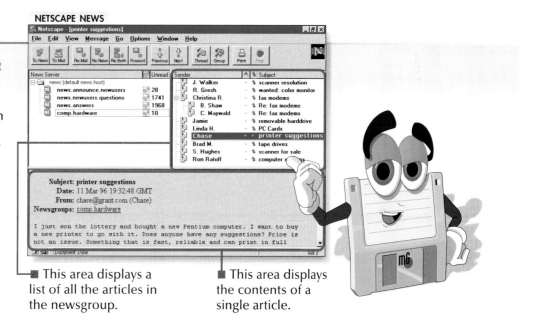

■ This area displays a list of all the articles in the newsgroup.

■ This area displays the contents of a single article.

SUBSCRIBE TO NEWSGROUPS

You subscribe to a newsgroup you want to read on a regular basis.

If you no longer want to read the articles in a newsgroup, you can unsubscribe from the newsgroup at any time.

MODERATED NEWSGROUPS

Some newsgroups are moderated. In these newsgroups, a volunteer reads each article and decides if the article is appropriate for the newsgroup. If the article is appropriate, the volunteer posts the article for everyone to read.

Moderated newsgroups may have the word "moderated" at the end of the newsgroup name (example: sci.military.moderated).

In an unmoderated newsgroup, all articles are automatically posted for everyone to read.

MAIN NEWSGROUP CATEGORIES

alt (alternative)

General interest discussions that can include unusual or bizarre topics.

Examples

alt.fan.actors
alt.music.alternative
alt.ufo.reports

biz (business)

Business discussions that are usually more commercial in nature than those in other newsgroups. Advertising is allowed and lists of job openings are available.

Examples

biz.books.technical
biz.jobs.offered
biz.marketplace

comp (computers)

Discussions of computer hardware, software and computer science.

Examples

comp.lang.pascal.borland
comp.security.misc
comp.sys.laptops

K12 (kindergarten to grade 12)

Discussions of topics concerning kindergarten to grade 12 students.

Examples

k12.chat.elementary
k12.ed.life-skills
k12.ed.math

MAIN NEWSGROUP CATEGORIES

misc (miscellaneous)
Discussions of various topics that may overlap topics discussed in other categories.

Examples
misc.consumers.house
misc.entrepreneurs
misc.taxes

news
Discussions about newsgroups in general. Topics range from information about the newsgroup network to advice on how to use it.

Examples
news.admin.misc
news.announce.newgroups
news.newsites

rec (recreation)
Discussions of recreational activities and hobbies.

Examples
rec.arts.movies.reviews
rec.food.recipes
rec.sport.football.pro

sci (science)
Discussions about science, including research, applied science and the social sciences.

Examples
sci.agriculture
sci.energy
sci.virtual-worlds

soc (social)

Discussions of social issues, including world cultures and political topics.

Examples

soc.college
soc.culture.caribbean
soc.politics

talk

Debates and long discussions, often about controversial subjects.

Examples

talk.environment
talk.philosophy.misc
talk.rumors

REGIONAL NEWSGROUPS

There are newsgroup categories that focus on topics of interest to people living in specific geographical regions.

Examples

aus Australia
bc British Columbia
ca California

NEWSGROUPS FOR BEGINNERS

There are three newsgroups that are helpful for beginners.

Examples

news.announce.newusers
news.answers
news.newusers.questions

WORK WITH ARTICLES

READ AN ARTICLE

You can read articles to learn the opinions and ideas of thousands of people around the world.

New articles are sent to newsgroups every day. You can browse through articles of interest, just as you would browse through the morning paper.

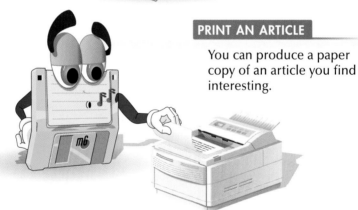

PRINT AN ARTICLE

You can produce a paper copy of an article you find interesting.

POST AN ARTICLE

You can post (send) a new article to a newsgroup to ask a question or express an opinion. Thousands of people around the world may read an article you post.

If you want to practice posting an article, send an article to the **alt.test** newsgroup. You will receive automated replies to let you know you posted correctly. Do not send practice articles to other newsgroups.

REPLY TO AN ARTICLE

You can reply to an article to answer a question, express an opinion or supply additional information.

Reply to an article only when you have something important to say. A reply such as "Me too" or "I agree" is not very informative.

Quoting

When you reply to an article, make sure you include part of the original article. This is called quoting. Quoting helps readers identify which article you are replying to.

Private Replies

You can send a reply to the author of an article, the entire newsgroup or both.

If your reply would not be of interest to others in a newsgroup or if you want to send a private response, send a message to the author instead of posting your reply to the entire newsgroup.

NEWSGROUP ETIQUETTE

Newsgroup etiquette refers to the proper way to behave when sending messages to a newsgroup.

WRITING STYLE

Thousands of people around the world may read an article you post to a newsgroup. Before posting an article, make sure you carefully reread the article.

ARTICLE

I just won the lottery. I bought a new Pentium computer. I want to buy a new printer to go with it. Does anyone has any suggestions? Price is probably not an issue but it might be. I would prefer something that are fast, reliable and can print in full color. Thanks in advance.

◯ -Grammar errors
？ -Misleading

Make sure your article is clear, concise and contains no spelling or grammar errors.

Also make sure your article will not be misinterpreted. For example, not all readers will realize a statement is meant to be sarcastic.

SUBJECT

The subject of an article is the first item people read. Make sure your subject clearly identifies the contents of your article. For example, the subject "Read this now" or "For your information" is not very informative.

READ ARTICLES

Read the articles in a newsgroup for a week before posting an article. This is called lurking. Lurking is a good way to learn how people in a newsgroup communicate and prevents you from posting information others have already read.

READ THE FAQ

The FAQ (frequently asked questions) is a document that contains a list of questions and answers that often appear in a newsgroup.

The FAQ prevents new readers from asking questions that have already been asked. Make sure you read the FAQ before posting any articles to a newsgroup.

POST TO THE APPROPRIATE NEWSGROUP

Make sure you post an article to the appropriate newsgroup. This ensures that people interested in your questions and comments will see your article.

Do not post an article to several inappropriate newsgroups. This is called spamming. Spamming is particularly annoying when the article serves a commercial purpose, such as selling a product or service.

CHAT

You can instantly communicate with people around the world by typing back and forth. This is called chatting.

Chatting is a great way to meet people and exchange ideas.

When chatting, the text you type immediately appears on the screen of each person involved in the conversation.

SAVE MONEY

You can use the chat feature to communicate with family, friends and colleagues in other cities, states or countries without paying long-distance telephone charges.

NICKNAMES

People participating in a conversation often choose nicknames. Do not assume people are really who they say they are.

CHANNELS

There are different chat rooms, or channels, that you can join. Each channel usually focuses on a specific topic. The name of a channel often tells you the theme of the discussion.

CHATTING ON THE INTERNET

Internet Relay Chat (IRC) is a popular chatting system on the Internet. IRC lets you chat privately or in groups. Popular IRC channels include 30+, Friendly and Hot Tub.

You need an IRC program to participate in IRC chats. You can get an IRC program at the following Web sites:

Global Chat

URL http://www.qdeck.com/chat/download.html

mIRC

URL http://www.emapnet.com/service/mirc/download.html

CHATTING ON THE WEB

There are sites on the Web that let you chat. Unlike chatting on the Internet, you do not need a special program to chat on the Web.

WebChat was the first chatting application on the Web and is still the most heavily trafficked Web site. There are hundreds of WebChat channels you can join. Popular channels include those designed for specific age groups, such as Pre-Teen Chat, Thirtysomething and Fifty Plus Chat.

You can chat on the Web at the following site:

WebChat

URL http://wbs.net

WEB SITES

A

ABORIGINAL PEOPLE

Aboriginal Star Knowledge Menu
Learn about medicine wheels, Native theology and astronomy.

URL http://indy4.fdl.cc.mn.us/~isk/stars/starmenu.html

Arte Maya Tz'utuhil Gallery
Paintings by and photographs of contemporary Mayan artists.

URL http://www.artemaya.com

Canadian Native Art
A beautiful collection of Canadian Native art.

URL http://www.netbistro.com/pg/Art/native

Take in some indigenous culture at our aboriginal people sites.

Native People Exhibit

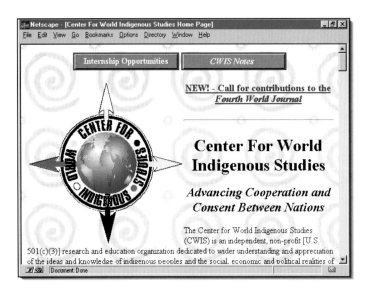

Center For World Indigenous Studies
This center is devoted to improving the understanding of indigenous culture.

URL http://www.halcyon.com/FWDP/cwisinfo.html

Earth Warriors
An organization dedicated to preserving the environment and Native sacred sites.

URL http://www.teleport.com/~dbullock/ewr.shtml

Fourth World Documentation Project
Learn about the struggles of indigenous people with this online library of texts.

URL http://www.halcyon.com/FWDP/fwdp.html

Indigenous Peoples Archive
Bibliographies and abstracts dealing with indigenous peoples and the environment.

URL gopher://minerva.forestry.umn.edu:70/11/trps/dat/04

Links to Aboriginal Resources

A large and comprehensive collection of links on aboriginal issues.

URL http://www.bloorstreet.com/300block/aborl.htm

National Museum of the American Indian

Smithsonian's newest museum celebrates the Native peoples of the Western Hemisphere and includes links to other Native sites.

URL http://www.si.edu/nmai

Native American Adventure

An interactive and informative journey through Native culture.

URL http://www.indians.org

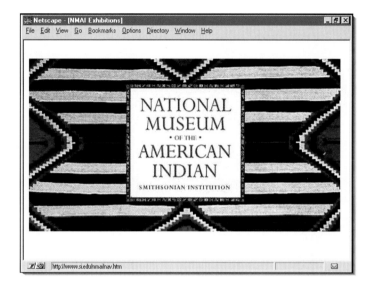

Native American Art Gallery

Dream catchers and feather earrings are among the many different kinds of Native crafts available for viewing or purchasing.

URL http://www.info1.com:80/NAAG

Native American Artists' Home Page

View artwork by Native American artists and find out how to order prints of your favorites.

URL http://www.artnatam.com

Native American History Archives

This site has many articles and documents related to Native history.

URL http://neal.ctstateu.edu/history/world_history/archives/archive47.html

Native Languages

Resources and links to help you learn more about a wide variety of indigenous languages.

URL http://web.maxwell.syr.edu/nativeweb/language/language.html

NativeTech

A showcase of the complex technologies and art developed by Native Americans.

URL http://www.lib.uconn.edu/NativeTech

NativeWeb

An excellent site for anyone interested in issues concerning indigenous peoples.

URL http://web.maxwell.syr.edu/nativeweb

RED INK

Electronic version of the scholarly magazine concerned with Native issues.

URL http://grad.admin.arizona.edu/AIGC/
RedInk/RED_INK.HOMEPAGE.HTML

Tandanya—National Aboriginal Cultural Institute

See selections of artwork from the Australian National Aboriginal Cultural Institute.

URL http://chopper.macmedia.com.au/Tandanya.html

Traditional Food, Health and Nutrition

Discover the benefits of traditional Native foods and try some practical Native recipes.

URL http://indy4.fdl.cc.mn.us/~isk/food/
foodmenu.html

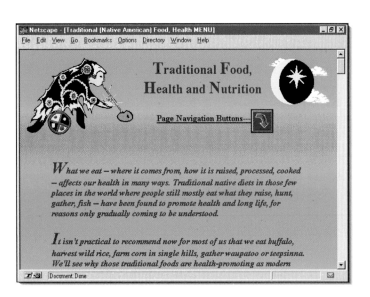

You won't sell yourself short with these advertising sites.

ADVERTISING

a small ad shop

This company is, well, a small ad shop. Take a look at some of its work at this unique, simple site.

URL http://www.asmalladshop.com

Advertising Age

The magazine that is the bible for the advertising industry keeps you up-to-date with the latest advertising news.

URL http://www.adage.com

Dahlin Smith White

The advertising agency for many technology companies such as Intel. Check out clients, staff and sample ads.

URL http://www.dsw.com

DDB Needham Interactive Communications

This branch of DDB Needham Worldwide produces multimedia and Internet-related work for companies such as Pepsi and American Airlines.

URL http://www.ddbniac.com

Fallon McElligott

Biographies of the people behind this successful company and some of their latest work.

URL http://www.fallon.com

Floathe Johnson

Find out about TechnoBranding and see this company's work for high-tech clients like Hewlett-Packard.

URL http://www.floathe.com

Foote, Cone & Belding Technology Group

A clean site from a firm that does great work for technology companies like Adobe.

URL http://www.dnai.com/fcb-tg

Herring/Newman

Tour the agency and see what they do all day or find out if you are an undiscovered advertising genius.

URL http://www.herringn.com

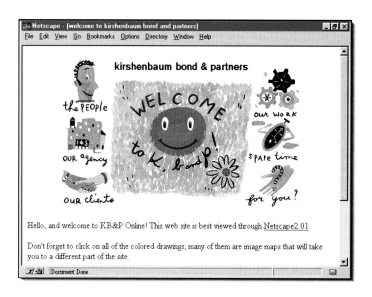

J. Walter Thompson

This key advertising company has clients such as Kellogg and Ford. Its large Web site includes company facts and some fun stuff.

URL http://www.jwtworld.com

Kingswood Kranium

A fun-filled site from this full-service marketing agency. If you dig deep enough you can actually find out about the company.

URL http://www.kingswood.com

Kirshenbaum Bond & Partners

This firm creates ads for Keds, Snapple and others. Check out the neat little extras on this site.

URL http://www.kb.com/index.html

StoogeNet

Just starting to do business on the Internet? From Promotion Pitfalls to Security Blunders, you can learn from the mistakes these guys have made.

URL http://stoogenet.com

A

AFRICA & THE MIDDLE EAST

Explore our African and Middle Eastern sites.

Africa News Online

This site is a good source of information about African current events, sports, culture and much more.

URL http://www1.nando.net/ans/ans.html

Africa Online: Newsstand

Links to African newspapers, magazines and other interesting services provided by Africa Online.

URL http://www.africaonline.com/ AfricaOnline/newsstand.html

Africa Resource Listings

An excellent collection of resources for those who may be planning a trip to Africa.

URL http://www.gorp.com/gorp/location/ africa/africa.htm

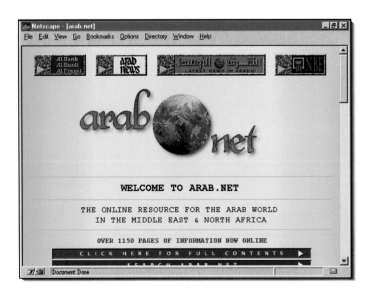

African Wildlife

Find information on African animals at this site.

URL http://www.wolfe.net/~scat

Arab.Net

More than 1,000 pages of information about the Arab world in North Africa and the Middle East.

URL http://www.arab.net

Eye on Africa

Updated daily, these African news items are collected from sources around the world.

URL http://www.webperfect.com/afrinet/news.html

Israel Foreign Ministry

Find out about Israeli culture, government, current events and much more.

URL http://www.israel.org

Jerusalem Post

Headlines and articles from one of Israel's leading newspapers.

URL http://www.jpost.co.il

Jordan

This site has lots of information on the Kingdom of Jordan, including politics, human rights and economics.

URL http://dec.iconnect.com/jordan

Jordan Star

The Middle East's first online English-language newspaper, *The Star* provides political, economic and cultural information each week.

URL http://arabia.com/star

Khaleej Times Online

One of the leading English-language newspapers in the Middle East.

URL http://khaleej.com

Lines in the Sand

An excellent online guide to peace and conflict in the Middle East.

URL http://www.tiger.ab.ca/mideast

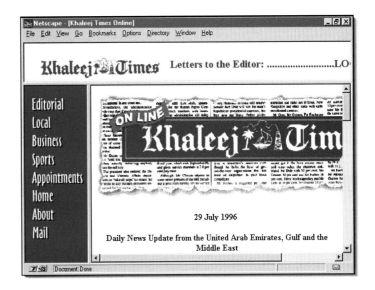

Saudi Arabia

This site includes general information, news releases and even a multimedia presentation.

URL http://imedl.saudi.net

South African Government of National Unity

Visit this site to learn more about the new, democratic South Africa.

URL http://www.polity.org.za/gnu

South African Mail & Guardian

The online version of one of South Africa's leading independent newspapers.

URL http://www.mg.co.za/mg

Zambian National WWW Server

Everything you ever wanted to know about Zambia may be found here.

URL http://www.zamnet.zm

Zambian Post

The first Zambian newspaper on the Web, *The Post* publishes news and information five days a week.

URL http://www.zamnet.zm/zamnet/post/post.html

AGRICULTURE

You will grow to love our agricultural sites.

Agricultural Genome Information Server (AGIS)

Searchable databases on the genomes of plants, animals and other organisms that are important to agriculture.

URL http://probe.nalusda.gov

Beekeeping Home Page

Everything you ever wanted to know about beekeeping.

URL http://weber.u.washington.edu/~jlks/bee.html

Department of Agriculture

This site provides information on U.S. government agencies, agricultural programs, department history and much more.

URL http://www.usda.gov

Global Entomology Agriculture Research Server (GEARS)

Multimedia information for the whole family about the role of insects, especially bees, in agriculture.

URL http://gears.tucson.ars.ag.gov

GrainGenes

A database of information on the genes of various grains as well as sugarcane.

URL http://wheat.pw.usda.gov/graingenes.html

Horticulture in Virtual Perspective

Useful information for plant lovers, including gardening tips, marketing trends and online courses.

URL http://hortwww-2.ag.ohio-state.edu/hvp/HVP1.html

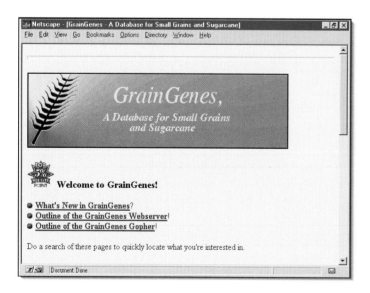

International Commission of Agricultural Engineering

This organization works to stimulate research in the field of Agricultural Engineering.

URL http://wworg.nlh.no/CIGR

Livestock Virtual Library

Useful, searchable information on all kinds of livestock for breeders and farmers.

URL http://www.ansi.okstate.edu/library

Tele-Garden

At this Web site you can control a robot that will plant, water, maintain and monitor plants.

URL http://www.usc.edu/dept/garden

ANIMALS

Amazing Fish Cam!

The fish cam allows you to see live pictures of colorful fish in an aquarium.

URL http://www1.netscape.com/fishcam/fishcam.html

THE AMAZING FISH CAM!

If you are running Netscape 1.1, check out
The Continuously Refreshing Fish Cam

American Association of Zoo Keepers (AAZK)

A great site for potential zoo keepers.

URL http://aazk.ind.net

Animal Resources

Sea World and Busch Gardens provide this site with information on dolphins, birds, endangered species and much more.

URL http://www.bev.net/education/SeaWorld/infobook.html

Cats Frequently Asked Questions

If there is anything you want to know about cats, you can probably find it here.

URL http://www.cis.ohio-state.edu/hypertext/faq/usenet/cats-faq/top.html

Common Birds of the Australian National Botanic Gardens

Illustrations, bird call recordings and descriptions of the birds that inhabit the botanical gardens.

URL http://155.187.10.12/anbg/birds.html

Cows Caught in the Web

Cow sounds, portraits, trivia and moooch mooore.

URL http://www.brandonu.ca/~ennsnr/Cows/Welcome.html

Dalmatian Plantation

Information on buying and breeding Dalmatians, with great links and pictures of cute Dalmatian puppies.

URL http://www.magpage.com/~kdee/dal.html

Electronic Zoo

Click on one of the animals on the home page to access pages of scientific information.

URL http://netvet.wustl.edu/e-zoo.htm

Ferret Central

This site answers all kinds of questions about ferrets as pets and provides numerous links along with a Ferret Photo Gallery.

URL http://www.optics.rochester.edu:8080/users/pgreene/central.html

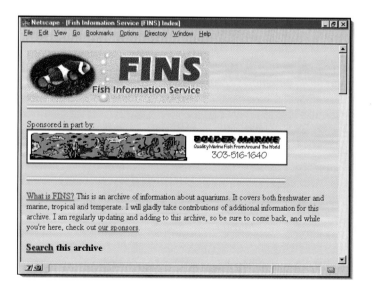

Fish Information Service (FINS)

This searchable archive of information on freshwater and marine aquariums includes fish picture catalogs.

URL http://www.actwin.com/fish/index.cgi

Flea News

Learn more about this tormentor of the animal kingdom.

URL http://www.ent.iastate.edu/FleaNews/AboutFleaNews.html

Good Vibrations

Gifts for animal lovers. Shop for T-shirts and sweats with cat, dog, horse and wildlife designs.

URL http://www.good-vibrations.com

Herp Haven

If you want to have a frog, newt, snake or lizard as a pet, slither over to this herpetology center for help.

URL http://www.herphaven.com

Horse Country

Lots of pictures and information on horses and horseback riding are stored at this site.

URL http://www.pathology.washington.edu/Horse/index.html

Horsemen's Yankee Pedlar

An online newspaper dealing with the world of horses.

URL http://www.sai.com/pedlar

LlamaWeb

All about llama farming, breeding, care, uses, eating habits and much more.

URL http://www.llamaweb.com/degraham

National Zoo

The site where you can explore the Smithsonian Institution's National Zoological Park, including a behind-the-scenes look.

URL http://www.si.edu/organiza/museums/zoo/homepage/nzphome.htm

NetPets

Order pet supplies on the Web or look at a database of dog breeds and other pet information.

URL http://www.netpets.com

Go wild in our animal sites.

NetVet

NetVet is a comprehensive resource center for veterinary medical information.

URL http://netvet.wustl.edu/vet.htm

Office of Protected Resources

The Blue Whale, Hawaiian Monk Seal, Green Sea Turtle and Gulf Sturgeon are only a few of the endangered marine species listed at this site.

URL http://kingfish.ssp.nmfs.gov/tmcintyr/prot_res.html

Online Book of Parrots

This virtual book on parrots and parrot-like birds cannot be imitated.

URL http://www.ub.tu-clausthal.de/p_welcome.html

ANIMALS *continued*

Pet Shoppe

Order from a huge catalog of items for all sorts of pets.

URL http://www.petshoppe.com

Pet Supplies Online

Treats for your cat and dog, available online.

URL http://awa.com/pets

Pug Dog Home Page

Everything you ever wanted to know about this breed of dog.

URL http://www.camme.ac.be/~cammess/
www-pug/home.html

Rainforest Workshop

Learn about the insects, birds and other animals that inhabit temperate and tropical rainforests.

URL http://164.116.102.2/mms/
rainforest_home_page.html

Squidpage

A variety of information, pictures and recipes dealing with squid.

URL http://www.mindspring.com/~webrx/
squid/squid.html

Tennessee Aquarium

Take a tour of the world's largest freshwater aquarium.

URL http://www.tennis.org

Turtle Trax

Information on marine turtles and what you can do to help them.

URL http://www.io.org/~bunrab

Virtual Pet Cemetery

You can submit a story, poem or picture of your dearly departed pet to the world's first online pet burial ground.

URL http://www.lavamind.com/pet.html

Whale Adoption Project

You can help whale protection and conservation efforts by adopting a Humpback Whale.

URL http://www.webcom.com/~iwcwww/
whale_adoption/waphome.html

Whale-Watching-Web

Discover whales and whale watching at this multimedia site.

URL http://www.physics.helsinki.fi/whale

Wolf Park

This facility conducts research on the social behavior of wolves.

URL http://tigerden.com/Wolf-park/
Welcome.html

Wonderful Canine World

Your dog will give this site three paws out of four!

URL http://www.gae.unican.es/general/
dogs/dogs.html

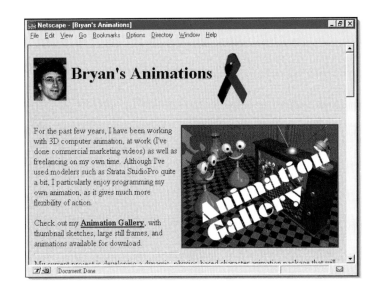

ANIMATION

1st Internet Gallery of GIF Animation

Have a look at the latest and greatest in online GIF animations.

URL http://www.reiworld.com/royalef/
galframe.htm

Animation FAQ

Answers to frequently asked questions from the newsgroup comp.graphics.animation. Covers everything from animation as a hobby to animation as a career.

URL http://www.ridgecrest.ca.us/fx/
cga-faq.html

Bryan's Animations

Bryan Beatty has created some high-quality animations of character movement, many of which are available from this page as .fli and .mpg files.

URL http://www.oas.omron.com/bryan/
anims.html

Our animation sites will get things moving.

Demo Version of Imagine

Imagine is a 3-D modeling, rendering and animation package for the PC. Try out this free demo version.

URL http://www.coolfun.com/html/
showroom.html#imdemo

Example Facial Animations

Computer models of human and animal faces are presented in this collection of animations.

URL http://www.cs.ubc.ca/nest/imager/
contributions/forsey/dragon/anim.html

Fractal Movie Archive

One of the largest collections of fractal animations on the Web.

URL http://www.cnam.fr/fractals/anim.html

GeoSync Sci-Fi

Tune into an original science fiction film being broadcast over the Internet.

URL http://www.netaxs.com/~legend/geosync

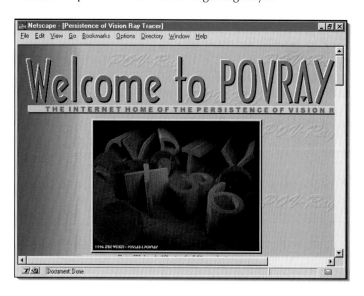

GifBuilder

GIF animations are an easy way to include moving pictures in your Web pages. GifBuilder is a utility for creating them on the Macintosh.

URL http://iawww.epfl.ch/Staff/Yves.Piguet/
clip2gif-home/GifBuilder.html

Kiernan's Suspended Animation Page

A collection of .mpg animations made using the animation package, Wavefront.

URL http://www.unm.edu/~kholland

Persistence of Vision Ray Tracer (POV-Ray)

Ray-tracing creates photo-realistic images by modeling where light rays would bounce and reflect in a picture. This is the home page of POV-Ray, the best free ray-tracing package.

URL http://www.povray.org

Softimage

Learn all about Microsoft's popular animation program, Softimage 3-D.

URL http://www.microsoft.com/softimage

Sparkle

This is a free MPEG movie player for the Macintosh.

URL http://charlotte.acns.nwu.edu/
internet/apps/mac/sparkle

SPmorf

Create your own transformation animations with this morphing software.

URL http://www.eskimo.com/~scott/
spmorf.html

WebExplorer Animation Collection

Cruise by and pick up an animation for your OS/2 WebExplorer Web browser.

URL http://eev11.e-technik.uni-erlangen.de/
animationen.html

APPLIANCES & HOME ELECTRONICS

47st. Photo

This New York store includes cameras as well as stereo, video and computer equipment.

URL http://www.47stphoto.com

Plug into our appliance and home electronics sites.

Beeper & Stereo Store Car Audio Catalog

A selection of new and used items, with most brands available for online ordering.

URL http://www.carstereo.com

Bose

Learn about the technology behind Bose's quality speakers and check out the product display.

URL http://www.musicwest.com/Sponsors/
Bose/bose.html

Consumer Direct Electronics

A busy site with audio, security and entertainment products for the home along with phones, microwaves and more.

URL http://www.wholesalece.com

Consumer Elektronics Warehouse

Refurbished stereo and consumer electronics available for order through e-mail.

URL http://iaswww.com/cew.html

Direct Sales, Inc.

Items sold here include camcorder batteries, security systems, audio/video components and storage units.

URL http://www.ishops.com/direct

DSS Satellite Store

Get answers to all of your questions about these satellite dishes, then check out the satellite services and pricing information.

URL http://ngwwmall.com/shops1/
dss_systems

Maytag

Remodeling or just replacing appliances? Look for current deals along with tips on kitchen design and appliance use. Pictures and product specifications are also offered here.

URL http://www.maytag.com

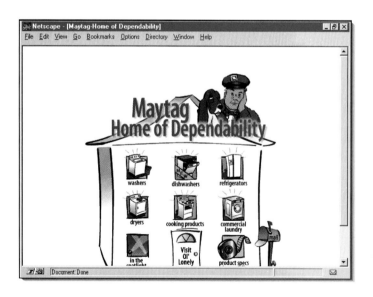

Nobody Beats the Wiz

Check out the weekly audio, video, home office and computer specials from this U.S. East Coast superstore.

URL http://www.nbtw.com

One Call

These mail-order specialists offer a huge range of audio and video equipment from companies such as RCA, JVC, Kenwood and Toshiba.

URL http://www.onecall.com

Soundstage

Complete with photos, this site offers high-end speakers, cables and accessories as well as classifieds and a user forum for your questions.

URL http://www.soundstage.com

the good guys!

This leading U.S. retailer of electronic products lets you browse through the monthly specials or explore the WOW! multimedia superstore in Las Vegas.

URL http://www.thegoodguys.com/index.html

AQUATICS

Divers Alert Network
Information on safety, education and research in scuba diving worldwide.
URL http://www.dan.ycg.org

MarineData Internet
At this site you can find information about boats, marine engines, yachting, motorboating and the marine industry in general.
URL http://www.marinedata.co.uk/start.html

Ocean World
European Web site dedicated to sailing, racing, motorboating and other sea activities.
URL http://www.oceanworld.com

ScubaWorld Online
Outstanding Web resource on scuba diving.
URL http://www.scubaworld.com

Swimming Science Journal
An electronic journal containing articles on coaching competitive swimming.
URL http://rohan.sdsu.edu/dept/coachsci/swimming

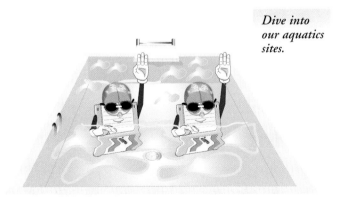

Dive into our aquatics sites.

SWIMnews ONLINE
A great source for news, stories, and world and regional records in swimming.
URL http://www.swimnews.com

United States Swimming
Official site of the governing body for amateur swimming in the United States.
URL http://www.usswim.org

United States Water Polo
Official site of the governing body for the sport of water polo in the United States.
URL http://www.ewpra.org/uswp

Water Skier's Web
A comprehensive water-skiing resource, covering a variety of techniques.
URL http://waterski.net

65

A

ARCHAEOLOGY

Dig into our archaeology sites.

Ancient World Web

Learn all about the latest discoveries.

URL http://atlantic.evsc.virginia.edu/julia/AW/breaking.html

Archaeology on the World Wide Web

Southampton University's guide to many interesting archaeological resources.

URL http://avebury.arch.soton.ac.uk/NetStuff/archplaces.html

ArchNet

An excellent resource page with many links and a search tool.

URL http://spirit.lib.uconn.edu/archaeology.html

Excavation of the Ancient Turkish City of Çatalhöyük

A guide to the ongoing excavations of what is believed to be the world's first urban center.

URL http://catal.arch.cam.ac.uk/catal/catal.html

Great Kiva 3-D Model

Go on a guided tour of this 3-D reconstruction of an ancient home.

URL http://www.sscf.ucsb.edu/anth/projects/great.kiva/greatkiva.html

Institute of Egyptian Art and Archaeology

A beautiful site with many images, including a photo tour of this ancient, desert nation.

URL http://www.memst.edu/egypt/main.html

Prehistoric Cave Paintings

Images and commentary on the discovery of well-preserved cave art in the south of France.

URL http://www.culture.fr/culture/gvpda-en.htm

Seven Wonders of the Ancient World

An incredibly informative and beautiful online tour.

URL http://pharos.bu.edu/Egypt/Wonders

Stonehenge in 3-D

Several computer-generated graphics showing what the mythic site may have looked like centuries ago.

URL http://wantree.com.au/~kevin/henge.html

Unguided Tour of Pompeii

Visit this buried Roman city online.

URL http://enterzone.berkeley.edu/ez/e2/articles/frankel/tour1.html

ART DEALERS & ANTIQUES

American Coin & Stamp Home Page

Browse through the catalog and then place a bid for the next auction of coins, stamps and other items.

URL http://www.wid.com/coin

Antique and Collectible Exchange

The original online antique marketplace offers a great way to buy and sell your antiques and collectibles.

URL http://www.worldint.com/ace

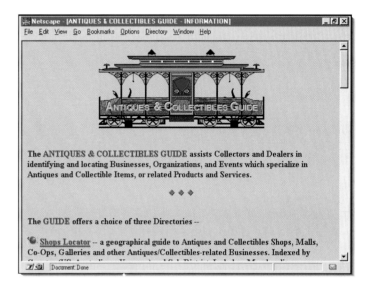

Antique Link

An excellent one-stop site for anyone in the market for antiques, with a searchable antique dealer listing, a buyer and seller database and much more.

URL http://www.antiquelink.com

Antique Mall

Want to buy or sell valuable or hard-to-find items? Try here first.

URL http://www.wwwebmaster.com/AntiqueMall

Antiques and Collectibles Guide

Find antique and collectible dealers by geographic location or by the items they stock.

URL http://www.tias.com/amdir/info.html

Antiques and The Arts Weekly

One of America's leading antique magazines, known for its auction listings and industry news, is now online.

URL http://www.thebee.com/aweb/aa.htm

ANTKonLINE

A wealth of 20th century artifacts, including art deco, advertising materials, arts and crafts, toys and more.

URL http://www.suba.com/ANTKonLINE

ArtSource1

Limited edition, signed and numbered prints by many artists are available at this site.

URL http://nvi.com/ArtSource1

Australian Aboriginal Art

Paintings, totems and carvings from Arnhemland, Central Australia and the Daly River areas.

URL http://www.aaia.com.au/#TOP

Find some oldies but goodies in our art dealer and antique sites.

Bingham Gallery Online

Specializing in works by deceased American artists, this gallery displays available art online.

URL http://www.binggallery.com

Christie's

Review listings of upcoming auctions from the world's oldest fine art auctioneer.

URL http://www.christies.com

G.S. Converse & Co. Great Antique Clocks

Browse through a catalog of antique clocks from around the world.

URL http://www.pond.com/~gsc

Incredible Collectibles

This antique store has an online catalog containing descriptions, prices and photographs, as well as an online museum displaying glassware and china.

URL http://www.tias.com/stores/IC

Internet Arts & Antiques

A great place to track down antiques for sale, with an area where you can place an ad for that perfect piece you have been looking for.

URL http://www.wdsi.com/antiques.html

Learn About Antiques & Collectibles

New to collecting? Find lots of useful information here to help you get started.

URL http://www.ic.mankato.mn.us/antiques/
Antiques.html

Monte Cristo Antique Mall

A host of antiques and collectibles, including paper goods and scientific items. Use the U.S. Patent Dater to find out how old your items are.

URL http://www.montecristo.com

Paris to Province

This antique gallery specializes in 18th and 19th century English, French and Italian antiques.

URL http://www.paris-to.com

Pegasus Antiques

Browse through the extensive online catalog or see what this company is interested in buying.

URL http://www.antiqueshop.com

Ship Art International, Inc.

Rates and information for people interested in shipping art, antiques and other delicate items across the U.S.

URL http://ourworld.compuserve.com/
homepages/ShipArt

Sotheby's

Find out about this famous auction firm or try an interactive Auction Adventure.

URL http://www.sothebys.com

Susi's A Gallery for Children

Browse through a catalog of art that you can stick on the wall or wear on your wrist, and then order items online.

URL http://www.susigallery.com

William Doyle Galleries

Online auction catalogs, highlights from upcoming auctions, and other services from appraisals to restoration.

URL http://www.doylegalleries.com

ART GALLERIES

Age of Enlightenment

Visit France's national museums and learn more about the Age of Enlightenment.

URL http://mistral.culture.fr/lumiere/
documents/files/imaginary_
exhibition.html

Browse through our art gallery sites.

Art Crimes: The Writing on the Wall

This gallery of graffiti art from cities around the world includes shows, interviews and more.

URL http://www.gatech.edu/graf/index.html

Art of Tibetan Sand Painting

Check out the pictures and movies documenting the creation of a sand painting by Tibetan monks.

URL http://www.chron.com/mandala

ArtServe

More than 16,000 images related to the history of art and architecture. Choose from classical art, Islamic architecture and more.

URL http://rubens.anu.edu.au

Dia Center for the Arts

This organization covers many areas of the arts, from poetry and dance to painting and sculpture.

URL http://www.diacenter.org

Electric Gallery

This gallery organizes its fantastic art into nine categories, including Amazon, Haitian and Jazz & Blues.

URL http://www.egallery.com

Gallery 360

Take a 3-D tour of this virtual gallery of digital art, which includes sculpture and paintings.

URL http://www.sfgate.com/gallery360

Gallery for the Digital Arts

Check out exhibits of some great computer-generated artwork.

URL http://web.sirius.com/~stas/Gallery/exhibit.html

Jack Øvacs—People's Gallery

Have your photography, paintings and drawings displayed at this site for the world to see.

URL http://www.netm.com/art

McMichael Canadian Art Collection

This Canadian art gallery features work by the Group of Seven and Native artists.

URL http://www.mcmichael.com

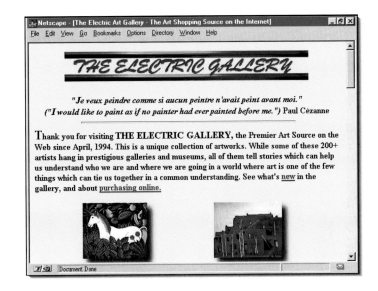

National Heritage Board of Singapore

Here you will find a great collection of Asian art, cultural information and images.

URL http://www.museum.org.sg

National Museum of African Art

Check out the collections at this museum and learn all about the various art forms in Africa.

URL http://www.si.edu/organiza/museums/africart/homepage/nmafa.htm

National Museum of American Art

View almost 1,000 works of art from across the United States.

URL http://www.nmaa.si.edu

Rock & Roll Digital Gallery

Check this site frequently to view the latest exhibition of rock and roll artwork.

URL http://www.hooked.net/julianne/index.html

The Blue Dot

Unlike any other art gallery you will ever visit. Online exhibits, poetry and lots of unconventional features.

URL http://www.razorfish.com/bluedot

The Cafe

More than an art gallery, this is a cyber-hangout where you can look at art, watch movies, chat with other art lovers or read some great poetry.

URL http://www.virtualcafe.com

Virtual Art Galleries

This site will take you on a journey through art galleries around the world that showcase masters such as Leonardo di Vinci. Not bad for only $4.95 and you don't have to pay for airfare!

URL http://www.helpline.com/powerpak/catpak/00000059.html

WebMuseum

A huge collection of some of the world's best art.

URL http://sunsite.unc.edu/louvre

ASIA

Central Asia Resource Project

An informative list of links and resources on Central Asia, with focus on the republics of Uzbekistan, Turkmenistan, Tajikistan, Kyrgyzstan and Kazakstan.

URL http://www2.hawaii.edu/~abichel

China Today

Information on China's government, culture, trade, entertainment and more.

URL http://www.chinatoday.com

Hong Kong Government Information Center

Pictures, government offices, news updates and a lot more on Hong Kong.

URL http://www.info.gov.hk

India

This site offers business and contact information, public notices and online consular forms to help you in your dealings with India.

URL http://www.indianconsulate-sf.org

Japanese Information

All kinds of information on Japan, such as Japanese proverbs, government and customs.

URL http://www.ntt.jp/japan/index.html

Korea Window

A unique site that offers an abundant amount of information on Korea.

URL http://www.kois.go.kr

Republic of Turkey

Politics, culture, current news and more on the country that bridges Europe and Asia.

URL http://www.turkey.org/turkey/index.html

Sri Lanka

Sri Lanka's Embassy in Washington offers help with tourist and immigration matters and provides general information and news releases on Sri Lanka.

URL http://wheat.symgrp.com/symgrp/srilanka

Taiwan

An excellent source of recent events and in-depth information about Taiwan.

URL http://gio.gov.tw

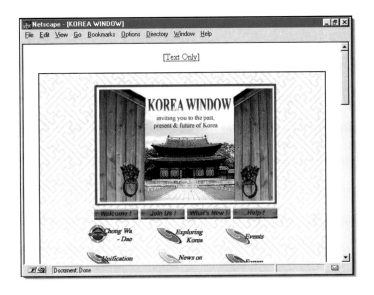

Speed through our auto racing sites.

AUTO RACING

American Racing Scene

This online magazine devoted to the IndyCar and NASCAR racing scenes supplies you with up-to-the-minute results, points standings, photos galore and more.

URL http://www.racecar.com

goracing.com

Graphics-intensive information center on different racing circuits for autos, cycles and boats.

URL http://www.goracing.com

Indianapolis Motor Speedway

The official Web site for the world's best-known race track. Get complete race coverage and Indy Racing League information, including driver biographies.

URL http://www.brickyard.com

International Motor Sports Association

The site of the world's top organization for professional sports car racing provides comprehensive information on several different racing series.

URL http://www.imsaracing.com

NASCAR Online

This official NASCAR site may be the best auto racing site on the Web.

URL http://www.nascar.com

National Corvette Museum

Enjoy one of North America's most popular sports cars.

URL http://BowlingGreen.KY.net/corvette

SCORE International

Check out truck racing photos, statistics and race results from the SCORE Off-Road Desert Championship Series.

URL http://www.score-international.com

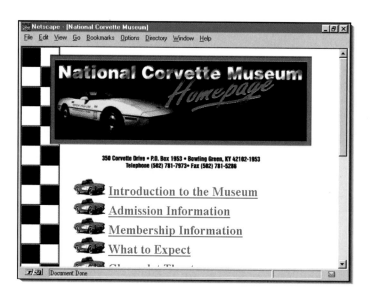

Thrust SSC News

The site for the Thrust SSC Project to set the world land speed record.

URL http://thrustssc.digital.co.uk

AUTOMOBILES

@Toyota

In this virtual showroom you will find information on cars and dealers, the Toyota racing program, *The Hub* online magazine, auto industry news and more.

URL http://www.toyota.com

4WD: Four Wheel Drive and All Wheel Drive

An Internet magazine for 4WD and AWD fans that has sections with news and technical details for every brand you can think of.

URL http://www.sofcom.com.au/4WD/4WD.html

American Emergency Vehicles

Forget the sensible station wagon. Have you considered buying an ambulance?

URL http://www.ambulance.com

Atlas Motor Vehicle

A live motorcycle auction with five language options for international fans.

URL http://www.atlasmv.com

Auto Trader Online

A pretty cool site if you are searching for a car.

URL http://www.traderonline.com/main.html

Auto-By-Tel

Lease or purchase a new car online.

URL http://www.autobytel.com

Autoscape

From Acura to Volvo, you will find dealers across the United States. Or check the technical details of any vehicle sold in North America.

URL http://www.autoscape.com

BMW Canada Inc.

Enter some information and the online consultant will recommend which model of BMW is right for you.

URL http://www.bmw.ca

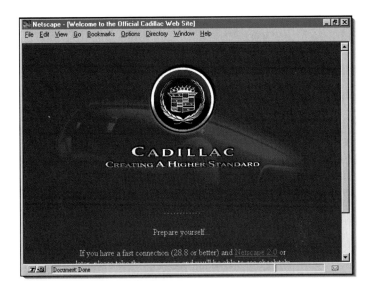

Go cruising through our automobile sites.

BMW of Germany

You will find the BMW Art Cars and lots of technical goodies here.

URL http://www.bmw.de/HOMHOME.html

BMW of North America, Inc.

Full information on various models with a listing of U.S. dealers and a link to the BMW Car Club of America.

URL http://www.bmwusa.com/index.html

Cadillac

Information on the newest Cadillac models and upcoming events sponsored by the upscale car maker.

URL http://www.cadillac.com

Car-Link

Buy or sell used cars using listings that include color pictures, or order brochures for new cars.

URL http://www.car-link.com

AUTOMOBILES *continued*

Car.Net

Shop for a car using the city, dealer name or make index, or visit the Porsche Museum.

URL http://www.car.net

Chrysler Technology Center

See Chrysler's latest technology and concept cars without having to line up at your local auto show.

URL http://www.chryslercorp.com

DealerNet: The Virtual Showroom

New cars, used cars, boats and RVs. Dealers from across the U.S. showcase their wares here.

URL http://www.dealernet.com

Dream Vehicles

Hot formula race cars and a train that doesn't need rails.

URL http://www.shadow.net/~aaadream

Ford Worldwide Connection

Check out all the Ford families of cars, along with U.S. dealer locations.

URL http://www.ford.com

Freeways by Alamo Rent A Car

Reserve a car online and check the weather for where you are headed.

URL http://www.freeways.com

Frequently Asked Questions About The Lemon Law

Buying a car in the United States? You should know about the Lemon Law.

URL http://www.directnet.com/
~rbrennan/lemon.html

General Motors

A comprehensive site from the world's largest car maker.

URL http://www.gm.com/index.htm

Goodyear Tires

Find the best tire for your car and the nearest dealer. Or check out a blimp near you.

URL http://www.goodyear.com

Harley-Davidson Canada

Check out the motorcycle museum or cruise through photos and information on current models.

URL http://www.harleycanada.com

Honda

Honda in America, with a timeline, monthly specials, a virtual plant tour and more.

URL http://www.honda.com

Infiniti

Visit this very stylish site to find a fine automobile and order a brochure.

URL http://www.infinitimotors.com

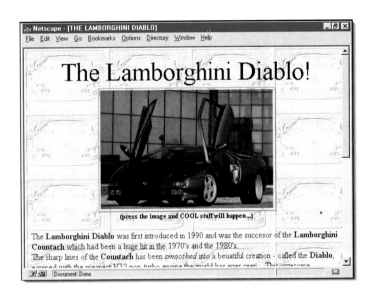

Lamborghini Diablo

What can you accomplish in four seconds? The Lamborghini Diablo can go from 0 to 62 mph in that time. Learn more about this car at this speedy site.

URL http://www.bastad.se/~johan/diablo/diablo.html

Lexus Center of Performance Art

Let Alex, the tour guide, show you everything Lexus has to offer.

URL http://www.lexususa.com

Lotus Cars

Dealers across the United States and Canada and great photos of the Lotus Esprit and other models.

URL http://www.lotuscars.com

Mazda Online

New and used cars and winter driving tips.

URL http://www.mazdacars.com

Mercedes-Benz

The world of Mercedes, from the latest luxury models to the Formula 1 circuit.

URL http://www.mercedes-benz.com

Miller Motorcars—Ferrari Dealership

Look for your dream Ferrari, new or used.

URL http://www.starweb.net/milmot/ferrari.htm

Nissan Motors

Explore the world of Nissan in four languages or go on the Pathfinder African Adventure.

URL http://www.nissanmotors.com

Pirelli

Tires, cables and the famous Pirelli Calendar.

URL http://www.pirelli.com

Rent-A-Wreck

Do not let the name fool you. This company does millions of dollars of business each year.

URL http://www.rent-a-wreck.com/raw

Rolls Royce of Beverly Hills

In addition to Rolls Royce, you will find Lamborghini, Bentley, Lotus and more here.

URL http://www.clark.net/pub/networx/autopage/dealers/de001.html

SAAB: Find Your Own Road

Fans of this great Swedish car will find current models and U.S. dealer information.

URL http://www.saabusa.com

Saturn Site

Check out the cars, find a dealer or order a brochure. Be sure to check out the progress of the Saturn Cycling Team.

URL http://www.saturncars.com

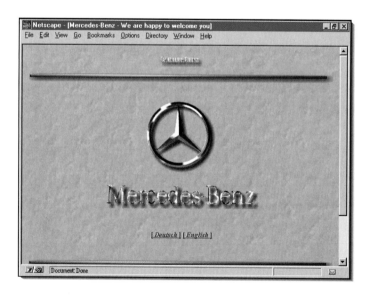

Special Car Journal

Find out about more than 4,000 cars for sale or articles on new models from makers like Ferrari and Mercedes.

URL http://www.specialcar.com

Subaru Online

Check out a dealer close to you, read the Drive Newsletter or take the Subaru Trivia Challenge.

URL http://www.subaru.com

Volkswagen

From the Beetle to the Passat, see 40 years of Volkswagen history.

URL http://www.vw.com

Volvo

New models, North American dealers, the legendary safety record and Volvo's European delivery program.

URL http://volvocars.com

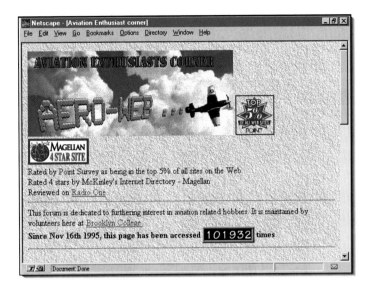

AVIATION & AEROSPACE

Aviation Enthusiasts Corner

Trying to find out where you can see a B-52 bomber or A-6 Intruder? Use the aircraft and museum locators at this site.

URL http://www.brooklyn.cuny.edu/rec/air

Aviation Home Page

Zoom in on information of interest to pilots and enthusiasts with this resource page.

URL http://www.cco.net/~gwilkerson/aviation.html

Daimler-Benz

An important company in the world of aerospace and aviation.

URL http://www.daimler-benz.com/index.html

AB

AVIATION & AEROSPACE *continued*

Internet Aerospace Links

A variety of links related to the aerospace industry.

URL http://www.galcit.caltech.edu/~padam/
htmls/AeroLinks.html

Kitfox Archives

Tired of flying in 747s and 767s? Before you build your own airplane, check out the information at this site.

URL http://dunkin.Princeton.EDU/.kitfox

Landings

Links to simulators, newsgroups, airshows and more.

URL http://www.landings.com

San Diego Aerospace Museum

Find out about aviation and aerospace history with an online tour of the museum and its exhibits.

URL http://www.globalinfo.com/noncomm/
aerospace/Aerospace.HTML

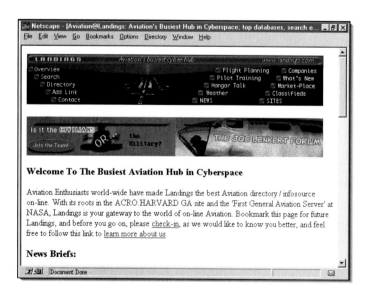

Fly high in our aviation and aerospace sites.

WWW Virtual Library—Aerospace

Browse through this virtual library to find information on aerospace.

URL http://macwww.db.erau.edu/
www_virtual_lib/
aeronautics.html

ANKS

1st National Bank of Pryor

Buying a plane? This bank may be just the lender you are looking for.

URL http://www.1st-of-pryor.com

American Express

Apply for a card, book your next trip or locate American Express offices around the world.

URL http://www.americanexpress.com

Bank of America

Economic news and money tips as well as information on services from home banking to investment strategies.

URL http://www.bankamerica.com

Bank of Boston

Search financial news from around the world or find the nearest bank machine.

URL http://www.bkb.com

Bank of New York

The leading depositary bank in the world.

URL http://www.iql.com/bankofny

Bankers Trust

Get Windows-based financial training games or check out global economic newsletters.

URL http://www.bankerstrust.com

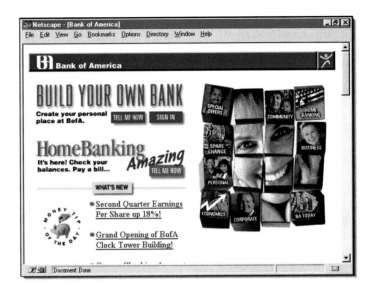

Invest some time in our bank sites.

BankNet Electronic Banking Service

The world's first Internet banking service. Although based in the U.K., customers from all over the world are accepted.

URL http://mkn.co.uk/bank

Boatmen's Bank of Rolla

After more than 100 years in business, this bank is now on the Internet.

URL http://www.rollanet.org/
~boatmens

Capital Bank

A Louisiana bank with special rates for its Web customers.

URL http://www.capbank.com

Chase Manhattan Corporation

The largest bank in the United States, with financial services in 52 countries.

URL http://www.chase.com

B

Tired of being held up in line? Bank from home with these sites.

Citibank

The site of this major U.S. bank has information on branches around the world.

URL http://www.citibank.com

DigiCash

This company specializes in electronic payment products and has developed the ecash system for the Internet.

URL http://www.digicash.com

Fannie Mae

Whether you are a money lender or a home buyer, this site offers all the home mortgage information your heart desires.

URL http://www.fanniemae.com

Fifth Third Bank

Want to know how long you will have that car loan? Try out the loan calculator!

URL http://www.53.com

First Chicago NBD

Try the easy-to-use Financial Planner, which takes you from the pre-teen years to the retirement years.

URL http://www.fcnbd.com

First of America Bank

This bank has a search tool that will help you find specific information.

URL http://www.foa.com

First Union

Apply for a MasterCard online or read about several other banking services.

URL http://www.firstunion.com

HomeOwners Finance Center

Check out this mortgage broker's daily rates or use the financial tools provided.

URL http://www.homeowners.com

Huntington Banks

Choose a credit card, plan for your retirement and more.

URL http://www.huntington.com

J.P. Morgan

Information on all of the firm's financial services, combined with market data.

URL http://www.jpmorgan.com

KeyBank U.S.A.

Need a boat loan? This is one of the leading marine lenders in the United States.

URL http://usa.nia.com/keybank

Mellon

Banking and investment services are just a click away.

URL http://www.mellon.com

Norwest

Find the locations of Cirrus bank machines throughout the world or view a collection of artwork.

URL http://www.norwest.com

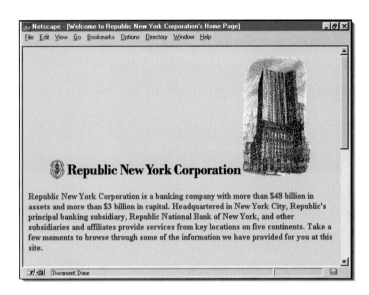

Netscape - [Welcome to Republic New York Corporation's Home Page]

File Edit View Go Bookmarks Options Directory Window Help

§ Republic New York Corporation

Republic New York Corporation is a banking company with more than $48 billion in assets and more than $3 billion in capital. Headquartered in New York City, Republic's principal banking subsidiary, Republic National Bank of New York, and other subsidiaries and affiliates provide services from key locations on five continents. Take a few moments to browse through some of the information we have provided for you at this site.

Document: Done

Online Banking and Financial Services Directory

A listing of more than 1,000 banks, credit unions and investment services companies that have sites on the Web.

URL http://www.orcc.com/banking.htm

RAM Research Group

Looking for the best deal on a credit card? Search through more than 10,000 financial institutions.

URL http://www.ramresearch.com/choices.html

Republic New York Corporation

A banking corporation that provides services on five continents.

URL http://www.rnb.com

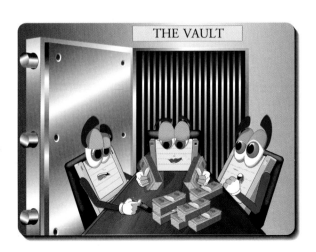

THE VAULT

B

Wells Fargo

Try the online banking at the merged Wells Fargo/First Interstate Bank.

URL http://www.wellsfargo.com

BASEBALL

Baseball Online

An online publication loaded with information on college, minor and major league baseball.

URL http://199.72.8.130

Baseball Server

Visit this site for detailed information on scores, news and standings, as well as baseball feature articles.

URL http://www2.nando.net/SportServer/baseball

Baseball Weekly

A thorough, weekly baseball magazine.

URL http://www.usatoday.com/bbwfront.htm

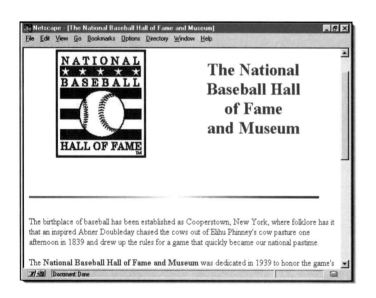

Chicago White Sox Baseball

Follow the progress of the Chicago White Sox on live Internet radio.

URL http://www.audionet.com/sox.htm

Internet Baseball League

IBL is an electronic play-by-mail baseball league now entering its fifth year.

URL http://www.ibl.org

Internet's Baseball Cards Store

A great place to buy or sell baseball cards, with good prices and selection.

URL http://www.baseball-cards.com

Major League Baseball

ESPN hosts this site dedicated to the major league.

URL http://espnet.sportszone.com/mlb

National Baseball Hall of Fame and Museum

This site provides lots of valuable information about the hall of fame. Look for a new and expanded site coming soon.

URL http://www.enews.com/bas_hall_fame/overview.html

RealBaseball.com

Your source for scores, standings and press releases from independent minor leagues.

URL http://www.realbaseball.com

Society for American Baseball Research

Many links to baseball-related sites, information on research committees and more.

URL http://www.skypoint.com/~ashbury/ sabrhomepage.html

The Sports Network—Major League Baseball

Check out this searchable collection of baseball information, covering news, scores, standings, statistics and more.

URL http://www.sportsnetwork.com:80/ filter/filter.cgi/mlb/mlb.html

Top Baseball News

USA Today brings you this daily listing of headlines from the world of baseball.

URL http://www.usatoday.com/sbfront.htm

BASKETBALL

Basketball Highway

Information and resources for basketball coaches.

URL http://www.bbhighway.com

Carolina Pros Home Page

Brainchild of the Boston Celtics' Rick Fox, this is the organization of people who have played basketball under coach Dean Smith at the University of North Carolina.

URL http://CarolinaPros.com

Journal of Basketball Studies

Magazine providing statistical analyses of the game from a coaching perspective.

URL http://cmr.sph.unc.edu/~deano/bball/ index.html

Slam dunk your way through our basketball sites.

B

NBA Interactive Schedule

Check a listing of today's games or search for upcoming games.

URL http://wintermute.sr.unh.edu/
cgi-bin/nba-page

NBA On NBC

This site provides information on NBC T.V.'s coverage of NBA games, including schedules and action photos.

URL http://nbaon.nbc.com

NBA.com

The official site for the National Basketball Association.

URL http://www.nba.com

On Hoops

Outspoken commentary on the NBA.

URL http://www.onhoops.com

Prep Stars Recruiter's Handbook

Provides scouting reports on America's top high school prospects.

URL http://www.bballrecruit.com/
prepstars

BIOLOGY

Biodiversity and Biological Collections

This Web server has links and a search tool to help you find information on biological specimens.

URL http://muse.bio.cornell.edu

Biologist's Control Panel

This site contains a large collection of biological databases, search tools and other information of interest to biologists.

URL http://gc.bcm.tmc.edu:8088/bio

CELLS alive!

This highly graphical site, complete with a flapping cell, has interesting tidbits of information on cells.

URL http://www.comet.chv.va.us/quill

Course/Tutorial on Cell Biology

Here is a great place to study various aspects of cellular biology.

URL http://lenti.med.umn.edu/~mwd/cell_www/cell.html

Developmental Studies Hybridoma Bank (DSHB)

The DSHB was established to supply researchers with antibodies that are useful for studies in developmental and cell biology.

URL http://www.gdb.org/Dan/DSHB/dshb.intro.html

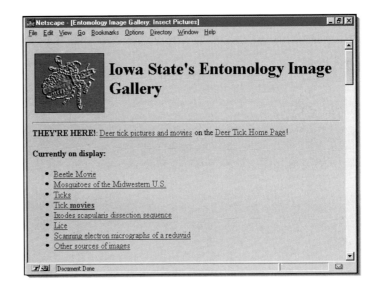

Entomology Image Gallery: Insect Pictures

Pictures and movies of insects: ticks, mosquitoes, beetles, lice and more.

URL http://www.ent.iastate.edu/imagegallery.html

Our biology sites are alive with excitement.

Integrated Microscopy Resource (IMR)

Descriptions of the different kinds of microscopes available for use by research scientists.

URL http://www.bocklabs.wisc.edu/imr/imr.html

Kids Web—Biology and Life Sciences

This site provides general information on biology and life sciences.

URL http://www.npac.syr.edu/textbook/kidsweb/biology.html

Malaria Database

An important resource for scientists studying tropical diseases.

URL http://www.wehi.edu.au/biology/malaria/who.html

B

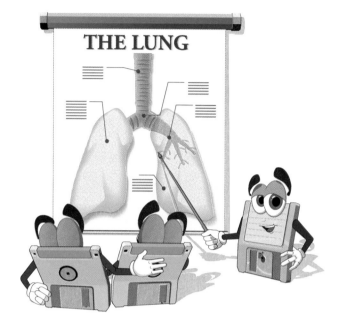

Microbial Underground

Microbiology, molecular biology, medical information and an online course in medical bacteriology.

URL http://www.qmw.ac.uk/~rhbm001

Monarch Watch

This site, dedicated to the conservation of the Monarch butterfly, will teach you about its biology and how to raise Monarchs at home!

URL http://monarch.bio.ukans.edu

MuscleNet

This colorful Italian site deals with muscle biology and neuromuscular disorders.

URL http://www.bio.unipd.it/~telethon/index.html

Neurosciences on the Internet

A searchable index of neuroscience Web resources and original neuroscience material.

URL http://ivory.lm.com/~nab

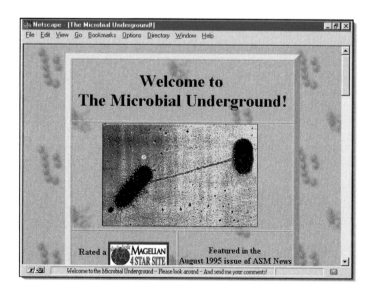

Pharmaceutical Information Network

If you want information on prescription drugs or on pharmacies in general, look here.

URL http://pharminfo.com

Virtual Frog Dissection Kit

No mess, no smell, no death—virtual frog dissection!

URL http://www-itg.lbl.gov/vfrog

Yuckiest Site on the Internet

Satisfy your intense curiosity about cockroaches at this Web site.

URL http://www.nj.com/yucky

BIZARRE

50 Greatest Conspiracies of All Time

Read excerpts from this fascinating conspiracy book. Big Brother really *is* watching.

URL http://www.conspire.com

Addicted2: Stuff

Celebrating people's unusual pastimes and strange obsessions with material objects.

URL http://www.morestuff.com

Airsickness Bags

Pictures and information on this person's extensive collection of international airsickness bags.

URL http://www.pvv.unit.no/~bct/spypose

Amazing Magic 8 Bob, Ph.D.

Ask Wise Bob a question and he will give you an answer to your problem.

URL http://inp.cie.rpi.edu/cgi-bin/bob

Amazing Rubberband Ball

A ball made entirely of rubberbands that were donated, found or stolen.

URL http://www.easttexas.com/pdlg/theball.htm

Bathroom Wall

A place to write down your thoughts without actually being a vandal.

URL http://www.photografius.com/bathroom.html

Beard Research

In the interest of science, this fellow shaved off half his beard one winter to see if facial hair actually helped keep his face warm.

URL http://mudhead.uottawa.ca/~pete/beard.html

Bill Gates Personal Wealth Clock

Find out just how rich the owner of Microsoft really is.

URL http://www.webho.com/WealthClock

Brent's Useless Time Script 2

You can find out how many seconds are left in this year, the correct time in Edmonton, Canada, the number of seconds since you were born and other not-so-interesting facts.

URL http://www.law.ualberta.ca/brent/time2.html

B

Capt. James T. Kirk Sing-a-long Page

You can listen to, and sing along with, William Shatner as he sings such classics as *Mr. Tambourine Man* and *Lucy in the Sky with Diamonds*.

URL http://www.ama.caltech.edu/users/mrm/kirk.html

Celebrities Barefoot

If you have a foot fetish, check out this photo collection of barefoot famous people.

URL http://www.tensornet.com/~thrasher/Celebs

Center for the Easily Amused

These hard-working experts have created the Ultimate Guide to Wasting Time.

URL http://www.amused.com

Chia Pet Zoo

A humorous, photographic tribute to Chia Pets.

URL http://www.accessone.com/~jonathin

Bring some fun into your life with our bizarre sites.

Church of the SubGenius

Let Bob guide you down the true path of Slack.

URL http://sunsite.unc.edu/subgenius

Confession Booth

A virtual confession booth with an easy-to-fill-out sins form.

URL http://anther.learning.cs.cmu.edu/priest.html

Contortion Home Page

A page dedicated to some very flexible individuals.

URL http://www.escape.com/~silverbk/contortion

Corpses for Sale

View a ghastly gallery of life-like models of decaying human corpses and then order one for home delivery!

URL http://distefano.com

Cyrano Server

Fill out the form and Cyrano will compose a love letter for you.

URL http://www.nando.net/toys/cyrano.html

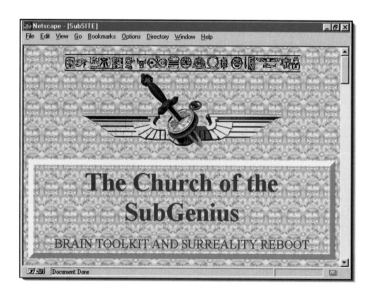

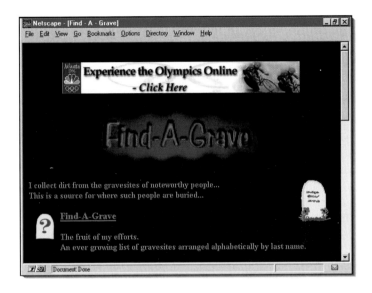

Death Clock

Enter a few facts about yourself and this kind site will tell you how many seconds you have left on Earth.

URL http://www.ucs.usl.edu/~rkc7747/death.html

Eraser Art

See what one man with a little talent, too much time and an obsession with erasers can accomplish when he puts his mind to it.

URL http://www.middlebury.edu/~carruthe/my_art.shtml

EVIL Little Brother Excuse Generator

Need a really good excuse? This site will provide you with one.

URL http://www.dtd.com/excuse

Feeble Gourmet

The incredibly detailed lunch log of a government employee.

URL http://nosferatu.nas.nasa.gov/~rat/gourmet

Find-A-Grave

This guy collects dirt from the gravesites of noteworthy people and will guide you to some of their final resting places.

URL http://www.orci.com/personal/jim/index.html

Hairy Human Home Page

One man's obsession with his body hair and the many facts and research he has collected on the subject.

URL http://www.luna.co.uk/~charles

Interactive Ego Booster

This site tries to help people feel upbeat and sure of themselves.

URL http://web.syr.edu/~ablampac/ego/index.html

B

BIZARRE *continued*

iPizza

This electronic pizza kitchen will prepare a bizarre pizza, perhaps topped with ants and light bulbs, and deliver it to a friend by e-mail for free.

URL http://www.internetuniv.com/pizza/ipizza.htm

Land O' Useless Facts

Get a daily dose of useless trivia or browse through the extensive archives of useless facts.

URL http://www-leland.stanford.edu/~jenkg/useless.html

MeatMation

Some very strange art constructed entirely out of meat.

URL http://www.cais.net/frisch/meatmation

Mirsky's Worst of the Web

This man has dedicated his life to finding the worst sites on the Web and guiding you to them.

URL http://mirsky.com/wow

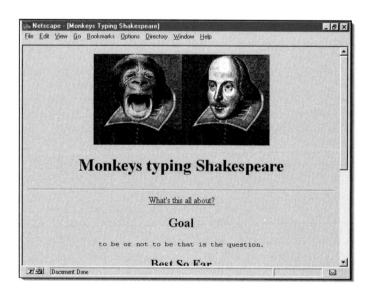

Monkeys Typing Shakespeare

See if this virtual monkey can actually manage to type "to be or not to be that is the question."

URL http://bronte.cs.utas.edu.au/monkey

Museum of Bad Art

This site is a celebration of bad art in all its forms.

URL http://glyphs.com/moba

Paranoia Home Page

This page is dedicated to promoting freedom of thought on the Internet.

URL http://www.paranoia.com

Piercing Mildred

Before you get that nose ring, it may be a good idea to practice your body piercing skills here.

URL http://streams.com/pierce

Plastic Princess Page

Everything you ever wanted to know about collecting plastic dolls, such as Barbie, including price guides and a listing of doll shows.

URL http://d.armory.com/~zenugirl/barbie.html

Really Big Button That Doesn't Do Anything

This site contains a button that does absolutely nothing when pressed.

URL http://www.wam.umd.edu/~twoflowr/button.htm

Roadkills-R-Us

Looking for a really good recipe for roadkill tacos? This site has one for you.

URL http://www.rru.com

Rude Things in My Fridge

Every month this bachelor invites you into his fridge to see decaying and rotting food.

URL http://www.wbm.ca/users/kgreggai/html/fridge.html

SCHWA

Learn how to survive an alien invasion, purchase alien protection and warning devices and read about the movement that might save your life.

URL http://fringeware.com/SchwaRoot/Schwa.html

Our bizarre sites will take you into another dimension.

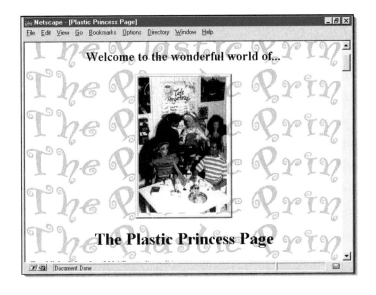

Welcome to the wonderful world of...

The Plastic Princess Page

Shrine to Toast

A celebration of the wonders of toast.

URL http://www.teleport.com/~cramsay/shrine.html

Strange Case of the Lost Elvis Diaries

Read a new chapter every week in this wildly comic tale of a reporter's search for Elvis Presley's legendary lost diaries.

URL http://home.mem.net/~welk/elvisdiaries.html

Strange Stories

Learn about the doomsday machine, read an anonymous letter about the Roswell UFO crash or browse through the collection of odd facts.

URL http://www.csn.net/~stephenl/strange.htm

Strawberry Pop-Tart Blow-Torches

How to turn a breakfast food into an industrial tool.

URL http://www.cbi.tamucc.edu/~pmichaud/
toast

Talk to My Cat

Type in what you want to say and the computer in this man's home will actually say it to his cat.

URL http://queer.slip.cs.cmu.edu/cgi-bin/
talktocat

Todd's Gallery of Pathetic Human Regret

Share in one guilt-ridden young man's life.

URL http://www.eden.com/~tfast/
regret1.html

Top Tips

The place to go if you want silly tips on doing just about anything.

URL http://www.emtex.com/toptips

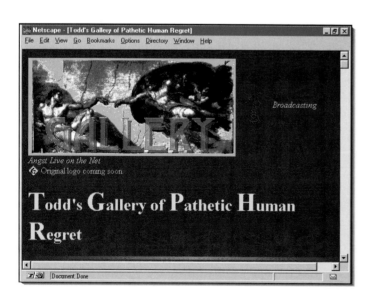

Tres Bizarre

A daily trip through some of the stranger sites on the Web.

URL http://ucunix.san.uc.edu/%7Esolkode/
tres_bizar

UFO Folklore

Tales, facts and common misconceptions about the strange things that go on in our skies.

URL http://www.qtm.net/~geibdan

Ugly Page Maison

Easily one of the ugliest and most annoying pages on the Web.

URL http://www.ai.univ-paris8.fr/~apb/
home.html

Underground Net

If it is bizarre, unusual or just plain out-of-this-world, you will probably find it here.

URL http://bazaar.com

Useless WWW Pages

Your travel guide to the most useless and weird sites on the Web.

URL http://www.chaco.com/useless

Virtual Kissing Booth

Pucker up and get in line for some cyber-smooching.

URL http://www.whitehawk.com/vkb

Vomitus Maximus Museum

Some very disturbing art awaits you here if you have the stomach for it.

URL http://www1.primenet.com/vomitus

Wall O' Shame

True stories reflecting the decay of civilization.

URL http://www.milk.com/wall-o-shame

Yuckiest Site on the Internet

Join a worm and a cockroach on a journey into their worlds.

URL http://www.nj.com/yucky

Netscape - [Virtual Kissing Booth]
File Edit View Go Bookmarks Options Directory Window Help

Virtual Kissing Booth

Hawaiian Summer Edition!

Movies... Movies... **The HAMMER** **Entertainment Center**
And even more MOVIES!!! (Click Here!)

Welcome to the Hawaiian Summer edition of the Virtual Kissing Booth! In this issue, Kelli shows off her hot summer looks, along with a few outfits she picked up on a recent trip to Hawaii. There is also a surprise **mystery smoocher** lurking in the shadows. If you're persistent, maybe you'll find out who it is.

Document: Done

BOARD GAMES

Game Cabinet

A monthly magazine that includes a collection of game rules and strategies.

URL http://www.gamecabinet.com

GNU WebChess

This award-winning online game provides varying skill levels from beginner to expert.

URL http://www.delorie.com/game-room/chess

Kasparov vs. Deep Blue

Details on the chess match between the world's top human chess player and the world's top computer.

URL http://www.chess.ibm.park.org

B

BOARD GAMES *continued*

Monopoly

Spend some time at this Web site dedicated to the famous board game.

URL http://www.monopoly.com

United States Chess Federation

The Web site for the governing body of chess in the United States.

URL http://www.websong.com/uscf

WebBattleship

Sink your opponent's ships before your opponent sinks yours.

URL http://info.gte.com/gtel/fun/battle/ battle.html

World Wide Web Ouija

Close your eyes, put your hand on the mouse and let the Ouija board answer your questions.

URL http://www.math.unh.edu/~black/cgi-bin/ ouija.cgi

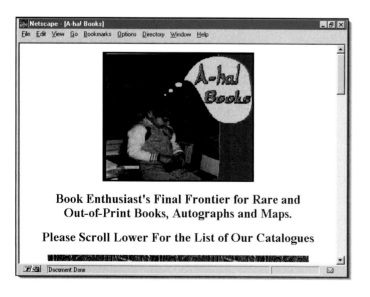

BOOKS

ABC Bücherdienst

Search and order from a list of more than one million titles from Germany, the U.S., Spain and the Netherlands.

URL http://www.telebuch.de/us/index.htm

A-ha! Books

Order from a daily updated catalog of rare and out-of-print books.

URL http://www.lightlink.com/tokman

Amazon.com Books

Order from a catalog of more than one million titles.

URL http://www.amazon.com

Audiobook Source

More than 5,000 books on tape! Choose a bestseller or browse through the sale bin.

URL http://www.audiobooksource.com/ absource

BookWeb

Find links to bookstores around the world and information on books, authors and the book industry.

URL http://www.ambook.org

Cookbook Store

Since 1983, this store has been providing the best selection of food and wine books. Order a featured book or check out the links.

URL http://www.cook-book.com

Crazy Books

An online source for underground books on subjects from debts and drugs to dumpster diving.

URL http://www.crazybooks.com

Fodor's

Planning a vacation? Check out this online catalog from one of the premier publishers of travel guides.

URL http://www.fodors.com

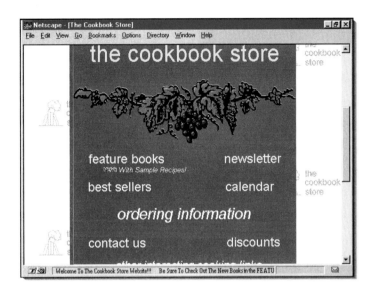

IDG Books Online

Explore hundreds of books from the knowledge publisher—including the bestselling Simplified™, Teach Yourself Visually and ...For Dummies® series.

URL http://www.idgbooks.com

maranGraphics

Learn about the world's most user-friendly computer books at this site. Then find out how to order your own copies.

URL http://www.maran.com

Nautical Mind

Books, software and videos for naval buffs.

URL http://www.nauticalmind.com

Pandora's Books

Look to this site for thousands of out-of-print science fiction, fantasy, horror and mystery books.

URL http://portal.mbnet.mb.ca/
pandora

B

BOOKS *continued*

Penguin U.S.A.
This well-known publisher has something for everyone.

URL http://www.penguin.com

Virtual Book Shop
Search the catalog of rare and collectible books from around the world.

URL http://www.virtual.bookshop.com

BOTANY

Australian National Botanic Gardens
Explore the amazing plant life of Australia.

URL http://www.anbg.gov.au/anbg/index.html

Base Angiosperm Listing
A list of the flowering plants, with images and information on each family.

URL http://www.isc.tamu.edu/
FLORA/cronang.htm

Plant yourself in front of our botany sites.

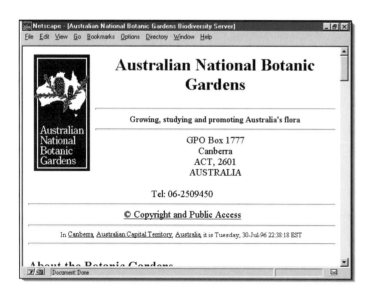

British Trees
Interesting information on the native trees of Great Britain.

URL http://www.u-net.com/trees

Burpee
Since 1876, Burpee has been providing seeds by mail. Now you can request a catalog and place an order via the Internet.

URL http://garden.burpee.com

Carnivorous Plant Database
Search the handy database or view the slide shows on the many plants that eat insects.

URL http://www.hpl.hp.com/bot/cp_home

Coyote Creek
Herbs, flowers, shrubs, vines and trees that you can order online for shipment throughout the United States.

URL http://www.tyrell.net/~dreid

Garden Store

Online ordering of bulbs, shrubs, perennials, wildflowers and more.

URL http://www.gardenstore.com

Gourmet Gardener

An online catalog of herbs, vegetables and edible flowers as well as books and gifts for gardeners.

URL http://metroux.metrobbs.com/tgg/catalog.htm

InterUrban WaterFarms

If you are thinking of hydroponic gardening, look here for information and supplies.

URL http://www.viasub.net/IUWF/3.html

kinderGARDEN

This site is especially for children who want to explore the world of gardening.

URL http://aggie-horticulture.tamu.edu/kinder/index.html

Lawn Genie

Irrigation products for your lawn or garden. The free design service helps you plan the right sprinkler system.

URL http://www.lawngenie.com

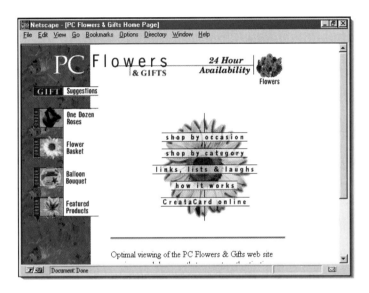

National Agricultural Library Image Database Project

This library is a database of pictures and information on plants, plant pests and plant diseases.

URL http://promenade.lis.pitt.edu

Orchid House

If you want to grow the exotic orchid, this is the site to see.

URL http://sciserv2.uwaterloo.ca/orchids.html

PC Flowers & Gifts

Order flowers, plants, teddy bears and other gifts for all occasions. Flower delivery available for the United States, Canada and more than 150 other countries.

URL http://www.pcflowers.com

B

BOTANY *continued*

Plant & Insect Parasitic Nematodes

An aid for the identification and research of these tiny, parasitic worms.

URL http://ianrwww.unl.edu/ianr/plntpath/nematode/wormhome.html

Redwood City Seed Company

Seeds for endangered vegetables, specialty plants and peppers, including the "World's Hottest Pepper."

URL http://www.batnet.com/rwc-seed

Rhododendron Page

Paradise for flower lovers.

URL http://haven.ios.com/~mckenzie/rhodo05.html

SBE's Exotic Tropical Plant Seed Catalog

Hundreds of unusual seeds from all over the world, plus a universal seedbank.

URL http://www.datasync.com/sbe/Welcome.html

Select Seeds Antique Flowers

A selection of antique flower varieties, including a sweet pea first bred in 1884. Copy the catalog onto your computer or order a printed copy through the mail.

URL http://trine.com/GardenNet/SelectSeeds

Time Life Gardening Library

A wonderful resource where you can search the Time Life Electronic Encyclopedia for pictures and plant-growing instructions.

URL http://pathfinder.com/vg/TimeLife

BOXING/MARTIAL ARTS/ BODYBUILDING

American Center for Chinese Studies (ACCS)

This non-profit organization is dedicated to the development of mind, body and spirit.

URL http://www.kungfu.org

CyberDojo

An outstanding resource providing information for the karate community.

URL http://www.ryu.com/CyberDojo

Gracie U.S.A. Jiu-Jitsu Home Page

Find out all about the Gracie style of Jiu-Jitsu created by Brazilian Carlos Gracie.

URL http://www.gracie.com

International Judo Federation

Looking for the latest news on the Olympic Games and other international Judo competitions? This site will satisfy your curiosity.

URL http://www.ijf.org

MuscleNet—The Virtual Gym

Bodybuilders can come here to post messages, find out about upcoming contests or link to tons of other bodybuilding sites.

URL http://www.musclenet.com

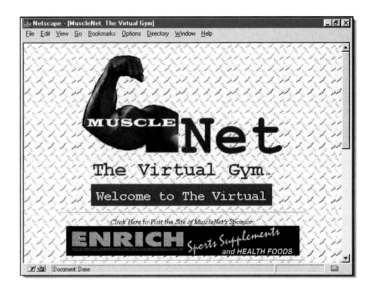

Survey of Black Belt Costs and Benefits

An online survey of the costs and benefits of gaining a black belt at various schools, both American and international.

URL http://cswww2.essex.ac.uk/Web/karate/misc/black-belt.html

Sweet Science

Here you can catch Phrank Da Slugger's commentary on recent boxing news, read an article from the *Boxing Times* or check the guide to U.S. televised fights.

URL http://www.sweetscience.com

Tae Kwon Do Reporter

Enthusiasts will find coverage of competitive Tae Kwon Do as well as informative reports and training tips.

URL http://www.tenerten.com/tkdrpt

Top Rank Boxing

View video clips from fights, read about upcoming fights and discuss boxing with others in the Fan Forum.

URL http://www.toprank.com

C

CAMPING

Campground Directory

A state-by-state listing of American campgrounds, with links to camp sites in Canada and the U.K.

URL http://www.holipub.com/camping/director.htm

Campground Online

This online magazine has a wealth of resources for RVers and campers, including a campground directory with pictures and descriptions.

URL http://www.channel1.com/users/brosius

Camping Checklist

A handy list of everything you need to pack for a camping trip.

URL http://www.billboard.com/Mike_Smith/Crisis_Kits/Camping_list

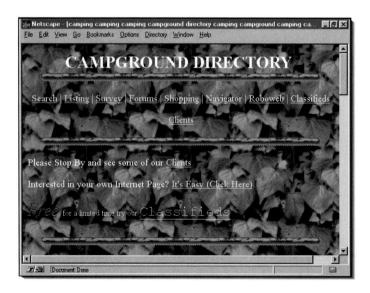

Camping Frequently Asked Questions

Ask a question about camping or read through other people's questions and answers.

URL http://www.jwa.com/CAMPING/FAQS/faqs.html

CampSoft

This handy software helps you manage your camp or conference center.

URL http://www.ints.com/campsoft.html

Jesse Brown's Outdoors

You can order camping gear from the online outpost of this well-known North Carolina outdoor equipment store.

URL http://www.jessebrown.com/store.html

KOA

The home page of Kampgrounds of America has information about camp locations and things to do.

URL http://www.koakampgrounds.com

Modem-Friendly Campgrounds

Want to check your e-mail while on holiday? This site lists campgrounds that encourage computer use and have phone lines available.

URL http://web2.nafe.com/roads/camping/roads_phones.html

ParkNet

The online presence of the National Park Service features information about the national parks of America, including park history, geography, nature and preservation.

URL http://www.nps.gov

Roads to Adventure

A terrific site that lets travelers use the Internet as a tool for researching their next adventures.

URL http://www.tl.com

Wrolin Camping 'Round The World

An alphabetically indexed list of links for international campgrounds.

URL http://www.wrolin.com/campindx.htm

 CARDS

Bridge Companion

Want to improve your bridge-playing skills? This site offers informative articles and exercises to help.

URL http://www.phoenix.net/~tbc

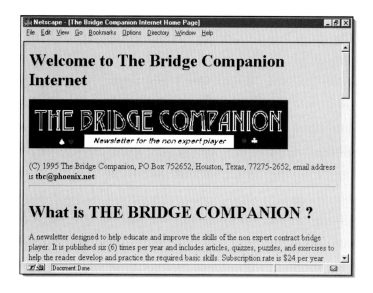

Welcome to The Bridge Companion Internet

THE BRIDGE COMPANION
Newsletter for the non expert player

(C) 1995 The Bridge Companion, PO Box 752652, Houston, Texas, 77275-2652, email address is **tbc@phoenix.net**

What is THE BRIDGE COMPANION ?

A newsletter designed to help educate and improve the skills of the non expert contract bridge player. It is published six (6) times per year and includes articles, quizzes, puzzles, and exercises to help the reader develop and practice the required basic skills. Subscription rate is $24 per year

Card Games

A huge collection of rules for card games from around the world.

URL http://www.cs.man.ac.uk/card-games

Collectible Card Games

Everything you ever wanted to know about collectible trading card games—and more!

URL http://www.itis.com/other-games

Discount Games

This large collectible card game distributor has an interesting site on the Web. Check out new releases or order your favorite games online.

URL http://www.discountgames.com/ great_hall.html

DOS Card Games

This collection of popular computer card games is for DOS users.

URL http://webspace.com/pub/wvoyager/ cardsd.htm

Our card sites will deal out loads of fun.

Macintosh Card Games

A collection of more than 50 card games for Macintosh computers.

URL http://www.gamesdomain.co.uk/
directd/macgames/card/card.html

Playing-Cards Frequently Asked Questions

This collection of information on playing-cards will interest collectors, researchers and game players alike.

URL http://www.cs.man.ac.uk/
playing-cards/faq.html

Pretty Good Solitaire

A software package of 60 single-player card games for Windows.

URL http://users.aol.com/GoodSol/
pgs.html

Turn of a Friendly Card

Visit this online store for all of your collectible card game needs.

URL http://www.netwalk.com/~turn

Windows Card Games

Find many popular card games for Windows.

URL http://softsite.com/win3/gam/
cardex.htm

ZByte High Tech Playing Cards

ZByte playing-cards are the cards of the future! Learn how to play your favorite games with these cards.

URL http://www.insist.com:80/zbyte/
indexo.shtml

CATALOGS & MAIL ORDER

Ballard Designs

Browse through the online catalog of home furnishings, decorative accessories and gifts.

URL http://www.ballard-designs.com

Catalog Mart

The easiest and fastest way to get just about any catalog available in the U.S. Choose from more than 10,000—all free!

URL http://catalog.savvy.com

Netscape - [Pretty Good Solitaire]

File Edit View Go Bookmarks Options Directory Window Help

Pretty Good Solitaire

Shareware Solitaire for Windows 3.1 and 95
by Tom Warfield

The Solitaire Wizard — Click here to create your own solitaire games!

Document: Done

Catalog Orders Headquarters

You can order catalogs from a variety of specialty categories, such as weddings, Christmas cards and office supplies.

URL http://Catalog.Orders.com/co/index.html

Catalog Site

At this site you can order catalogs from more than 100 companies that sell everything from auto accessories to workout equipment.

URL http://www.catalogsite.com

Fingerhut Online

Fingerhut offers a wide variety of products including jewelry, electronics, clothing and much more.

URL http://www.fingerhut.com

Gift Catalogs

Don't fret over finding the perfect gift for someone who has everything! These catalogs will give you some great ideas!

URL http://www.giftcatalog.com

These catalog and mail order sites deliver hours of entertainment.

Hammacher Schlemmer

This company, started in 1848, was the first to sell steam irons and electric shavers. Visit this site and see what is new these days.

URL http://www2.pcy.mci.net/marketplace/hamshlem

Lands' End

Need some help picking out an outfit? This site features a Shopping Advisor you can e-mail for help.

URL http://www.landsend.com

L.L. Bean

Sporting gear and apparel for those who love the outdoors.

URL http://www.llbean.com

Mall of Catalogs

Get on the mailing lists of more than 1,600 mail order catalog companies.

URL http://www.csn.net/marketeers/mallofcatalogs

Nasco

Choose from numerous catalogs in categories such as educational teaching aids, farm supplies and laboratory sampling equipment.

URL http://www.nascofa.com

Sharper Image Catalog

A company offering unusual and creative gifts.

URL http://www.sharperimage.com

Shop at Home

Search by name, keyword or category for a catalog of interest.

URL http://www.shopathome.com

Spiegel

Check out this extensive inventory of home accessories, electronics, fashion and kids products.

URL http://www.spiegel.com/spiegel

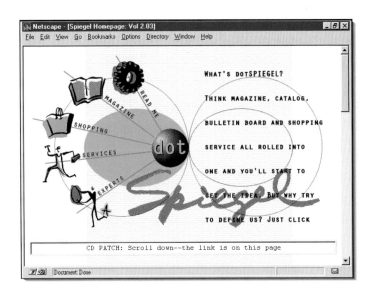

Tilley Endurables

It all started with a hat, but this company now sells a huge selection of travel and adventure clothing to customers around the world.

URL http://www.exportcanada.com/ cheetah/tilley/til-home.html

Wild Man Crowley

Clothing and footwear from companies including Woolrich, Columbia, Danner and Rockport. Order online or by phone.

URL http://www.wmcrowley.com

CELEBRITIES

Audrey Hepburn

This amazing woman and her achievements, both on and off the screen, are presented through links, quotations and images.

URL http://mypage.direct.ca/j/jechen/ index.html

Celebrities & Attractions Magazine

A large list of celebrities, cast lists from T.V. shows and more.

URL http://www.infomagic.com/~hlr/ celebs/magazine/index.html

Celebrity Chronicle

Read about brushes with famous people or submit your own account of a close encounter of the celebrity kind.

URL http://www.polaris.net/~merlin/fame.html

Celebs on the Web

This site contains an ever-expanding list of celebrities' personal home pages and e-mail addresses. Drop your favorites a line!

URL http://home.earthlink.net/~grumpus/celebs1.html

Chat Soup

Chat with celebrities online or just check up on the tastiest tidbits from past conversations.

URL http://www.chatsoup.com

Clint Eastwood

Go ahead, make his day! Check out photographs, audio clips, a biography and more.

URL http://www.pyramid.net/eastwood

De Niro Museum

A tribute to one of the most talented actors of our time, Robert De Niro.

URL http://www.cs.bc.edu/~kawashim/deniro.html

Dead Celebrities

A tribute to celebrities who died after 1969 and before their time, including such greats as John Candy and Kurt Cobain.

URL http://www.directnet.com/~mgemme

Demi Moore

A large collection of images of this very photogenic actress.

URL http://www.diskriter.com/demi

Gillian Anderson Home Page

Many articles, interviews, sound recordings and pictures of Gillian Anderson, along with links to other X-Files sites.

URL http://gpu3.srv.ualberta.ca/~mlwalter/GAHP.html

Harrison Ford

Articles, images and sound clips relating to the star of some of the most successful films of all time.

URL http://www.smartlink.net/~deej7/ harrison_ford.html

Heather Locklear Internet Fan Club

A popular Web site for this star's fans.

URL http://www.locklearweb.com

James Dean

This site features many pictures and insights into the life of James Dean.

URL http://www.jdean.com

Marilyn Monroe

Take a virtual tour through this legend's life, complete with pictures and links to memorabilia resources.

URL http://www.ionet.net/~jellenc/ marilyn.html

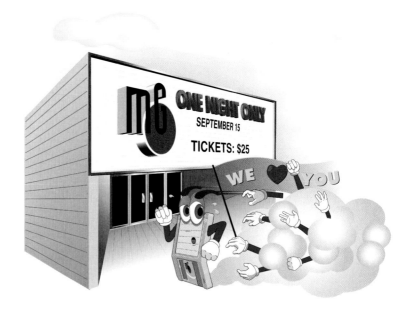

Plastic People

Before and after shots of celebrities who have undergone plastic surgery.

URL http://199.232.114.17/People/~loux/ plastic.htm

Sandra Bullock

More than 600 pictures of this popular actress, as well as interviews, video clips and more.

URL http://www.matrix.de/sandra-bullock

Supermodel.com

Lots of information and many pictures of the world's top fashion models.

URL http://www.supermodel.com

Tom Cruise

Everything you ever wanted to know about the star of *Mission Impossible* and *Top Gun*.

URL http://www.cyberhighway.net/~phlacin/ cruise.html

Winona Ryder

Articles, facts, current news, sound and video clips along with more than 500 pictures of the actress.

URL http://www.qp.com/winona

CHAT

AlphaWorld

To become a citizen of this chat site, just visit the immigration office.

URL http://www.worlds.net/alphaworld

Globe Chat

A popular and established Web chat site.

URL http://www.theglobe.com/theglobe/
onlinechat

iChat

This program makes it easy to access Internet chat systems.

URL http://www.ichat.com/client.html

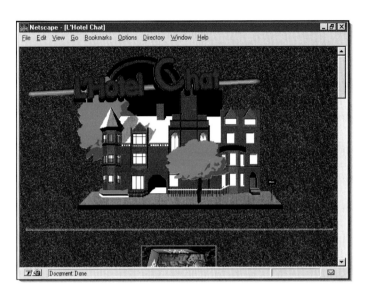

You will want to spread the word about our chat sites.

Internet TeleCafe

Billing itself as the Internet's largest social chat environment, the TeleCafe features an easy-to-use interface.

URL http://www.telecafe.com/telecafe

L'Hotel Chat

Multiroom chatting set in a five-star hotel on the coast of Monaco.

URL http://chat.magmacom.com/lhotel/
hotel.html

mIRC

A fully featured Internet Relay Chat program for Windows.

URL http://www-2.nijenrode.nl/
software/mirc

The Palace

A multifaceted chat center from Time Warner—participate in dozens of virtual discussions around the Web or create your own online social environment.

URL http://www.thepalace.com

Tribal Voice

This site offers PowWow, a unique Windows program that allows up to seven people to chat, transfer files and cruise the Web as a group.

URL http://www.tribal.com/powwow

WebChat

This Web chat program lets you easily incorporate images, video clips, audio clips and links into your chat.

URL http://www.irsociety.com/webchat.html

WebChat Broadcasting System (WBS)

A large and very active Web chat server—join discussions on just about any topic imaginable.

URL http://www.irsociety.com

Worlds

A 3-D graphical chat environment with sound effects and background music!

URL http://www.worlds.net

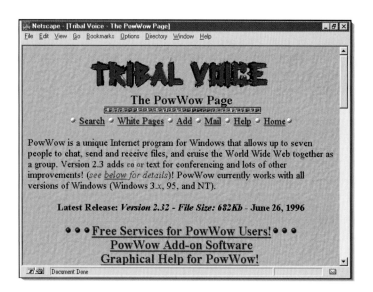

You'll get a reaction out of our chemistry sites.

CHEMISTRY

American Chemical Society (ACSWeb)

Information about the society, articles from chemical journals, a software catalog, membership application and more.

URL http://www.acs.org

Animations

This chemistry site contains pictures, slide shows, movies and 3-D presentations of molecules and chemical structures.

URL http://www.pc.chemie.th-darmstadt.de/molcad/movie.html

Atlas of Side-Chain and Main-Chain Hydrogen Bonding

The Atlas displays information on various aspects of hydrogen bonding in proteins.

URL http://www.biochem.ucl.ac.uk/~mcdonald/atlas

Microworlds

An interactive science tour covering the Advanced Light Source, bullet-proof polymers and more.

URL http://www.lbl.gov/MicroWorlds/MicroWorlds.html

Periodic Table of the Elements

Click on an element in the Periodic Table to get information about that element.

URL http://mwanal.lanl.gov/CST/imagemap/ periodic/periodic.html

Stanford Linear Accelerator Center (SLAC)

Points of interest about the linear accelerator at Stanford University are provided for both the general public and more scientific users.

URL http://www-slac.slac.stanford.edu

Undergraduate Organic Chemistry Laboratory Experiments

This site contains examples of the kinds of chemistry experiments done by students at the university level.

URL http://www.dartmouth.edu/academia/ chem/chemexp

Wilson Group

This chemistry research site will help you visualize molecules.

URL http://www-wilson.ucsd.edu

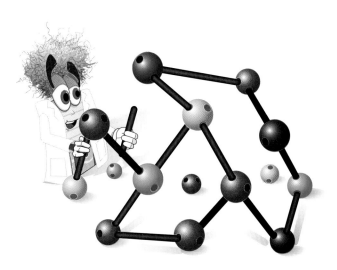

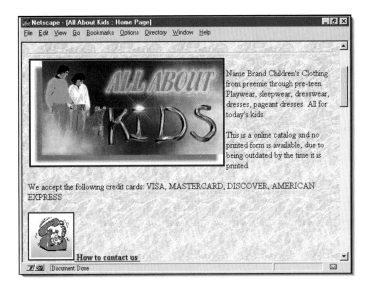

CLOTHING

Airwalk

If you board, bike or just thrash through life, this is the footwear and site for you.

URL http://www.airwalk.com

All About Kids

Clothes and accessories for children from babies to pre-teenagers.

URL http://allaboutkids.com

Angel of Fashion

Follow the links to what are considered to be the Web's best fashion sites.

URL http://www.wp.com/SST/angel.html

Armani Exchange

A look at Giorgio Armani's more relaxed clothing.

URL http://www.armaniexchange.com

Benetton

Benetton is known for its controversial ads. Visit this hip, colorful site to find out more.

URL http://www.benetton.com

Birkenstock Express

An online catalog with more than 30 styles of Birkenstock shoes and sandals.

URL http://www.footwise.com/ur

College Outfitters Online

Clothes, accessories, books and more for the student in all of us.

URL http://www.inet.thequad.com/co/
home.html

Cosmopolitan

For now, the Italian version of Cosmo is the only one on the Internet, but some discussions are in English.

URL http://www1.internetforce.com/
cosmopolitan/maggio/english.html

Costume Page

Costume events, tailoring, organizations and art links make this site an excellent resource for those interested in costumes.

URL http://members.aol.com/nebula5/costume.html

Cowboy Trail

Howdy partner! Looking for authentic western clothing? You've found the site, so sit a spell and surf a bit.

URL http://www.cowboytrail.com

Culture Zone

Fashion is more than just clothes...it's an attitude! Explore alternative fashion culture here.

URL http://www.culturezone.com/current

CyberSwell Pleasure Center

Hip fashions and the ever-cool Hush Puppies shoes.

URL http://www.cyberswell.com/dummy.html

Designers Direct

Fashions from Guess, Calvin Klein and Levi's are available online.

URL http://www.DesignersDirect.com

Digital Fashions

Sexy lingerie, swimsuits and hosiery for women as well as underwear for men—all available for order online.

URL http://www.dti-tech.com

Fashion Internet

A stylish online magazine that lets you see what will be in next season and gives you the scoop on the fashion industry.

URL http://www.finy.com/toc.html

Fashion Page

All the latest fashion news, tips and interviews with industry personalities can be found on the pages of this electronic magazine.

URL http://www.charm.net/~jakec

Fashion.Net

Whether you are looking for fashion industry connections or just fashion, style and beauty resources, this is the site for you.

URL http://www.fashion.net

Filson Quality Outdoor Clothing

This company specializes in outdoor clothing and has been in business for over 98 years. If you like the outdoors, you'll love this site.

URL http://www.halcyon.com/ool/filson/clothing.html

Fruit of the Loom

Underwear on the Internet—what will they think of next?

URL http://www.fruit.com

Genius T-Shirts

Unique shirts featuring great men and women throughout history. Choose from Einstein, Beethoven, Emily Dickinson and more.

URL http://www.a1.com/shirt/t-shirt.html

Georges Marciano

An online catalog of men's and women's fashions along with a virtual tour of the store on Rodeo Drive.

URL http://GeorgesMarciano.com

Green For Jeans

Buyers and sellers of used Levi's. More than 20,000 pairs are bought and sold each month.

URL http://www.green4jeans.com

Guess

Go behind the scenes at a Guess photo-shoot or send a digital postcard to a friend.

URL http://www.guess.com

Hypermode

Virtual reality, hip articles and professional photography will please the fashion fanatic.

URL http://www.hypermode.com

Our clothing sites are dressed for success.

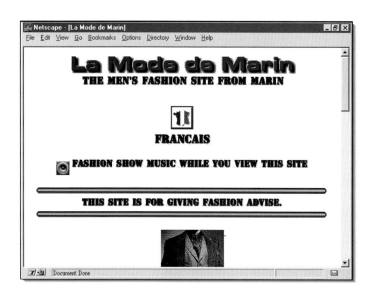

Indian Motorcycle

One of the most popular lines of clothing today.

URL http://www.indian.on.ca

JCPenney

Take a peek at what one of America's largest department store chains has to offer.

URL http://www.jcpenney.com

Joe Boxer

Enter the Joe Boxer carnival of goodies for men, women, boys and girls and get yourself some virtual clean undies online.

URL http://www.joeboxer.com

La Mode de Marin

Clothes make the man, so go ahead guys, pick up some fashion tips from this site!

URL http://acs5.gac.peachnet.edu/~jmeyer/index4.html

Levi's

Comfy, cotton and very cool. Visit this jeans manufacturer's hip site to check out the Denim Dictionary or try the history quiz.

URL http://www.levi.com

Lumière

Makeup experts, fashion tips, feature articles and fashion photography, with some nifty tricks that will make your computer screen come to life.

URL http://www.lumiere.com

Net.Wear Apparel

An online catalog of T-shirts and baseball caps to wear as you surf the Internet.

URL http://www.netwear.inter.net

Nicole Miller

Dresses, ties and scarves. Search for a Nicole Miller store near you.

URL http://www.nicolemiller.com

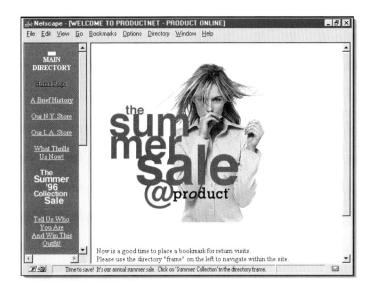

Prison Blues

After more than 100 years of making their own clothes, prisoners in Oregon are now making denim clothing for people outside the prison walls.

URL http://www.big-house.com

Product

A delightfully simple line of clothing for women.

URL http://www.productnet.com

Shirt and Tie Museum

Spice up your wardrobe with a novelty tie! This fabulous collection features ties with just about everything, from Elvis to a mackerel.

URL http://www.shirtandtie.com

Starter

The popular manufacturer of sports clothes is now on the Web.

URL http://www.starter.com

CLOTHING *continued*

The Look Online

This site features runway photos, articles, a list of New York fashion events and more.

URL http://www.lookonline.com

Vogue

Clothes for women can be found at this site.

URL http://www.shopinvogue.com

Wool

See this season's color, fabric and styling directions for men and women.

URL http://www.woolmark.com

COMICS

Al Gore's Cartoon Gallery

A collection of the U.S. vice-president's favorite political cartoons about his public life.

URL http://www.whitehouse.gov/WH/EOP/ OVP/html/Cartoon.html

Comic Strip

A great site to find your favorite comics, such as *Alley Oop*, *Peanuts*, *Dilbert* and *The Born Loser*.

URL http://www.unitedmedia.com/comics

Comics du Jour

Check out new comics every day.

URL http://internet-plaza.net/zone/comics

ComicsWorld

This site offers everything for comic book enthusiasts and collectors, from news releases and interviews to contests and more.

URL http://www.comicsworld.com/cw/index.html

Dark Horse Comics

Preview some comics online or find out what is happening in the comics industry.

URL http://www.dhorse.com

DC Comics

Check out a new comic, listen to an original Superman radio broadcast and much more.

URL http://www.dccomics.com

Far Side Daily

This site provides a different *Far Side* comic each day.

URL http://www.ausweb.com.au/FarSide

FDR Cartoon Archive

This huge collection of political cartoons created during the presidency of Franklin D. Roosevelt is both educational and fun.

URL http://www.wizvax.net/nisk_hs/ departments/social/fdr_html/ FDRmain.html

Fitzban's Guide to DC Comics

News and links to information on the DC universe, including heroes such as Batman, Supergirl and Green Lantern.

URL http://expert.cc.purdue.edu/~fizban/ dc/dc.html

Marvel Comics

Learn about the past and future of this comic book giant or check out links to other sites.

URL http://garnet.berkeley.edu/~net-dq/ project.html

Personal Hotlist

Create your own funny pages by selecting which comic strips you want to read each day.

URL http://www.uta.fi/yhteydet/personalhl.html

Super Marketing

Remember Sea Monkeys? How about Stretch Armstrong? This site's collection of comic book ads is sure to entertain and amuse you!

URL http://www.steveconley.com/ supermarketing.htm

The Inkwell

Check out some of the best editorial cartoonists in the U.S.

URL http://www.unitedmedia.com/inkwell

Virtual Comics

Take a peek at these interactive comics, complete with multimedia effects.

URL http://www.virtualcomics.com

C

Crack the Safe

Play any of the games of skill and knowledge offered at this site for loads of fun.

URL http://www.sunsetdirect.com/contest/index.html

Cyberpet's Writers Contest

This site invites kindergarten to grade 9 students to enter a writing contest and win up to $400.

URL http://www.cyberpet.com/cyberdog/happeng/contstw.htm

Jolly Joker Free For All Treasure Hunt

Ahoy matey! Climb aboard to solve the mystery of the Jolly Roger!

URL http://jollyroger.com/free.html

Our contest sites are sure to win your approval.

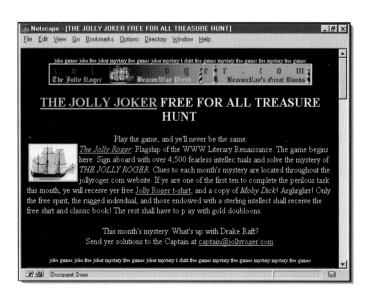

PrizeLINK

Learn how you can win up to $1 million instantly, just for answering questions and surfing the Web.

URL http://prizes.com/prizelink

Riddler.Com

One of the best places on the Web for free contests, trivia and prizes.

URL http://www.riddler.com

sandbox.net

Compete with players worldwide for the chance to win cool prizes in these intriguing, interactive adventure games.

URL http://www.cyberhunt.com

SETI Asimov Memorial Limerick Contest

This limerick contest is held in honor of Isaac Asimov, the great sci-fi writer and avid limericist!

URL http://www.setileague.org/awards/limerick.htm

SEXTANT Cyberspace Odyssey

This site offers an exciting new mission every day.

URL http://www.boldlygo.com

ThreadTreader's WWW Contests Guide

A great resource for contest enthusiasts, complete with lists of raffles, sweepstakes and more!

URL http://www.4cyte.com/ThreadTreader

WORLDVILLAGE CONTEST PAGE

Several games and contests with opportunities to win great software prizes.

URL http://www.worldvillage.com/wv/ contests.htm

WWW Contests

Information and links to many contests and sweepstakes on the Web.

URL http://www.umr.edu/~rchaplin/ contest.html

Yoyodyne

Play some cool games and maybe you'll win some great prizes, like a T-shirt or even a trip to the Caribbean.

URL http://www.yoyo.com

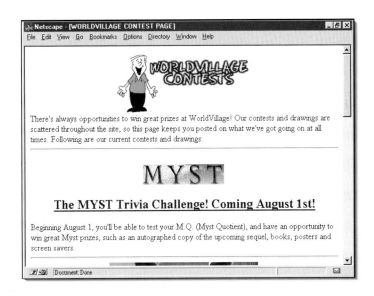

CYCLING

Bicycle Commuting Page

A page full of tips for people making the move to bicycle commuting.

URL http://www.spies.com/~ceej/Facts/ Distractions/bikes.html

Bicycle Helmet Safety Institute

A non-profit, consumer-funded institute that serves as a technical resource for bicycle helmet information.

URL http://www.bhsi.org

Bicycles Frequently Asked Questions

Answers to frequently asked questions posted to a cycling newsgroup.

URL http://www.cis.ohiostate.edu/hypertext/ faq/usenet/bicycles-faq/top.html

Bicycling Community Page

A great collection of bicycling resources.

URL http://danenet.wicip.org/bcp

Bicycling Hall of Fame

Read about the history of cycling, browse through the photo gallery and find out who belongs to the Hall of Fame.

URL http://www.nj.com/bike/hof/induct.hof.html

Bike Trails

An online magazine for bicycle enthusiasts. Check out the lists of trails or read about a bike club near you.

URL http://community.net/~necknox/home.html

Cyber Cyclery

A comprehensive resource for bicycling, covering news, racing events, products, shops, associations and more.

URL http://cyclery.com

Cyberider Cycling

This site is devoted to all aspects of cycling and includes links to other cycling sites.

URL http://blueridge.infomkt.ibm.com/bikes

Mountain Bike Resources Online

A site dedicated to getting you out of the house and into the mountains.

URL http://www.mbronline.com

VeloNet

An electronic information desk for cyclists.

URL http://cycling.org

VeloNews Interactive

A well-designed site covering everything about the world of bicycle racing.

URL http://www.velonews.com/VeloNews

DANCE

BalletWeb

Many pictures of dancers along with an Electric Ballerina that uses computer animation to illustrate basic ballet steps.

URL http://users.aol.com/balletweb/
balletweb.html

Belly Dance

Learn more about this ancient dance style.

URL http://cie-2.uoregon.edu/bdance

CHAINS

A celebration and exploration of West African music and dance.

URL http://found.cs.nyu.edu/andruid/
CHAINS.html

CyberDance—Ballet on the Net

A great source for links to ballet and modern dance information on the Internet.

URL http://www.thepoint.net/
~raw/dance.htm

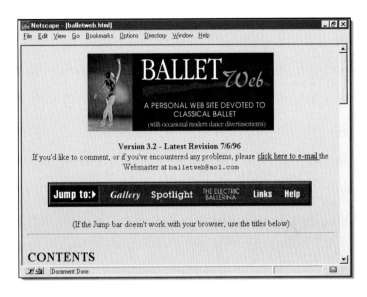

DancePages Directory

Listings of choreographers, companies and dancers worldwide.

URL http://emporium.turnpike.net/~dpd/
index.htm

Dancescape

Your guide to the world of competitive ballroom dancing.

URL http://wchat.on.ca/dance/pages/
dscape1.htm

Waltz through our dance sites.

Dancing on a Line

An excellent online magazine with feature articles, photo galleries and reviews of the international dance scene.

URL http://www.danceonline.com

Dictionary of Common Ballet Terms

Learn all about pliés, arabesques and pirouettes here.

URL http://www.bway.net/~dajoncs/
ballet/pbt/language

D

DANCE *continued*

Ernesto's Tango Page

Put a rose between your teeth before you visit this site.

URL http://www.ims.uni-stuttgart.de/
phonetik/ernst/tango/ebtango.html

Information Super Dance Floor

A great resource for those who want to learn the latest country music dance step.

URL http://www.apci.net/~drdeyne

National Ballet of Canada

Canada's premier ballet company.

URL http://www.ffa.ucalgary.ca/nbc/
nbc_main.html

Square and Round Dance Page

Interested in square or round dancing? This site will tell you which clubs to visit and much more.

URL http://pages.prodigy.com/sq.dance

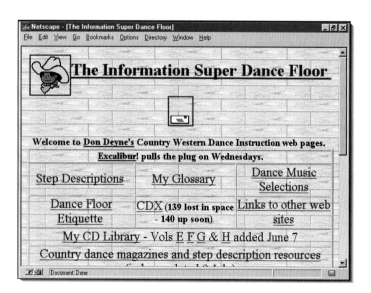

DEPARTMENT STORES

Dillard's Online!

Find great gift ideas, a complete wedding planning guide and dozens of recipes from the employees.

URL http://www.azstarnet.com/dillards

Federated Department Stores, Inc.

Find out what is hot in more than 400 stores, including Macy's, Bloomingdale's and The Bon Marché.

URL http://www.federated-fds.com

Fred Meyer

A fun and witty site from this Portland-based chain, where the concept of one-stop-shopping began.

URL http://www.fredmeyer.com

JCPenney

Find the JCPenney store nearest you or order from the online catalog.

URL http://www.jcpenney.com

Kmart

Browse through the latest circular from the store that has more than 2,000 locations across America.

URL http://www.kmart.com

L.L. Bean

Check out products and services offered by this sporting gear and apparel company.

URL http://www.llbean.com

Mercantile Stores Company, Inc.

Use the free personal shopping service, available in more than 100 U.S. stores.

URL http://www.mercstores.com

Neiman Marcus

Get the latest news from the fashion world or find out what is happening at Neiman Marcus this month.

URL http://www.neimanmarcus.com

PNA: Us Against The Wal

Read about Gig Harbor's battle to keep Wal-Mart out of the small town.

URL http://www.harbornet.com/pna

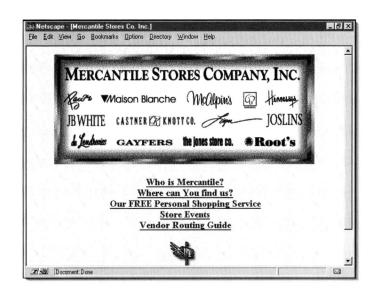

Price Costco

Find a location near you or browse through the mail order catalog.

URL http://www.pricecostco.com

Wal-Mart

Locate a store near you or check out the specials in this month's circular.

URL http://www.wal-mart.com

DISASTERS

Chernobyl and its Consequences

Read a document about the Chernobyl accident at this site.

URL http://polyn.net.kiae.su/polyn/manifest.html

Browse through our department store sites.

D

Emergency

A guide to emergency services and organizations that are available worldwide.

URL http://www.catt.citri.edu.au/ emergency/emergency.html

Federal Emergency Management Agency

The goal of this agency is to help you prepare for and cope with a natural disaster.

URL http://www.fema.gov

Geographical Survey Institute

Information on recent Japanese earthquakes and major disasters.

URL http://www.gsi-mc.go.jp

Internet Disaster Information Network

Up-to-date information on current disasters as well as information on disasters of the past.

URL http://www.disaster.net

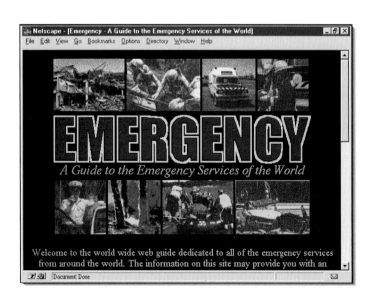

Los Angeles City Fire Department

Practical information on preventing fires and what to do in case of a fire.

URL http://www.ci.la.ca.us/department/ LAFD/index.html

Provincial Emergency Program

Another site to help you prepare, respond and recover from a natural disaster.

URL http://hoshi.cic.sfu.ca/~pep

TheEpicenter.com

Get information on how to prepare for an emergency such as a tornado, hurricane, flood or earthquake.

URL http://nwlink.com/epicenter

DRINKS

800 Spirits Corporate Gift Catalog

Order wines, liquors and other goodies online for delivery around the world.

URL http://owl.net:80/OWLspace/spirits

Bert Grant's World Famous Ales

Find out about a brewery that uses a batch of yeast that is more than 40 years old.

URL http://www.grants.com

Budweiser Online

Become an honorary beermaster or order cool Budweiser merchandise.

URL http://budweiser.com

Coca-Cola

Refresh yourself by visiting the entertaining site from this soft drink maker.

URL http://www.cocacola.com

Coopers Brewery Home Page

Find out about these fine Australian beers from a family-owned brewery in operation since 1862.

URL http://www.halcyon.com/conbev/coopers.htm

Finlandia Vodka

Menus and recipes that use this distinctive Finnish vodka.

URL http://www.lpg.fi/finlandia

Great American Beer Club

Join the club and get American microbrewed beers delivered to your door each month.

URL http://www.greatclubs.com/beerclub.html

Guinness Brewing

Visit this brewery in Dublin or check out The Local, an online pub.

URL http://www.guinness.ie

Jack Daniel's

Learn the story of the oldest registered distillery in the United States, wander through Lynchburg Square or grab the free screen saver.

URL http://www.infi.net/jackdaniels

DE

DRINKS *continued*

Jose Cuervo Tequila

Check out the history of tequila or pick up some Cuervo recipes.

URL http://www.cuervo.com

Liqueurs Online

Order fine wines, liqueurs and sake.

URL http://www.gpkg.com/liqueurs

Los Olivos Wine and Spirits Emporium

Order anything from seven-year-old sour mash bourbon to pear brandy.

URL http://www.sbwines.com

Molson Canadian I Am Online

Find out what it takes to make one of North America's favorite beers.

URL http://www.molson.com/canadian

Park Avenue Wine & Liquor Shop

Order superb French Bordeaux and Burgundies online.

URL http://www.intac.com/~avalon/wine.html

Pepsi

Hang around Pepsi World and win fabulous prizes!

URL http://www.pepsi.com

Perrier

Browse through the art gallery, read restaurant reviews or order Perrier merchandise.

URL http://www.perrier.com

Real Beer Page

Take a tour of some of the best microbreweries in the world.

URL http://realbeer.com

Republic of Tea

Order a wide variety of teas online and learn how to make a cup of tea correctly.

URL http://eMall.Com/Republic/Tea.html

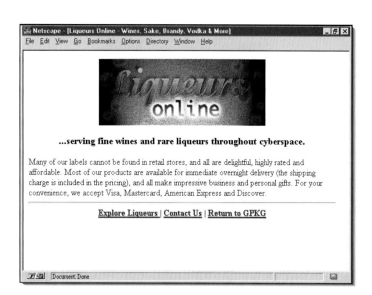

Rogue Ales—Oregon Brewing Company

Visit the site of this Oregon microbrewery specializing in ales to find out what makes its products special.

URL http://RealBeer.com/rogue

Sam's Wine Warehouse

Order wine or single malt scotch online.

URL http://www.sams-wine.com

Snapple

Enter the SnappleSphere and find out why Snapple wants to be number three. You can also check out the contests and special offers.

URL http://www.snapple.com

Stoli Central

Learn about spirits from around the world, create and name your own vodka cocktail and more.

URL http://www.stoli.com

Refresh yourself with our drink sites.

Zima

Check out the well-stocked fridge for a host of "cold links."

URL http://www.zima.com/index.html

EARTH SCIENCES

Byrd Polar Research Center

Look here for information on polar environments and polar research.

URL http://www-bprc.mps.ohio-state.edu

Global Hydrology and Climate Center

Find out about global studies on the role of water and water vapor in world climates.

URL http://wwwghcc.msfc.nasa.gov

E

GLOBE Visualizations

Provides global climatic data on temperature, cloud cover, precipitation and more.

URL http://globe.gsfc.nasa.gov/globe

Great Lakes Information Management Resource

This site is an information resource on the environment of the Great Lakes Region.

URL http://www.cciw.ca/glimr/

Hydrology-Related Internet Resources

Read the hydrology primer or find out about water-related sciences.

URL http://etd.pnl.gov:2080/hydroweb.html

International Data Center

The IDC will be involved in international monitoring for compliance with nuclear test ban agreements.

URL http://www.cdidc.org:65120

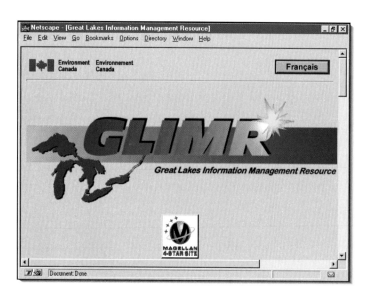

JASON Project

A great place for students and teachers to participate in an electronic field trip and discover their environment.

URL http://seawifs.gsfc.nasa.gov/
scripts/JASON.html

Kids Web—Geology and Earth Sciences

Earthquake information, ocean floor research, volcano images and more can be found at this site.

URL http://www.npac.syr.edu/textbook/
kidsweb/geology.html

NSF Geosciences Integrated Earth Information Server

For a global vision of the earth sciences and instructional materials for teachers, visit this National Science Foundation site.

URL http://atm.geo.nsf.gov

Southern California Earthquake Center

An archive and distribution center of seismological data. Check out the cool SeismoCam.

URL http://scec.gps.caltech.edu

Southern California Earthquake Center @ UCLA

This center does research on crustal deformation, crustal structure and fault behavior and motion.

URL http://scec.ess.ucla.edu

Texas WaterNet

This research facility deals with questions of water quality, wetlands management, agricultural waste treatment, pollution and more.

URL http://twri.tamu.edu

Ultimate Field Trip

Great photographs of the Earth from space with explanations and comments by NASA astronaut Kathryn D. Sullivan.

URL http://ersaf.jsc.nasa.gov/uft/uft1.html

University of Chicago Shock Wave Lab

Click on sections of the blueprint of the Shock Wave Lab to find out how the shock wave gun works.

URL http://geoleo.uchicago.edu/Lab

Welcome to the University of Chicago Shock Wave Lab

Here's a picture the shock wave lab. You are looking at the University of Chicago 80 mm

DEF

Virtual Antarctica

Take a virtual tour of Antarctica!

URL http://www.terraquest.com/antarctica

VolcanoWorld

A great site to explore volcanoes.

URL http://volcano.und.nodak.edu/vw.html

EDUCATION

AcademicNet

A great resource for educators interested in using multimedia technology for higher education.

URL http://www.academic.com

Academy One

One of the best sources of educational resources on the Web.

URL http://www.nptn.org:80/cyber.serv/AOneP/academy_one/menu.html

129

E

EDUCATION *continued*

Check out these classy education sites.

Adult Distance Education Internet Surf Shack

Links and information for continuing your education or getting that diploma online.

URL http://www.helix.net/~jmtaylor/ edsurf.html

AskERIC

This award-winning site offers information on education and maintains an online library of lesson plans for teachers.

URL http://ericir.syr.edu

Berklee College of Music

Get full information about the world's largest independent music college.

URL http://www.berklee.edu

Canada's SchoolNet

Find a wealth of resources and opportunities to work online with teachers and students from around the world.

URL http://schoolnet2.carleton.ca

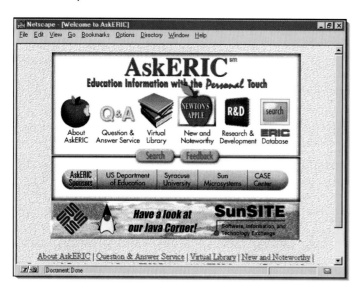

City University of New York

This university is made up of 21 post-secondary institutions and enrolls more than 200,000 students each year.

URL http://www.cuny.edu

Classroom Connect

An excellent resource for K12 educators to access information, including an online Teacher Contact Database.

URL http://www.classroom.net

College Board Online

Get the test question of the day from the creators of the SAT and prepare yourself for a college education.

URL http://www.collegeboard.org

CollegeNET

Search for information on colleges and universities or check out available financial aid.

URL http://www.collegenet.com

Cornell University

Tour the campus and get information about undergraduate, graduate and professional programs.

URL http://www.cornell.edu

EdWeb

This site about educational reform and information technology was named one of the 50 Best Places to Go Online by *NetGuide Magazine*.

URL http://k12.cnidr.org:90

Evergreen State College

Information about everything this Washington State college has to offer, from admissions to recreation.

URL http://www.evergreen.edu

FastWEB

A guide to finding university and college scholarships.

URL http://www.studentservices.com/fastweb

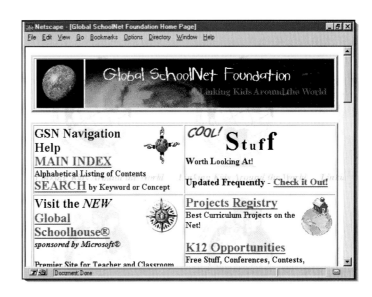

FinAid: The Financial Aid Information Page

This site tells you where and how to get financial aid and how to avoid scams.

URL http://www.cs.cmu.edu/afs/cs.cmu.edu/user/mkant/Public/FinAid/finaid.html

Foreign Language Resources on the Web

A great collection of resources for people interested in other languages and cultures.

URL http://www.itp.berkeley.edu/~thorne/HumanResources.html

Georgetown University

Check out admissions and programs at the main campus or the schools of law and medicine.

URL http://www.georgetown.edu

Global SchoolNet Foundation

This site is dedicated to bringing students from around the world together for a variety of exciting projects.

URL http://www.gsn.org

EDUCATION *continued*

Harvard University

Review the course catalog online, see a map of the campus and learn about this Ivy League school.

URL http://www.harvard.edu

Hawaii Pacific University

Get a warm welcome from the president of this university known for its marine science program.

URL http://www.hpu.edu

Kaplan: Get a Higher Score

Prepare for college admission tests and practice a job interview.

URL http://www.kaplan.com/index.html

KidLink

This project, aimed at involving children ages 10 to 15 in a global dialog, has brought together more than 60,000 kids from 85 countries.

URL http://www.kidlink.org

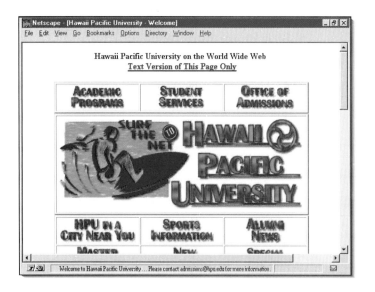

Kidopedia

An encyclopedia written by kids from all over the world.

URL http://rdz.stjohns.edu/kidopedia

Kids' Space

This outstanding site lets kids from around the world share their art, writing and music with each other.

URL http://plaza.interport.net/kids_space

New School for Social Research

This school offers distance learning for adults around the world. Complete your BA without leaving your keyboard.

URL http://www.dialnsa.edu

New York University

Find information on admissions, financial aid and campus facilities at this Greenwich Village-based university.

URL http://www.nyu.edu

Peterson's Education Center

This fantastic site offers information about educational opportunities at all levels.

URL http://www.petersons.com

Princeton Review

Get help preparing for the SAT, LSAT, GMAT and other tests.

URL http://www.review.com

Queen's College, University of Oxford

Find out all about the programs and academic life at this 600-year-old college in England.

URL http://info.ox.ac.uk/~queesys

Quest

The home for NASA's "Internet in the Classroom" project offers support and services for schools and teachers.

URL http://quest.arc.nasa.gov/index.html

Stanford University

Find information on admissions and programs at this 100-year-old school located in the foothills of San Francisco. As well, you can take an impressive picture tour of Stanford.

URL http://www.stanford.edu

Summerhill School

Information on this "free school," founded in 1921 by A.S. Neill.

URL http://ourworld.compuserve.com/homepages/summerhill

Teacher's Edition Online

This site offers many resources for educators, including lesson plans, tips on classroom management and job opportunities.

URL http://www.teachnet.com

DEF

E

EDUCATION *continued*

Teachers Helping Teachers

Share your teaching tips and ideas with others or get some new ideas from teachers around the world.

URL http://www.pacificnet.net/
~mandel/index.html

Teaching and Learning on the Web

Search this large collection of sites that focus on technology in education.

URL http://www.mcli.dist.maricopa.edu/
tl/index.html

TESTPREP.COM

A complete SAT test preparation course with more than 700 practice problems.

URL http://www.testprep.com

Touro College Law Center

Find the top 10 reasons to apply to Touro and information about academic and summer programs.

URL http://www.tourolaw.edu

Study our education sites.

University of California, Berkeley

Online information on undergraduate and graduate admissions, campus information, a schedule of classes and more.

URL http://www.berkeley.edu

University of Illinois at Urbana-Champaign

Find out about courses offered, the campus, the community and more.

URL http://www.uiuc.edu

University of Texas at Austin

Check out the admission, registration and housing information, or look over the student organizations and personal Web pages.

URL http://www.utexas.edu

Vanderbilt University

Get an online look at academic and student life at this Nashville-based university, established in 1875.

URL http://www.vanderbilt.edu

Virtual Online University

This site is dedicated to providing distance education on the Internet, from kindergarten to university level.

URL http://www.athena.edu

Yale University

Find out about programs and campus life at Yale.

URL http://www.yale.edu

ENERGY

Energy Efficiency and Renewable Energy Network

The United States Department of Energy provides an abundance of information on renewable energy and energy-efficient technologies.

URL http://www.eren.doe.gov

Fusion Energy Education Site

A place for the whole family to learn about nuclear fusion and plasma physics, with a Fusion Museum, a slide show and more.

URL http://FusEdWeb.pppl.gov

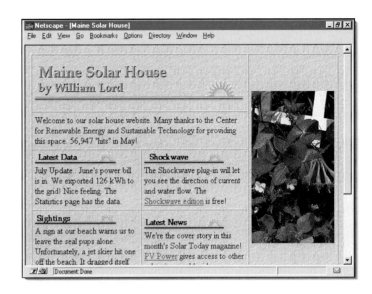

Netscape - [Maine Solar House]

File Edit View Go Bookmarks Options Directory Window Help

Maine Solar House
by William Lord

Welcome to our solar house website. Many thanks to the Center for Renewable Energy and Sustainable Technology for providing this space. 56,947 "hits" in May!

Latest Data
July Update.. June's power bill is in. We exported 126 kWh to the grid! Nice feeling. The Statistics page has the data.

Shockwave
The Shockwave plug-in will let you see the direction of current and water flow. The Shockwave edition is free!

Sightings
A sign at our beach warns us to leave the seal pups alone. Unfortunately, a jet skier hit one off the beach. It dragged itself

Latest News
We're the cover story in this month's Solar Today magazine! PV Power gives access to other

Document: Done

Maine Solar House

Anecdotal descriptions of building, owning and maintaining a solar-powered home.

URL http://solstice.crest.org/renewables/wlord/index.html

National Energy Research Supercomputer Center

NERSC provides high-performance computing and networking services to the energy research community across the United States.

URL http://www.nersc.gov

Office of Scientific and Technical Information

Access to scientific and technical information available from the U.S. Department of Energy.

URL http://apollo.osti.gov/html/osti/ostipg.html

Online Renewable Energy Education Module

A multimedia education tutorial on renewable energy including solar, geothermal, hydro, wind and biomass energy.

URL http://solstice.crest.org/renewables/re-kiosk/index.shtml

E

ENGINEERING

AEC InfoCenter

An information center for the architectural, engineering and construction industries.

URL http://www.aecinfo.com

Audio Web Home Page

A resource page for audio engineers and enthusiasts, including articles from the world's leading audio publications.

URL http://www.audioweb.com

Bluestone

Bluestone is involved in advanced development technology for computer applications.

URL http://www.bluestone.com

Marshall Space Flight Center

This NASA center uses engineers to fulfill its mission of developing and maintaining space transportation and propulsion systems.

URL http://www.msfc.nasa.gov

U.S.–Japan Technology Management Center

Click on the map at this site for information on Japanese technology and engineering.

URL http://fuji.stanford.edu

ENTERTAINMENT

Biz: Entertainment CyberNetwork

Entertainment news updates every hour, exclusive multimedia interviews and more.

URL http://www.bizmag.com

clickT.V.

This interactive entertainment magazine helps you get the most out of your T.V. time.

URL http://www.clickTV.com

CNN Showbiz News

Find out what's new in Hollywood or check out the latest home video and video game releases.

URL http://www.cnn.com/SHOWBIZ/index.html

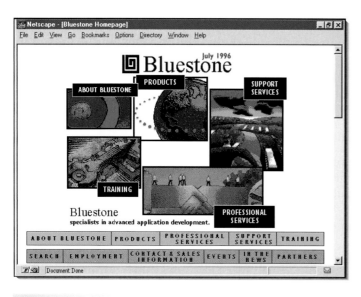

Crash Site

This entertaining site contains lots of weird and wonderful stuff.

URL http://www.crashsite.com/Crash

Entertainment Weekly

Articles about the top names in the business as well as reviews of the latest movies.

URL http://pathfinder.com/ew

Fix

An electronic magazine covering the music, movie and food scenes.

URL http://www.boston.com/thefix

Gigaplex

This online magazine dedicated to arts and entertainment is full of great pictures and video.

URL http://www.gigaplex.com

Globe

A fantastic entertainment site with live chats, games, surveys and much more!

URL http://www.theglobe.com

Hollywood Online

Great news, video clips of upcoming films and sound recordings of interviews with your favorite stars.

URL http://www.hollywood.com

Jam!

Complete entertainment coverage with a Canadian twist.

URL http://www.canoe.ca/Jam

Movienet

Find local show times listed by city as well as previews of movies coming soon to a theater near you.

URL http://www.movienet.com

E

You will sing the praises of our entertainment sites.

Mr. Showbiz

A very informative and interesting look at the world of entertainment.

URL http://www.mrshowbiz.com

People Magazine

Find out more about your favorite celebrities and get the latest entertainment news.

URL http://pathfinder.com/people

SALON

The magazine where politics and entertainment meet.

URL http://www.salon1999.com

t@p online

A hip look at entertainment, culture, sports and technology.

URL http://www.taponline.com

TV Guide Online

The classic guide to television is online.

URL http://www.iguide.com/tv

T.V. Net

T.V. listings from around the world, links to your favorite shows and more for the true couch potato.

URL http://tvnet.com

T.V.1

This site lets you customize T.V. listings to display only shows that interest you.

URL http://www.tv1.com

USA Today Life

Entertainment news and reviews from one of America's leading newspapers.

URL http://www.usatoday.com/life/lfront.htm

Vibe Online

This weekly entertainment and culture magazine covers fashion, movies, music and more.

URL http://www.vibe.com

ENVIRONMENT

40 Tips to Go Green

A list of practical things you can do at home, on the road, while shopping and at work to help save the environment.

URL http://www.ncb.gov.sg/jkj/env/greentips.html

African Bird Club

A club dedicated to the protection and preservation of African birds.

URL http://www.netlink.co.uk/users/aw/abchome.html

Agency for Toxic Substances and Disease Registry

Check out the large amount of searchable information on toxic substances and their health risks.

URL http://atsdr1.atsdr.cdc.gov:8080

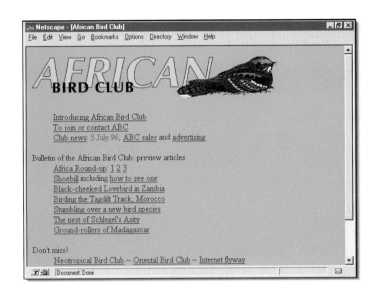

Arid Lands Newsletter

This newsletter deals with various aspects of arid lands research and management.

URL http://ag.arizona.edu/OALS/ALN/ALNHome.html

Chernobyl and its Consequences

Information on the 1986 accident at the Chernobyl Nuclear Power Plant.

URL http://polyn.net.kiae.su/polyn/manifest.html

Coyote's Way

A site for activists who want the latest news on environmental matters.

URL http://gladstone.uoregon.edu/~ambiente

EcoMall

EcoMall has information on a variety of environmental issues, including solar energy, vegetarianism, activism and more.

URL http://www.ecomall.com

E

ENVIRONMENT *continued*

EcoNet

This organization is involved in the preservation of the environment and offers resources to other groups working toward the same goal.

URL http://www.econet.apc.org/econet

EcoNet's Endangered Species Resources

EcoNet supplies United States government documents and other information about endangered species around the world.

URL http://www.econet.apc.org/endangered

EE-Link—Environmental Education on the Internet

A resource center for students and teachers involved with environmental education.

URL http://nceet.snre.umich.edu

Environmental Monitoring From Space

Find out how satellite data is used to monitor the density of green plants and determine a "Greenness Index" for Australia.

URL http://www.erin.gov.au/sat_pics/ndvi.html

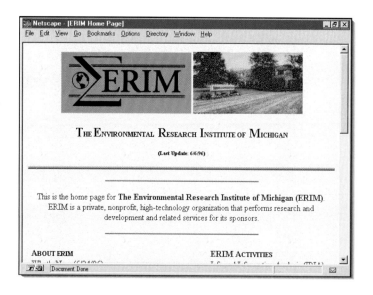

Environmental Research Institute of Michigan

This private, nonprofit institute will be of interest to scientists and researchers in the field of imaging technologies.

URL http://www.erim.org

Fabulous Kakapo

A site dedicated to the preservation of the flightless Kakapo, the world's largest and rarest parrot.

URL http://www.resort.com/~ruhue/kakapo.html

GreenWheels Electric Car Company

If you are looking for information, pictures and other resources dealing with electric cars, try this Web site.

URL http://northshore.shore.net/~kester

International Global Atmospheric Chemistry Project

Find answers to questions on the chemical composition of the atmosphere.

URL http://web.mit.edu/igac/www

John Muir Exhibit

Discover the history of this naturalist, conservationist and founder of the Sierra Club.

URL http://ice.ucdavis.edu/John_Muir

Measurement of Air Pollution from Satellites

Read a fascinating explanation of how the space shuttle and satellites can be used to measure air pollution.

URL http://stormy.larc.nasa.gov/overview.html

National Pollution Prevention Center for Higher Education

This center makes educational materials on pollution prevention available to university professors.

URL http://www.snre.umich.edu/nppc

Progressive Directory

The Institute for Global Communications (IGC) helps environmental and social movements by providing them with computer networking tools.

URL http://www.igc.apc.org/index.html

Rainforest Action Network

This beautiful site promotes the preservation of the Earth's rainforests.

URL http://www.ran.org/ran

Recycler's World

Read information relating to the recycling of paper, tires, metals and more.

URL http://www.recycle.net/recycle/index.html

Save The Earth Foundation ArtRock Auction

The proceeds from this auction of posters autographed by rock stars go to the Save the Earth Foundation.

URL http://www.commerce.com/save_earth

Science and the Environment

Topics at this site include clean air and water, recycling, health, population and agriculture, alternative energy and more.

URL http://www.cais.net/publish/stories/allstory.htm

ENVIRONMENT *continued*

Travel through our Europe sites.

Science and the Environment—Voyage Publishing

This site provides news summaries of environmental issues for high school and university teachers and students.

URL http://www.cais.net/publish

Suisun Marsh Natural History Association

This association is dedicated to preserving the Suisun Marsh and saving wildlife.

URL http://community.net/marsh

U.S. Environmental Protection Agency

A huge amount of indexed and searchable information on the EPA and its programs.

URL http://www.epa.gov

World Conservation Monitoring Center

The WCMC provides information on environmental conservation efforts worldwide.

URL http://www.wcmc.org.uk

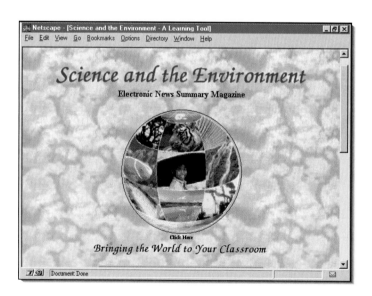

EUROPE

Belgium

Tidbits of information on Belgium, including types of Belgian beer.

URL http://www.belganet.be/~belganet

Croatia and Bosnia and Herzegovina

Learn about the people and governments of these nations.

URL http://www.xs4all.nl/~frankti/indexeng.html

Denmark

Plan a holiday in Denmark with the help of this site.

URL http://www.sima.dk/denmark

Europa Home Page

This site offers information on the European Union's goals and policies.

URL http://www.cec.lu

Geneva News and International Report

Articles from Switzerland's leading English language magazine.

URL http://w3.iprolink.ch/gnir

German Embassy, Ottawa

Germany's Embassy in Ottawa, Canada, offers information on German government, economics and tourism.

URL http://www.DocuWeb.ca/Germany

Global Russian Network

You can learn about Russian news, business and more at this site.

URL http://www.russianet.com

Greece

The Hellenic Culture home page is maintained by Greece's Ministry of Culture.

URL http://www.culture.gr

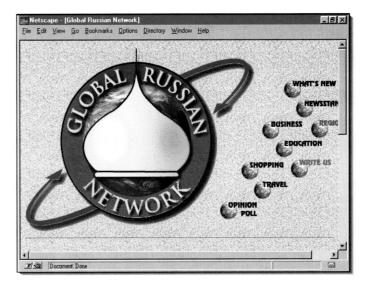

Greenland Guide

A guide to this remote island and how to have an arctic adventure you will never forget.

URL http://www.greenland-guide.dk

Iceland Connection

Discover this small near-arctic nation.

URL http://www.arctic.is

Ireland

Explore many aspects of Ireland through this site's Virtual Pub and guided tour.

URL http://www.visunet.ie

Italy

An informative home page maintained by Italy's Embassy in the United States.

URL http://www.italyemb.nw.dc.us/italy/index.html

EUROPE *continued*

Northern Ireland Government Server

At this site, you can search through government departments and read recent news about Northern Ireland.

URL http://www.nics.gov.uk

PA News Center

This informative source of news and headlines is maintained by Britain's Press Association.

URL http://www.pa.press.net

Poland

The official government Web site for the Republic of Poland.

URL http://www.urm.gov.pl

Russia Today

Take a look at what is happening in Russia today with this site's thorough coverage of Russian politics.

URL http://www.russiatoday.com

Russian and East European Studies (REESWeb)

This virtual library provides extensive links to information about Eastern Europe and Russia.

URL http://www.pitt.edu:81/~cjp/rees.html

Si, Spain

An information center for Spanish current affairs, history, culture and language.

URL http://www.DocuWeb.ca/SiSpain

United Kingdom

This site helps you locate government offices, services and officials in the United Kingdom.

URL http://www.open.gov.uk

Vatican

The official home page of the Holy See.

URL http://www.vatican.va

Virtual Finland

A complete and thorough guide to Finland and the Finnish people, covering national symbols, history, education, way of life and more.

URL http://www.vn.fi/vn/um

FISHING

All Coast Sportfishing

A magazine dedicated to our fishermen friends, with pictures, a kids' corner, information on chartering boats and more.

URL http://www.sport-fish-info.com

All Outdoors

This site provides the latest news on outdoor equipment.

URL http://www.alloutdoors.com

Anglers Online

This site offers links and information on everything from fishing gear to current fishing reports.

URL http://www.inetmkt.com/fishpage/index.html

Black Bass Foundation

This nonprofit group is trying to help preserve black bass fisheries and the sport of bass fishing in America.

URL http://www.wmi.org/blkbass

Federation of Fly Fishers

A great source of information on flyfishing clubs, conservation and more.

URL http://www.ool.com/fff

Fly Hook Comparison Chart

If you are interested in the technical aspects of fly hooks, then this is the site for you.

URL http://www.ofps.ucar.edu/~john/fish/tips/hooks.html

New Zealand Fishing

Heading to New Zealand soon? This site will help you plan your dream fishing vacation.

URL http://fishnz.co.nz

F

FISHING *continued*

Outdoors Online

An electronic magazine dedicated to outdoor sports, with emphasis on flyfishing.

URL http://www.ool.com

Rolling Your Own Sushi

If you have always wanted to learn to roll your own sushi, you have come to the right place!

URL http://www.rain.org/~hutch/sushi.html

University of Washington School of Fisheries

The University of Washington's fisheries program has links to several research projects.

URL http://www.fish.washington.edu

VFS Magazine

The first Internet journal of flyfishing features interesting articles and photography.

URL http://www.flyshop.com/VFSM

Virtual Flyshop

Check out this site for flyfishing information or plan your next flyfishing vacation.

URL http://www.flyshop.com

World of Fishing

A well-designed fishing site featuring books, videos, marine dealers, fishing news and much more.

URL http://www.fishingworld.com/Entry.html

FOOD

American Spoon Foods

Specialty food products with fruits, nuts, sauces and condiments are available by mail or from a store near you.

URL http://www.spoon.com

Anne's Favorite Recipes

Recipes from Chef Anne and the Hawthorne Lane Restaurant in San Francisco, adjusted so you can try them at home.

URL http://www.hawthornelane.com/
hawthornelane/recipes.html

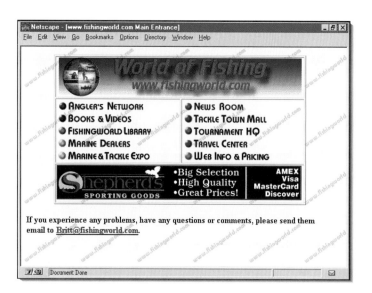

Antique Roman Dishes—Collection

Eat like a Roman emperor with these assorted recipes taken from an old Roman cookbook.

URL http://www.cs.cmu.edu/~mjw/recipes/
ethnic/historical/ant-rom-coll.html

Arabica Gourmet Coffee & Tea Club

Order quality coffee, tea and related accessories by e-mail.

URL http://www.arabica.com

Aunt Emma's Recipe World

Browse through the interesting recipes and drinks on this page, from Blow Me Down Tea to chicken salad.

URL http://web-star.com/Recipes/Recipe
Menu.html

Barbecue'n On The Internet

Everything you will need to make your next outdoor cooking experience a great one, from various barbecue cookers and techniques to recipes and photos.

URL http://www.nottingham.com/barbecue

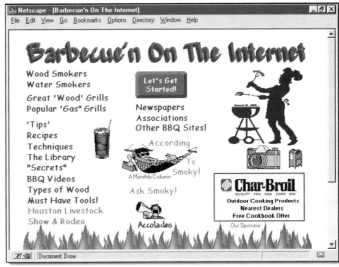

Barbecue'n On The Internet is a © copyright publication by Nottingham Internet Resources Houston, Texas 1996 All rights reserved.

Barrons Specialties—Gourmet Products

A place for lovers of wild rice. You will find wild rice facts as well as recipes and products to order.

URL http://northernnet.com/barrons

Bertrand Gourmet Store

A great selection of French food available online, from chocolates to cheeses.

URL http://www.lepanier.com

Best Food in the World

Mediterranean food is known for being both healthy and delicious. Dabble in recipes at this site.

URL http://www.phys.unsw.edu.au/~mettw/food

Cafe International

Order knives, cookware, oils and vinegars online or request a catalog from SUSCO, a leading U.S. restaurant supplier.

URL http://www.cafe-intl.com

FOOD *continued*

Campbell Soup Company

Recipes, menu planning and a whole ladle full of information on Campbell Soup brands.

URL http://www.campbellsoups.com/ Welcome1.html

Chocolatier Recipe Index

Exotic chocolate recipes are available here, complete with mouth-watering pictures.

URL http://www.godiva.com/recipes/ chocolatier/index.html

Christiane's Collection of Cooking Recipes

A group of nuclear chemists and physicists bring you this collection of great recipes.

URL http://quasar.physik.unibas.ch/~tommy/ nanni/recipes.html

Cooking with Caprial!

This chef not only has her own PBS T.V. series but also has a helpful site on the Web.

URL http://www.pacificharbor.com/pubmkt/cc

Copyright 1995 Campbell Soup Company. Campbell's is a registered trademark.

Copycat Recipes

Find recipes from KFC, the Olive Garden and Long John Silver's.

URL http://www.netins.net/showcase/ medea/copy.html

Creole and Cajun Recipe Page

Recipes and tips for cooking up the tasty cuisine New Orleans and Southern Louisiana are known for.

URL http://www.webcom.com/~gumbo/ recipe-page.html

CyberFood

Descriptive links to food and wine Web sites along with a review of computer cooking programs.

URL http://www.sjmercury.com/cybfood.htm

Deranged Spud Recipe Page

A new recipe for the humble potato every week.

URL http://www.primenet.com/ ~andspud/recipe.htm

Dinner Co-op

Find out how co-op dinners were started, check out more than 600 recipes or follow thousands of links to food-related Web pages.

URL http://gs216.sp.cs.cmu.edu/dinnercoop/home-page.html

Edibilia

A fantastic collection of links to many food and recipe sites.

URL http://www.ibmpcug.co.uk/~owls/edibilia.html

Epicurious Food

A great online magazine with a wealth of features for people who love to eat and drink.

URL http://www.epicurious.com/epicurious/home.html

FATFREE

This archive has more than 2,000 fat free and very low fat vegetarian recipes along with information on low fat diets and nutrition.

URL http://www.fatfree.com

Our food sites have good taste.

Ferris' Valley Groves

Juicy red grapefruit and lots of other goodies are available for order from this site.

URL http://www.valleygroves.com/valleygroves

Food Channel

A great starting point for food information, whether you are searching for industry trends, food fun, dining out advice or cooking help.

URL http://www.foodchannel.com

Food etc.

Every Friday this site will provide you with a new menu for next week's meals, with recipes and a grocery list to match.

URL http://www.foodetc.com

Food Lion

Read about special promotions and other events from the supermarket chain with more than 1,000 stores.

URL http://www.foodlion.com

DEF

F

FOOD *continued*

FoodNet

A great resource for information on food safety, nutrition and more.

URL http://foodnet.fic.ca

Frito Lay

Find a huge variety of chips for snack food lovers and the fabulous Dreamsite here.

URL http://www.fritolay.com

Godiva Online

Use the gift reminder service or enter the sweepstakes to win Godiva chocolates.

URL http://www.godiva.com

Handy Kitchen Tips

A funny and informative guide to what you should and should not do in the kitchen.

URL http://www.mcr.net/hotay/HKT/
HKT_Home.html

Healthy Choice

Health and fitness tips, menus, recipes and lots of news about food and health.

URL http://www.healthychoice.com

Herbs-n-Such World-Wide

Online herb shopping along with a database on herbs and herb use make this site a great resource.

URL http://www.accessnow.com/herbs/
welcome.html

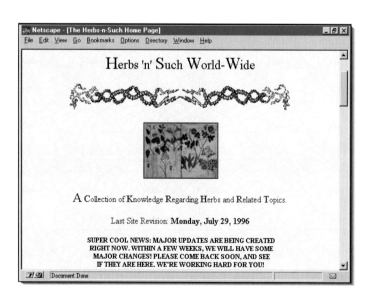

Hershey

Chocolate lovers, you have found paradise.

URL http://www.hersheys.com/~hershey

I Need My Chocolate

Chocolate information, recipes, links and more.

URL http://www.qrc.com/~sholubek/choco/start.htm

IGA

IGA shoppers around the world can enter the NetRaffle.

URL http://www.igainc.com

Insect Recipes

The recipe for Banana Worm Bread looks particularly tasty.

URL http://www.ent.iastate.edu/Misc/InsectsAsFood.html

Institute for Family Living

This organization, based in Washington, D.C., offers tips and information on how to feed your family for less.

URL http://www.radix.net/~ifl/welcome.html

™ ® *Kellogg Company © 1996 Kellogg Company*

Internet Chef

Join an online discussion of food, search for recipes or get tips and hints on preparing food and using utensils.

URL http://ichef.cycor.ca

Internet Epicurean

An online magazine with feature articles, recipe collections and a forum where you can ask questions and swap tricks of the trade.

URL http://internet.epicurean.com/latest

Kellogg's Cereal City

More fun than you will find in a box on the breakfast table!

URL http://www.kelloggs.com

Kitchen Link

This comprehensive list of Web links covers every cooking topic you can imagine.

URL http://www.frontiernet.net/~bcouch

FOOD *continued*

Kosher Express Recipes

A collection of kosher recipes focusing on Passover meals.

URL http://www.marketnet.com/mktnet/kosher/recipes.html

Kroger

Look for a store near you, search for your favorite food or try out the home shopping service.

URL http://www.foodcoop.com/kroger

Meal-Master Software & Recipes

Get more than 49,000 recipes and a free recipe-organizing program.

URL http://www.synapse.net/~gemini/mealmast.htm

Mentos

Links to the Mentos art gallery and a neat list of frequently asked questions.

URL http://www.mentos.com

Browsing through our food sites might just make you hungry.

Mimi's Cyber Kitchen

Here you will find all manner of food-related links, including recipes, cooking tips, instructions on growing your own produce and the medicinal values of some foods.

URL http://www.cyber-kitchen.com

Nabisco's Museum

Find out the history of your favorite cookies, crackers or cereals in Nabisco's Museum.

URL http://www.nabisco.com/museum

Pasta Home Page

Pasta lovers, this is your site! Find recipes, answers to popular questions and information on nutrition and pasta shapes.

URL http://www.ilovepasta.org

Pie Page

Recipes, tips and a step-by-step tutorial with pictures to help you make the perfect pie crust.

URL http://www.teleport.com/~psyched/pie/pie.html

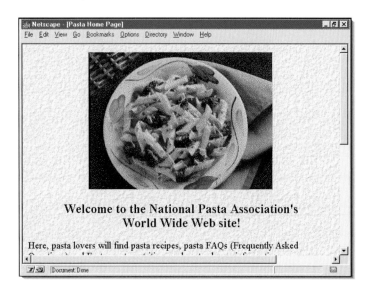

Policicchio Groves

Order grapefruit, oranges and gift baskets or join the fruit of the month club to get fresh fruit year-round.

URL http://www.vlmnet.com/groves

Ragú

This is a top-notch site with recipes, contests and guides to speaking Italian.

URL http://www.eat.com

Ready, Set, Dinner!

This free computer program offers recipes, a weekly meal planner and a grocery list generator.

URL http://www.potatoes.com

Recipe Archive Index

A large collection of recipes for almost anything you can think of: preserves, seafood, salads, candy and more.

URL http://www.cs.cmu.edu/~mjw/recipes

Recipe of the Week

A new recipe for the hungry Web surfer every week.

URL http://www.4-1-1.com/info/recipes.htm

Rolling Your Own Sushi At Home

This guide will help you prepare a variety of sushi at home.

URL http://www.netrunner.net/~pictures/sushi.html

Slikker Farms

Trying to find a gift for the person who has everything? Visit the site of this California farm to order gift baskets of fruits, nuts, syrups and more.

URL http://www.kern.com/slikker

SOAR: Searchable Online Archive of Recipes

With more than 22,000 recipes, you will be sure to find something to make for dinner.

URL http://soar.Berkeley.EDU/recipes

F

FOOD *continued*

Star Chefs

Interviews, biographies and recipes from some of the world's top chefs.

URL http://starchefs.com

Sugarplums

This culinary magazine offers gourmet recipes and tips as well as a special section on food and romance.

URL http://www.sugarplums.com

Sun-Maid

You do not need a grapevine to find the world's favorite raisin at this site.

URL http://www.sun-maid.com

Supermarket Connection

Find an online supermarket in your neighborhood and shop from home.

URL http://www.shopat.com

Tom's Recipes

Recipes for cookies, pies and dessert breads can be found here.

URL http://www-personal.umich.edu/
~brinck/recipe.html

Vegetarian Pages

News, famous vegetarians, recipes and much more.

URL http://www.veg.org/veg

Veggies Unite!

A great collection of vegetarian recipes, cooking tips, a veggie glossary and veggie events worldwide.

URL http://vegweb.com

West Side Fruitier

Exotic fruits in handmade baskets, available for delivery throughout the United States.

URL http://www.inch.com/~westside

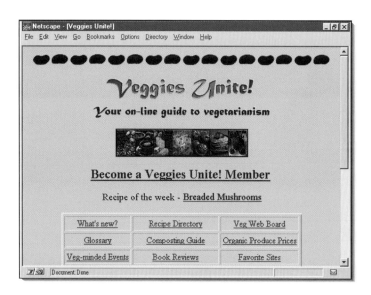

FOOTBALL

AllSports NFL News

A great source for the latest National Football League news.

URL http://www.allsports.com/cgi-bin/ sportnews.cgi?Sport=NFL

Canadian Football League

The official site of the CFL, featuring news, press releases, statistics, schedules and more.

URL http://www.cfl.ca

College Football

ESPN presents this great collection of information related to college football.

URL http://espnet.sportszone.com/ncf

Fantasy Insights

Home of the Fantasy Football League, a fun pastime for people who cannot get enough of football.

URL http://www.fantasyinsights.com

NFL Football

SportsLine U.S.A. brings you this thorough National Football League site.

URL http://www.sportsline.com/u/ football/nfl/index.html

NFL Latest News

Enjoy news items covering all aspects of the National Football League.

URL http://www.usatoday.com/sports/ football/sfn/sfn.htm

NFL Players, Inc.

This official site of the NFL players features a fan club, a trivia challenge and news about the team members.

URL http://www.nflplayers.com

NFL Stories

Daily football headlines from the FOX Broadcasting Company.

URL http://www.iguide.com/sports/ wire/sptfbpo.sml

Pro Football Expert

A software package that predicts the outcome of football games based on a large database of statistics.

URL http://www.he.tdl.com/~football

Proball Entertainment

One of the most entertaining sites available for football fans, featuring chatting, contests, standings and more.

URL http://tucson.com/proball/index.html

Team NFL

The home page of the National Football League.

URL http://www.nflhome.com

World League of American Football

Online coverage of the league that includes such teams as the Amsterdam Admirals and the Barcelona Dragons.

URL http://www.superbowl.com

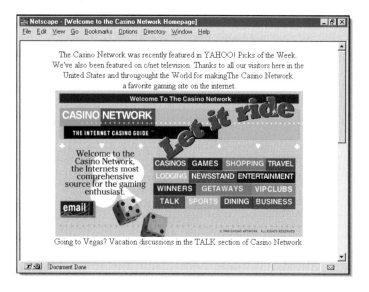

Take a chance on these gambling sites.

AMBLING

Atlantic City, New Jersey

Do you dream of playing poker in Atlantic City? If so, then this is the site for you.

URL http://www.plainsboro.com/~lemke/ ac/ac.html

Blackjack Review

An online journal covering the blackjack world.

URL http://www.conjelco.com/bjr/bjr.html

Card Player

This online magazine is devoted to gambling card games, with worldwide coverage of gaming news.

URL http://www.cardplayer.com

Casino Network

A comprehensive index of casino and gaming Web sites that includes information on entertainment, lodging, gaming and more.

URL http://www.casino-network.com

Casino Royale

Try your luck at this online casino!

URL http://www.funscape.com

DOR-Cino

A free interactive Web casino with slot machines, blackjack, poker, craps and horse racing.

URL http://www.dorcino.com

InterLotto

Feeling lucky? Visit this site and play the Internet's first online lottery.

URL http://interlotto.li

Internet Casinos

Strictly for entertainment, this site features online slot machines and more.

URL http://www.casino.org

Las Vegas Advisor

Planning a trip to Las Vegas? Be sure to check out this site's list of Las Vegas' Top Ten Values.

URL http://www.infi.net/vegas/lva

Las Vegas Gaming

Everything there is to know about staying and gambling in Las Vegas.

URL http://www.vegas.com

Rec.Gambling

A collection of frequently asked questions sent to various gambling newsgroups.

URL http://www.conjelco.com/faq/welcome.html

Sozobon Poker for Windows

Grab a demo of a Windows poker simulator that plays both Texas Hold'em and Seven Card Stud.

URL http://www.conjelco.com/sozobon.html

Sweepstakes Online

This site provides information on dozens of sweepstakes you can enter for big prizes.

URL http://www.sweepsonline.com

Trump Taj Mahal Poker

The world-famous poker room goes online.

URL http://www.trumptaj.com/games18.htm

GAMES—COMPUTER & VIDEO

3D Realms Web BBS

This game company has produced the titles Duke Nukem 3D, Terminal Velocity and Shadow Warrior.

URL http://www.3drealms.com

3DO

This creator of games gives you a behind-the-scenes look at its studio.

URL http://www.3do.com

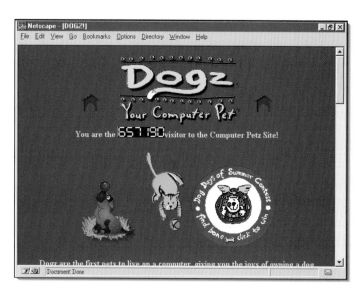

Apogee Web BBS

The creators of Wolfenstein 3D, Rise of the Triad and Raptor offer you demos, a virtual tour of the company and a chance to win software.

URL http://www.apogee1.com

Dogz

Get a free demo of a pet dog that lives on your computer desktop.

URL http://fido.dogz.com/dogz

DWANGO

This service allows you to play some of your favorite multi-player PC games, such as Doom, over the Internet.

URL http://www.dwango.com

Encyclopedia of MU*s Project: Dictionary Prototype

A glossary of terms related to the subculture of online MU*s such as MUD, MUSH and MOO.

URL http://www.eskimo.com/~hmcom/mud/wholedict.html

Frequently Asked Questions: MUDs and MUDding

Covers everything you might want to learn about the Multiple User Dimension, a popular online gaming pastime.

URL http://www.interplay.com/mudlist/mud/faq.html

Games Domain

Get games and game programming utilities or check out the online games magazine.

URL http://www.gamesdomain.co.uk

Happy Puppy

A huge collection of games, demos, strategy tips and more.

URL http://happypuppy.com

History of Classic Games

Memories of the classic home video games of 1972 to 1987.

URL http://www.owlnet.rice.edu/~dgb/museum/history/index.html

Id Software

Visit the creepy home page of the makers of the popular computer games Doom, Doom II and Quake.

URL http://www.idsoftware.com

Inside Mac Games Magazine

Get the latest news and demos of the best games for the Macintosh.

URL http://www.imgmagazine.com

Interplay

A well-known game publisher, Interplay produces software for PCs, Macs and gaming systems such as Sega and Nintendo. You can get free demos here.

URL http://www.interplay.com

Jagwire

Atari's official support site for the Jaguar gaming system.

URL http://www.atari.com/menu.html

Kali

Try out a demo of software that lets you play multi-user games over the Internet.

URL http://www.axxis.com/kali

Lights Puzzle

A simple yet challenging puzzle that you play on the Web.

URL http://www2.smart.net/
mcurtis-cgi-bin/lights.html

LucasArts Entertainment

The makers of the many well-known Star Wars games, such as Dark Forces, Rebel Assault and X-Wing.

URL http://www.lucasarts.com

Maxis

This company has produced the popular simulation series that includes SimCity, SimCity 2000, SimEarth and SimAnt.

URL http://www.maxis.com

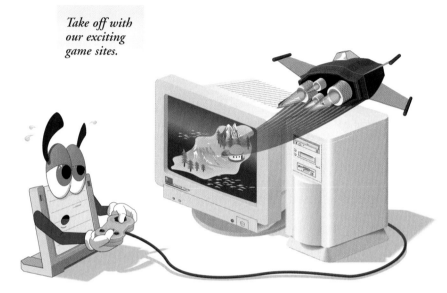

Take off with our exciting game sites.

MUD Connector

A nicely designed listing of more than 400 MUDs, each complete with a description and address.

URL http://www.absi.com/mud/
mud_home.html

MUD List

A comprehensive list of MUDs.

URL http://www.interplay.com/mudlist/
mud/listsel.html

Netropolis

An online game of international business intrigue.

URL http://www.delphi.co.uk/netropolis

NEXT Generation

The online version of the magazine that provides the latest information on games and the game industry.

URL http://www.next-generation.com

Nintendo Power

The official site of the popular video game entertainment company.

URL http://www.nintendo.com

PC Gamer Online

Find reviews, previews and gaming news at the online outpost of this computer gaming magazine.

URL http://www.pcgamer.com

Raven Software

You can grab demos of Raven's popular games, Heretic and Hexen, from this site.

URL http://www.ravensoft.com

Sega Online

Get the latest information from the makers of the popular Sega game system.

URL http://www.sega.com

Sony PlayStation

Explore Sony's official gaming system site.

URL http://www.scea.sony.com/playstation

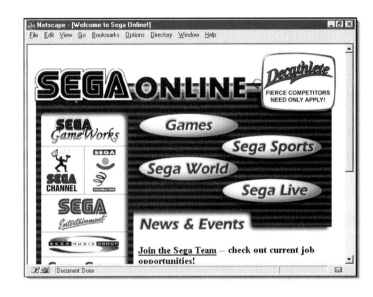

YOU DON'T KNOW JACK

A wacky trivia game from the makers of the After Dark screen saver.

URL http://www.berksys.com/www/
products/ydkj.html

GENEALOGY

Celtic Net Scottish Clans

A listing of all the Scottish clans, including images of their tartans and badges.

URL http://www.taisbean.com/
celticnet/clandirectory.html

Directory of Royal Genealogical Data

A database containing the genealogy of the British royal family and those who are linked to it by blood or marriage.

URL http://www.dcs.hull.ac.uk/
public/genealogy/royal

G

Everton's Genealogical Helper

This widely circulated magazine of genealogical research is now online.

URL http://www.everton.com

Genealogy Home Page

A well-organized source of links to the many genealogy resources available on the Web.

URL http://ftp.cac.psu.edu/ ~saw/genealogy.html

Genealogy Toolbox

An excellent starting point with many links and search tools to help you trace your roots.

URL http://genealogy.tbox.com/ genealogy.html

GenServ

This site charges a small fee to search more than 3.5 million names.

URL http://soback.kornet.nm.kr/~cmanis

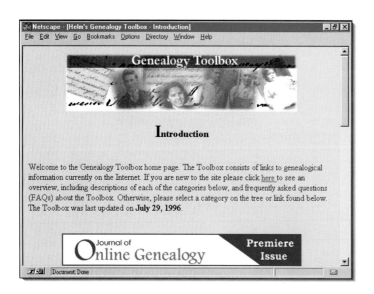

GenWeb Demo Page

At this site you can take a peek at what the future of genealogical research on the Web will look like.

URL http://demo.genweb.org/ gene/genedemo.html

IRLGEN

A guide to researching your Irish roots.

URL http://www.bess.tcd.ie/roots_ie.htm

Jeff Alvey's Heraldry Page

A great introduction to the history of coats of arms.

URL http://www.fred.net/jefalvey/ jeffhera.html

JewishGen

The official home of Jewish genealogy.

URL http://www.jewishgen.org

Maps Can Help You Trace Your Family Tree

A fact-filled page on how to use maps in your genealogical research.

URL http://info.er.usgs.gov/fact-sheets/genealogy/index.html

National Genealogical Society

This site offers many articles on how to conduct genealogical research.

URL http://genealogy.org/NGS/welcome.html

Roots Surname List Name Finder

A searchable list of thousands of last names that were submitted by genealogists.

URL http://www.rand.org/cgi-bin/Genea/rsl

Telephone Directories on the Web

Links to online phone books from around the world.

URL http://www.c2.org/~buttle/tel

U.K. and Ireland Genealogy

A helpful guide to researching your British and Irish ancestors.

URL http://midas.ac.uk/genuki

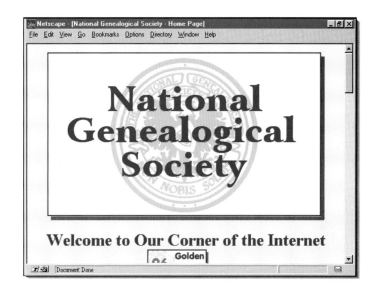

U.S. Census Bureau

This social, economic and demographic information will help you in your genealogy research.

URL http://www.census.gov

GENETICS

Agricultural Genome Information Server (AGIS)

Searchable databases of the genomes of plants, animals and other organisms that are important to agriculture.

URL http://probe.nalusda.gov

Cattle Genome Mapping Project

This site has diagrams and tables of chromosome mapping in cattle.

URL http://sol.marc.usda.gov/genome/cattle/cattle.html

G

GENETICS *continued*

Dog Genome Project

The project to map all of the chromosomes in dogs has an attractive site with genetic findings and general information on dogs.

URL http://mendel.berkeley.edu/dog.html

E. coli Genome Center

The aim of this genetics laboratory is to sequence the entire genome of the *E. coli* bacterium.

URL http://www.genetics.wisc.edu/Welcome.html

Human Genome Center for Chromosome 22

This center provides two searchable databases, one with sequencing information and one with mapping information.

URL http://www.cbil.upenn.edu/HGC22.html

Institute For Brain Aging and Dementia

This institute provides online information on Alzheimer's and related diseases.

URL http://teri.bio.uci.edu

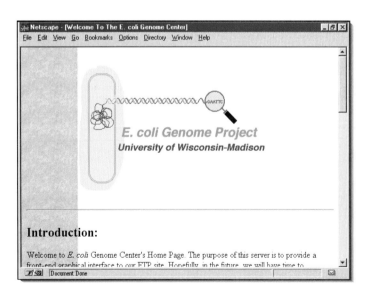

Mosquito Genomics WWW Server

This site offers access to mosquito genetic databases as well as mosquito images.

URL http://klab.agsci.colostate.edu

Mouse Genome Informatics

Search the Mouse Genome Database and the Gene Expression Database, or explore the Encyclopedia of the Mouse Genome's graphical genetic maps.

URL http://www.informatics.jax.org

Plant Gene Register

Search the full text of articles on plant genetics.

URL http://ophelia.com/Ophelia/pgr

Primer on Molecular Genetics (Department of Energy)

A primer on DNA, RNA, proteins, genes, chromosomes, mapping, linkage and more, along with a glossary of terms.

URL http://www.gdb.org/Dan/DOE/intro.html

Strange Mutants

Pictures of a headless fly, flies with mutated eyes and a fly with one eye and three antennae.

URL http://fly2.biology.uiowa.edu/Fly/Mutants.html

TBASE—The Transgenic/Targeted Mutation Database

A searchable catalog of information on the genetically altered animals that have been produced worldwide.

URL http://www.gdb.org/Dan/tbase/tbase.html

U.S. Poultry Gene Mapping

Find out about research being done to map the chicken genome.

URL http://poultry.mph.msu.edu

Virtual FlyLab

Do your own genetic experiments at Virtual FlyLab!

URL http://vflylab.calstatela.edu/edesktop/VirtApps/VflyLab/IntroVflyLab.html

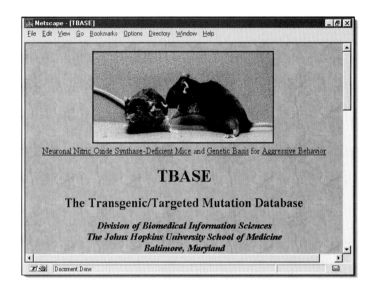

GEOGRAPHY

Ask-A-Geologist

General questions on earth sciences can be sent by electronic mail to a geologist.

URL http://walrus.wr.usgs.gov/docs/ask-a-ge.html

Canadian Atlas on SchoolNet

See maps, search for place names or test your knowledge of Canadian geography.

URL http://www-nais.ccm.emr.ca/schoolnet

City.Net

This site offers links to information on thousands of destinations around the world.

URL http://www.city.net

Color Landform Atlas of the United States

Geographical and pictorial images of all 50 states.

URL http://fermi.jhuapl.edu/states/states.html

Earth Viewer

Lets you look at the Earth from a variety of interesting perspectives.

URL http://www.fourmilab.ch/earthview/vplanet.html

GPS World

An Internet site for news and applications of the Global Positioning System.

URL http://www.advanstar.com/GEO/GPS

How far is it?

Simply enter two place names and this Web site will tell you the distance between them in miles and kilometers.

URL http://www.indo.com/distance

Maps in the News

This site offers you the chance to take a closer look at the countries, cities and other regions you hear about in the news.

URL http://www-map.lib.umn.edu/news.html

We will help you locate some great geography sites.

National Earthquake Information Center

Find out what's shaking on planet Earth.

URL http://wwwneic.cr.usgs.gov

Perry-Castañeda Library Map Collection

A wide selection of electronic maps of countries, cities and historical sites.

URL http://www.lib.utexas.edu/Libs/PCL/Map_collection/Map_collection.html

Planet Earth Home Page

This site has images, reference material and many great links to other pages dealing with our favorite planet.

URL http://www.nosc.mil/planet_earth/info.html

Project GeoSim

Free geography education software is provided at this site.

URL http://geosim.cs.vt.edu/index.html

Subway Navigator

Find the best routes in subway systems around the world.

URL http://metro.jussieu.fr:10001/bin/cities/english

Tide Tables for the United States

High and low tide information and tide predictions for all U.S. coastal regions.

URL http://www-ceob.nos.noaa.gov/makepred.html

Weather Image Grid

Many kinds of up-to-date weather maps.

URL http://hub.terc.edu/terc/edgis/w-grid.html

WebWeather

This site provides up-to-date weather information for all major cities in the U.S.

URL http://www.princeton.edu/Webweather/ww.html

World-Wide Earthquake Locator

Information on recent earthquakes and maps of where they took place.

URL http://geovax.ed.ac.uk/quakes/quakes.html

Xerox PARC Map Viewer

This site lets you zoom in to any point on the globe and take a closer look at a map of that area.

URL http://pubweb.parc.xerox.com/map

 GOLF

19th Hole

A site for the everyday golfer. Check out light-hearted golf articles, the golfer's lounge, newsstand and library or find golf equipment through the classifieds and pro shop listings.

URL http://www.sport.net/golf/home.html

ESPNET Golf Zone

ESPN hosts this site that features coverage of international golf tournaments. Get news, rankings, golf statistics and player information.

URL http://ESPNET.SportsZone.com/pga

Golf Channel Online

When the 24-hour cable golf channel is just not enough, come to the Web site.

URL http://www.thegolfchannel.com

Golf Heaven

Golf jokes, monthly draws for golf equipment, golf club information and more.

URL http://www.fairfield.com/golfheaven/intro.html

golf.com

A top-notch golf site with professional and amateur golf coverage alongside information on golf equipment, schools, resorts and more.

URL http://www.golf.com

Golfsmith

The online outpost of the popular golfing magazine.

URL http://www.golfsmith.com

*Our golf sites
are right on par.*

GolfWeb

Something for everyone interested in golf, including tournament results, a pro shop, a huge classifieds section and much more.

URL http://www.golfweb.com

Players' Exchange

Your one-stop source for golf information includes the latest tournament news, photos, games, golf history and more.

URL http://www.igolf.com

Rick Smith

This page offers golf tips from the golf instructor of the pros. You can also find out about his golf academy, instructional videos and his very own golf course designs!

URL http://www.ricksmith.com

USGA

The United States Golf Association features real-time scores during major golf tournaments, as well as a huge collection of golf information.

URL http://www.usga.org

Win Free Golf Balls

This site gives away three dozen quality golf balls each week. Answer the golf trivia question for a chance to win.

URL http://www.lagolf.com/balls/free.html

World Golf Pro Shop

This site offers the best in golf merchandise, a golf classifieds section and a golf art gallery.

URL http://worldgolf.com/proshop.html

Worlds of Golf

The people who write the rules on golf have a site with all member groups represented.

URL http://www.worldsofgolf.com

GOVERNMENT—UNITED STATES

Air Force

The sky is the limit for these people.

URL http://www.dtic.mil/airforcelink

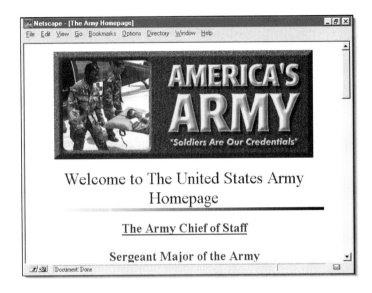

AllPolitics

A daily update on politics and politicians from *TIME* and CNN.

URL http://allpolitics.com

Arizona

Discover the Grand Canyon State.

URL http://www.state.az.us

Army

This site includes an online magazine and links to other sites related to the U.S. Army.

URL http://www.army.mil

California

Your cyber-gateway to the Golden State.

URL http://www.ca.gov

GHI

Campaign '96 Online

A comprehensive list of online information on the presidential and congressional races.

URL http://campaign.96.com

Capitol Watch Online

Information and links that will help you keep an eye on the politicians working for you.

URL http://www.capitolwatch.com

CapWeb

A comprehensive guide to the U.S. Congress.

URL http://policy.net/capweb/congress.html

Census Bureau

At this site you can find out how many people living in the U.S. have "Smith" as a last name.

URL http://www.census.gov

Elect to visit our government sites.

CIA

The official home page of the Central Intelligence Agency.

URL http://www.odci.gov/cia

Coast Guard

This site will provide you with information on the many ways the Coast Guard performs its missions at home and abroad.

URL http://www.dot.gov/dotinfo/uscg

Congressional E-mail Directory

A listing of the e-mail addresses of many congressional members as well as links to their home pages. Drop them a line and give them your opinion.

URL http://www.webslingerz.com/jhoffman/
congress-email.html

Constitution of the United States

"We, the people..." and the rest of this inspirational document can be found here.

URL http://www.ecst.csuchico.edu/
~rodmur/docs/USConstitution.html

Netscape - [United States Coast Guard Home Page]
File Edit View Go Bookmarks Options Directory Window Help

U.S. COAST GUARD

Welcome to the U.S. Coast Guard Home Page. Our goal is to provide the public with as much information as possible about the Coast Guard and its worldwide missions and activities.

Document: Done

CQs on the Job

Find out what floor speeches, bill introductions and committee votes your member of Congress has been responsible for recently in Washington.

URL http://voter96.cqalert.com/cq_job.htm

DEA

Looking for the latest statistics on speed abuse in the United States? The official site of the Drug Enforcement Administration is the place to look.

URL http://www.usdoj.gov/dea/deahome.htm

Declaration of Independence

The full text of this historic and revolutionary document.

URL http://www.ecst.csuchico.edu/~rodmur/docs/Declaration.html

DefenseLINK

Learn about the U.S. Department of Defense at this site.

URL http://www.dtic.dla.mil/defenselink

Democratic Party Online

Everything from budget battles to Party Central, where you can follow a link to Al Gore's political cartoon collection.

URL http://www.democrats.org

Department of Agriculture

Learn about the large number of services that help keep America's food supply abundant and safe.

URL http://www.usda.gov

Department of Commerce

This department was formed to promote American businesses and trade and is also responsible for such things as granting patents and predicting the weather.

URL http://www.doc.gov

Department of Education

Teachers and students alike will benefit from the information found here.

URL http://www.ed.gov

Department of Labor

More than 100 million American workers have wage protection, safety standards, pension rights and more due to the efforts of this department.

URL http://www.dol.gov

Department of State

This department is the leading U.S. foreign affairs agency and is responsible for implementing the president's foreign policies.

URL http://www.state.gov

Department of the Treasury

Money doesn't grow on trees. Visit this site to find out where it really comes from or browse through the extensive electronic library.

URL http://www.ustreas.gov

FBI

The Federal Bureau of Investigation offers lots of information about some of the more high profile cases it has dealt with.

URL http://www.fbi.gov

FBI's "Ten Most Wanted Fugitives"

Information on America's most wanted fugitives can be found here.

URL http://www.fbi.gov/toplist.htm

Federal Courts' Home Page

A great source for information regarding the Judicial Branch of the U.S. Government.

URL http://www.uscourts.gov

FedWorld

Links and information on a wide variety of government agencies and services.

URL http://www.fedworld.gov

Florida—Online Sunshine

This site will guide you through the State of Florida Legislature.

URL http://www.scri.fsu.edu/fla-leg

Forest Service

This is the site that Smokey the Bear calls home.

URL http://www.fs.fed.us

Grolier Online's The American Presidency

A comprehensive history of the presidency of the United States, organized for easy study by different reading levels.

URL http://www.grolier.com/presidents/preshome.html

Hawaii

Explore the Aloha State.

URL http://www.hawaii.gov

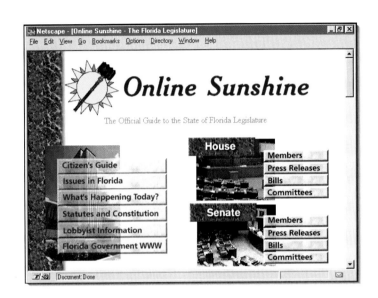

Highway 1

A non-profit corporation that uses innovative technologies to improve access to government information.

URL http://www.highway1.org

House of Representatives

This site provides information about House members, committees, organizations and more.

URL http://www.house.gov

House of Representatives Internet Law Library

More than 5,000 links to law resources on the Internet.

URL http://law.house.gov

Illinois

This site includes tours of the state museums as well as the usual government information.

URL http://www.state.il.us

Inaugural Addresses of the Presidents of the United States

The full text of every president's inaugural address can be found here.

URL http://www.columbia.edu/acis/bartleby/ inaugural/index.html

Indiana

Information about Indiana and a Kids' Net section.

URL http://www.state.in.us

IRS—The Digital Daily

The Internal Revenue Service's official site with a funny bone provides you with an easy, online way to file your taxes.

URL http://www.irs.ustreas.gov/prod/cover.html

Justices of the U.S. Supreme Court

Biographies of the judges who preside over the highest court in the land.

URL http://www.law.cornell.edu/supct/ justices/fullcourt.html

Louisiana

A great source for information on the Louisiana State Government.

URL http://www.state.la.us

Marine Corps

They go wherever they are needed— including the Internet.

URL http://www.usmc.mil

Massachusetts

The name may be hard to spell but the site will quickly guide you to the state government information you desire.

URL http://www.magnet.state.ma.us

Minnesota

A comprehensive and beautiful site dedicated to the North Star State.

URL http://www.state.mn.us/ welcome.html

NASA

Information on shuttle missions, the Hubble Telescope and much more can be found at the National Aeronautics and Space Administration site.

URL http://www.nasa.gov

National Debt Clock

And you thought your mortgage payments were a problem!

URL http://www.brillig.com/debt_clock

National Security Agency

At the NSA's site you can visit the National Cryptologic Museum or learn more about the availability of recently declassified material.

URL http://www.nsa.gov:8080

NavyOnline

This is the home cyber-port for the brave men and women who carry out America's missions on the oceans and seas around the globe.

URL http://www.navy.mil

Nevada

Take a gamble and visit this state's home page.

URL http://www.state.nv.us

New Hampshire

Links to information on the three branches of state government as well as to other Internet resources.

URL http://www.state.nh.us

New Jersey

Check out tourist attractions, colleges, universities and more.

URL http://www.state.nj.us

New York

The Empire State goes online!

URL http://www.state.ny.us

G

North Carolina
Visit the site of the Tar Heel State.

URL http://www.sips.state.nc.us

Oklahoma
Check out the Vacation Guide to learn about this state's tourist regions.

URL http://www.oklaosf.state.ok.us

Patent and Trademark Office
If you have just invented a better mousetrap, this is the place to go.

URL http://www.uspto.gov

Pennsylvania
Learn about the Keystone State's government, history, business and tourism.

URL http://www.state.pa.us

Find out about the state of things at our U.S. government sites.

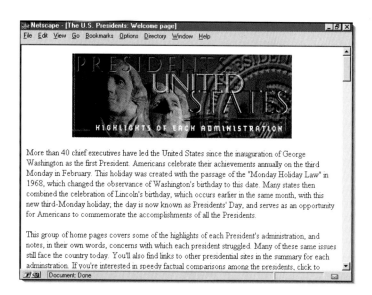

PoliticsUSA
An excellent site for political news and resources.

URL http://Politicsusa.com

Postal Service
You can access this site in sleet, snow and dark of night, all from the comfort of your computer.

URL http://www.usps.gov

President '96 Home Page
A campaign simulation where you become involved in the race for the White House!

URL http://www.pres96.com/index.html

Presidents of the United States
This group of home pages covers the highlights and struggles of each president's administration.

URL http://utkvx1.utk.edu/~razz2/uspres1.html

Reform Party

The home page of Ross Perot's grass-roots political party.

URL http://www.reformparty.org

Republican Main Street

This site has regular updates on Republicans in the news, video clips of T.V. appearances and even a schoolhouse where you can learn the history of the Republican Party.

URL http://www.rnc.org

Road to the White House

Information on the presidential candidates, links to a wide variety of political sites and a Virtual Voting Booth where you can cast your cyber-ballot.

URL http://www.ipt.com/vote

Rock the Vote

This hip site encourages young voters to get informed, take a stand and cast their votes.

URL http://www.rockthevote.org

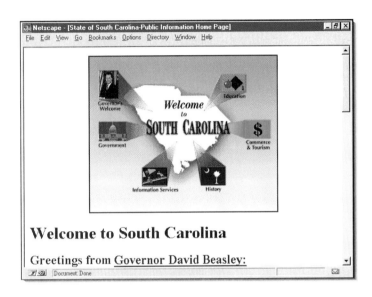

Senate

This site provides information about the members, committees and leadership of the Senate and its support offices.

URL http://www.senate.gov

South Carolina

State government, history, commerce, tourism and more.

URL http://www.state.sc.us

State and Local Government on the Net

A searchable site providing links to state and local government information available to you through the Web.

URL http://www.piperinfo.com/~piper/state/states.html

Tennessee

Don't miss the Tennessee Vacation Guide available online.

URL http://www.state.tn.us

Texas

The Lone Star State takes its place in cyber-space.

URL http://info.texas.gov/tih.html

Thomas: Legislative Information on the Internet

The Library of Congress maintains this site with information on hot bills, congressional records and how a law is made.

URL http://thomas.loc.gov

USSC Plus

You can find U.S. Supreme Court decisions dating back to 1967 at this site.

URL http://www.usscplus.com

Vermont

A delightful overview of the Green Mountain State.

URL http://www.cit.state.vt.us

Virginia

The Commonwealth of Virginia gives you a glimpse of its extraordinary natural beauty.

URL http://www.state.va.us

Vote Smart Web

Stay informed about the world of politics with this impressive collection of information, resources and links.

URL http://www.vote-smart.org

Washington

The source of information on all legislative activities in the state.

URL http://leginfo.leg.wa.gov

White House

Drop in for a visit and take a tour of the president's official residence.

URL http://www.whitehouse.gov

"Wisdom" of Dan Quayle

Interesting quotes from the former U.S. vice-president.

URL http://www.concentric.net/~salisar/quayle.html

GRAPHICS & FINE ARTS

Clip Art Connection

More than 2,000 samples of clip art as well as links to other sites, including a site with information on how to use clip art at home.

URL http://www.acy.digex.net/~infomart/clipart/index.html

Cool Science Image

Lots of incredibly cool pictures of insects, plants, planets and more.

URL http://whyfiles.news.wisc.edu/coolimages

Dystopian Vision Image Galleries

One of the best places to find pictures related to *Star Trek*, *Star Wars* and *Indiana Jones*.

URL http://koganuts.com./Galleries/index.html

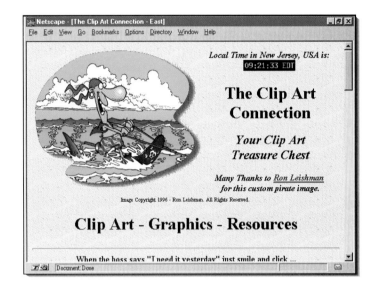

Fine Arts Images Archive

A collection of paintings from several eras.

URL http://pmwww.cs.vu.nl/archive/images/arts/.html

ImageServe

Thousands of European and Australian art and architecture pictures along with graphics-related links.

URL http://rubens.anu.edu.au/imageserve

NSSDC Photo Gallery

A great collection of images from space, complete with informative descriptions: pictures of the planets, asteroids, deep space objects and more.

URL http://nssdc.gsfc.nasa.gov/photo_gallery

GHI

GH

GRAPHICS & FINE ARTS *continued*

Steve's Image Library

A large collection of free icons you can use to create your own Web page.

URL http://www.widomaker.com/~spalmer

Swedish Sunet Archive

Pictures of just about everything you can imagine.

URL http://ftp.sunet.se/ftp/pub/pictures

TCD Image Archive

A good image collection organized by category.

URL http://www.maths.tcd.ie/pub/images/wee/images.html

Time Life Photo Sight

Pictures from Time Inc. magazines, as well as other photography-related stuff!

URL http://pathfinder.com/photo/sighthome.html

ZooNet Image Archive

A great collection of animal pictures. You will find everything from apes to zebras.

URL http://www.mindspring.com/~zoonet/gallery.html

HEALTH

Ability Online Support Network

An online service dedicated to connecting young people with disabilities to disabled and non-disabled peers and mentors.

URL http://www.ablelink.org

Achoo

A directory of health-related sites on the Internet.

URL http://www.achoo.com

Acupuncture Home Page

If you do not like needles, point your Web browser in another direction.

URL http://www.demon.co.uk/acupuncture/index.html

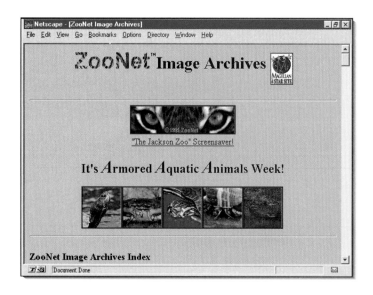

Aeiveos Home Page

Aeiveos does research with the aim of extending the human lifespan.

URL http://www.aeiveos.com

Aesthetic Concerns

Life-like prosthetic devices ranging from fingers and hands to toes and feet.

URL http://www.livingskin.com

AIDS Memorial Quilt

Each of the 32,000 panels in the quilt was made to remember the life of a person lost to AIDS.

URL http://www.aidsquilt.org

Alcoholics Anonymous Resources

Check out this site for AA online information.

URL http://matrix.casti.com:80/aa

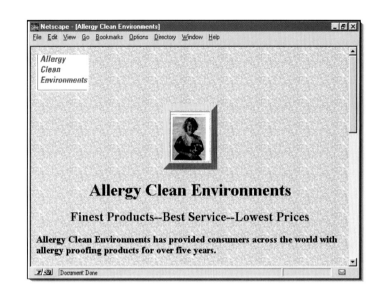

Allergy Clean Environments

This commercial site offers products that will be of interest to allergy sufferers.

URL http://www.w2.com/allergy.html

Alliance*U.S.A.

Information about a host of nutritional products designed to enhance your health.

URL http://www.csz.com/alliance.html

AmericaLens

Order contact lenses online and get delivery anywhere in the U.S. within three business days.

URL http://www.americalens.com

Autism Resources

At this site you will find an organized list of Autism resources on the Internet.

URL http://web.syr.edu/
~jmwobus/autism

H

HEALTH *continued*

Check up on our health sites.

Back Be Nimble

Hundreds of products to help relieve and prevent back, neck and body pain.

URL http://www.backbenimble.com

balance

An online fitness and health magazine.

URL http://hyperlink.com:80/balance

Bayer

The international chemical and health care company that invented Aspirin.

URL http://www.bayer.com/english/0000home.htm

Beeson Facial Plastic and Reconstructive Surgery

Contemplating a facelift or just a repair of that broken nose? Get answers to all your plastic surgery questions.

URL http://www.beeson.com

CancerGuide

A library of research and information compiled by someone who has survived cancer.

URL http://cancerguide.org

Centers for Disease Control and Prevention

Information on diseases, health risks, prevention strategies and much more.

URL http://www.cdc.gov

Children and Adults with Attention Deficit Disorders

The goal of this site is to better the lives of individuals with Attention Deficit Disorder.

URL http://www.chadd.org

ChronicIllnet

A site dedicated to chronic and terminal illnesses.

URL http://www.calypte.com

Columbia/HCA Healthcare Corporation

Health information on every topic under the sun—for all ages and every illness you can think of.

URL http://www.columbia.net

Cyber Pharmacy

A pharmacy that provides online information and services with mail or courier delivery throughout North America.

URL http://www.telepath.com/pharmacy

Deaf World Web

A list of social and cultural resources for the deaf in more than 30 countries worldwide.

URL http://deafworldweb.org/dww

DeathNET

This site features a collection of material related to the legal, moral, medical, historical and cultural aspects of human mortality.

URL http://www.rights.org/~deathnet

Doctor's Guide to the Internet

This site is great for both doctors and patients. You will find the latest medical news, as well as information on allergies, asthma, diabetes and much more.

URL http://www.pslgroup.com/docguide.htm

Eli Lilly and Company

Find out about treatments for diseases such as cancer and diabetes.

URL http://www.lilly.com

First Aid Online

Do you have a nosebleed or a sprained ankle? Learn simple first aid techniques at this site.

URL http://www2.vivid.net/~cicely/safety

Hat & Soul

A selection of hats specifically designed for women who have lost their hair due to chemotherapy.

URL http://www.hatandsoul.com

HEALTH *continued*

HealthSource

This site is designed to offer you the facts you need to live a long, healthy life.

URL http://www.doctors-10tv.com

Herbal Leader

A selection of natural health and wellness products available online.

URL http://www.multiplex.com/1/ a/HerbalLeader

International Food Information Council (IFIC) Foundation

This foundation supplies consumers with information on food safety, nutrition and health.

URL http://ificinfo.health.org

Lens Express

Order contact lenses, solutions, designer sunglasses and more.

URL http://www.lensexpress.com

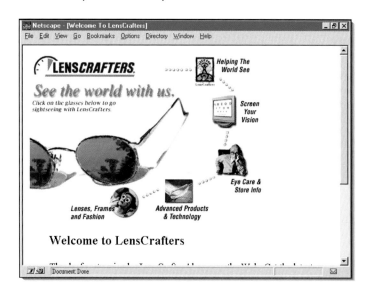

LensCrafters

Take the online eye test and see the latest trends in frames, lenses and sunglasses.

URL http://www.lenscrafters.com

Longevity Game

This interesting quiz calculates how long you will probably live based on data gathered by the life insurance industry.

URL http://www.northwesternmutual.com/ longevit/longevit.htm

MATRIX DERMATOLOGY RESOURCES

This site is guaranteed to make you itch and scratch with pictures and information on skin diseases and tumors.

URL http://matrix.ucdavis.edu

Medical Breakthroughs

Be informed with the up-to-date medical news at this site.

URL http://www.ivanhoe.com

Medical Oncology and Hematology Clinic

Lots of information about cancer treatments and links to other cancer-related sites.

URL http://www.fon-insight.com/mohc.html

Medscape

For health professionals and interested consumers.

URL http://www.medscape.com

National Institute for Occupational Safety and Health (NIOSH)

This government agency was established to promote safety and health at work through research and prevention.

URL http://www.cdc.gov/niosh/homepage.html

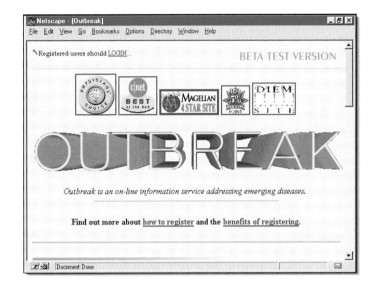

Nutrition Warehouse

Vitamins and nutritional supplements to help you stay healthy, build up your body or treat ailments.

URL http://www.nutrition-warehouse.com

Ohio Willow Wood Company

Orthotic and prosthetic components from a company that was started by a railwayman who lost his legs in a train accident.

URL http://www.owwco.com

OncoLink

Information on cancer, including causes, screening, prevention and support.

URL http://www.oncolink.upenn.edu

Outbreak

Online information on emerging diseases, such as Ebola and Mad Cow Disease.

URL http://www.objarts.com/outbreak

Paranoia Drugs Information Server

Read true stories of drug use, poetry and prose written by drug users and more.

URL http://www.paranoia.com/drugs

Patient's Guide to Carpal Tunnel Syndrome

Too much time spent typing on a keyboard can give you CTS. Find out how to diagnose and treat this condition.

URL http://www.sechrest.com/mmg/cts/ctsintro.html

PhRMA: America's Pharmaceutical Research Companies

See what drugs are currently in development by approximately 100 companies.

URL http://www.phrma.org

Prevention Online

A large resource of information on substance abuse prevention.

URL http://www.health.org

The Body

A multimedia resource on HIV and AIDS.

URL http://www.thebody.com

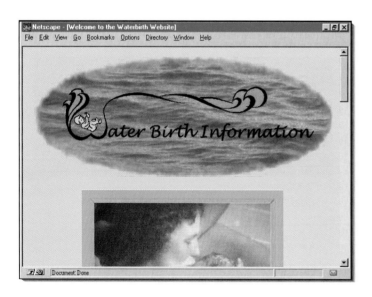

University of Washington Health Sciences Center

Page after page of health-related information.

URL http://www.hslib.washington.edu

Virginia Addiction Training Center

Information on drugs, alcohol and substance abuse.

URL http://freenet.vcu.edu/health/vatc/vatc.html

Virtual Hospital

A continuously updated health sciences library.

URL http://vh.radiology.uiowa.edu

Water Birth Information

Information on water-assisted deliveries.

URL http://www.well.com/user/karil

World Health Organization

Find out all about this important organization.

URL http://www.who.ch

1492: An Ongoing Voyage

An online exhibit examining the changes set in motion by Christopher Columbus and subsequent European explorers, conquerors and settlers.

URL http://sunsite.unc.edu/expo/ 1492.exhibit/Intro.html

Alexander Palace Time Machine

Step into this site for a virtual tour of the Tsar's Palace in St. Petersburg, Russia.

URL http://www.travelogix.com/emp/ batchison

Alexander the Great

Many images and interesting facts about Alexander the Great.

URL http://wso.williams.edu/~junterek

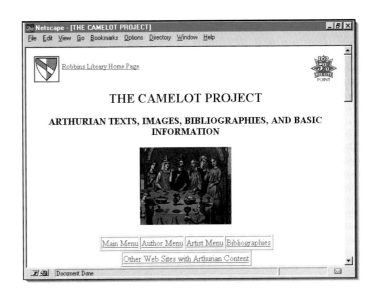

American Battlefield Protection Program

Learn about what is being done to preserve these landmarks.

URL http://www.cr.nps.gov/abpp/abpp.html

American Memory

A record of American culture and history that includes many images and sounds.

URL http://rs6.loc.gov/amhome.html

CACCF Search

A searchable database containing information on the 58,169 American casualties of the Vietnam War.

URL http://sersoft.clever.net/vietnam

Camelot Project

Everything you ever wanted to know about King Arthur and his court.

URL http://rodent.lib.rochester.edu/ camelot/cphome.htm

Our history sites are sure to become classics.

Distinguished Women of Past and Present

Biographies of women who have made significant contributions in science, politics, the arts and more.

URL http://www.netsrq.com/~dbois

EuroDocs

A collection of Western European historical documents.

URL http://library.byu.edu/~rdh/eurodocs

Exploring Ancient World Cultures

An online classroom where you can learn about eight ancient cultures.

URL http://cedar.evansville.edu/
~wcweb/wc101

Guide to the Monarchs of England and Great Britain

Pictures and biographies of the kings and queens who have ruled Britain over the years.

URL http://www.ingress.com/~gail

Historical Atlas of Europe and the Middle East

A great collection of maps and information covering ancient times to the present.

URL http://www.ma.org/maps/map.html

Historical Text Archive

A massive collection of resources on a wide range of topics.

URL http://www.msstate.edu/Archives/
History

History Reviews Online

A quarterly journal dedicated to reviewing history books.

URL http://www.uc.edu/www/history/
reviews.html

L'Chaim: A Holocaust Web Project

Lest we forget, this site contains personal accounts of the horrors as well as a virtual tour of a concentration camp.

URL http://www.charm.net/~rbennett/
l'chaim.html

Library of Congress Prints and Photographs

A large collection of images relating to U.S. history and culture.

URL http://lcweb.loc.gov/coll/print/guide

Modernism Timeline, 1890–1940

An ongoing project, which you can add to, dealing with modernism as a literary period.

URL http://weber.u.washington.edu/~eckman/timeline.html

Movietone News Online

View famous newsreels, send a postcard to a friend or rewrite history itself.

URL http://www.iguide.com/movies/movitone

Notable Citizens of Planet Earth

A fantastic resource containing biographies of more than 18,000 people from ancient times to the present.

URL http://www.tiac.net/users/parallax

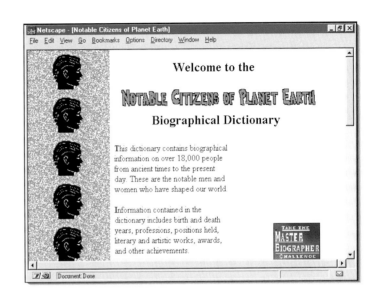

Remembering Nagasaki

Photographs and information about the bombing of Nagasaki.

URL http://www.exploratorium.edu/nagasaki/mainn.html

This Day in History

Learn what famous and not-so-famous events happened on this day in history.

URL http://www.historychannel.com/today

Twisted Freaks of History

This site contains documentary information on history's quirkier characters.

URL http://www.tiac.net/users/jclark/index.html

United States Civil War Center

Read information on the war between the Blue and the Gray.

URL http://www.cwc.lsu.edu/civlink.htm

HISTORY *continued*

WebAcropol

This site offers a guided tour of the famous Acropolis in Athens, Greece.

URL http://www.atkinson.yorku.ca/ exhibits/webacropol

World of the Vikings

Learn all there is to know about viking history and culture.

URL http://www.demon.co.uk/history/ index.html

World War I—Trenches on the Web

An impressive collection of images and documents about the Great War.

URL http://www.worldwar1.com

WWW Medieval Resources

Links to Web sites with medieval themes.

URL http://ebbs.english.vt.edu/medieval/ medieval.ebbs.html

The history of COMPUTERS

HISTORY OF COMPUTERS

Alan Turing Home Page

An extensive site dedicated to one of the founders of computer science.

URL http://www.wadham.ox.ac.uk/ ~ahodges/Turing.html

Apple II History

Read a detailed history of the Apple II computer, divided into 23 chapters.

URL http://www.hypermall.com/History

Calculating Machines

A history of non-electrical calculating devices, from the abacus to Pascal's machine.

URL http://www.duke.edu/~tj/hist/ calc_mach.html

Charles Babbage Institute

This research center at the University of Minnesota promotes studying and documenting the history of computing.

URL http://www.itdean.umn.edu/cbi/ welcome.htm

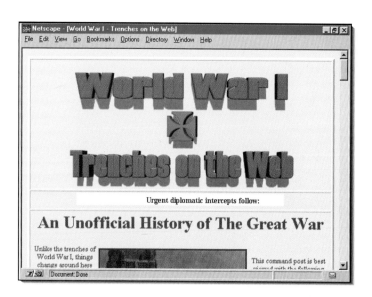

Chronology of Events in the History of Microcomputers

An overview of important events in microcomputer history, from 1926 to the present.

URL http://www.islandnet.com/~kpolsson/comphist.htm

Computer History and Folklore

Writings on the history of computers and the Internet.

URL http://yoyo.cc.monash.edu.au/~mist/Folklore

Computers: From the Past to the Present

This illustrated lecture of computing history includes ancient concepts of computer science.

URL http://www.cs.uregina.ca/~hoyle/Lecture

GENERATIONS

A virtual museum of home computer history.

URL http://www.dg.com/features/generations/generations.html

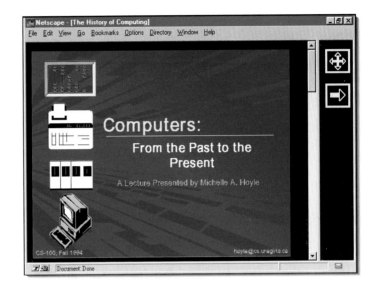

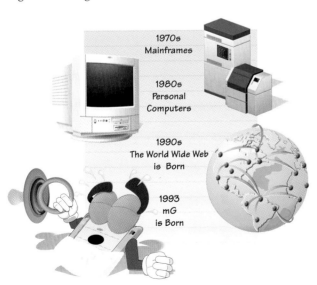

History of Computers During My Lifetime

A personal documentation of the history of computing, from the 1970s to today.

URL http://www.reflections.com.au/~jason/Articles/HistoryOfComputers/index.html

Hobbes' Internet Timeline

Complete coverage of Internet history.

URL http://info.isoc.org/guest/zakon/Internet/History/HIT.html

Internet

A brief history of the Internet by noted author Bruce Sterling.

URL http://www.eff.org/pub/Net_culture/internet_sterling.history

Obsolete Computer Museum

Ever wonder what happened to the Coleco Adam, the Commodore 64 and the Atari 800? They all rest in peace at this museum.

URL http://www.ncsc.dni.us/fun/user/tcc/cmuseum/cmuseum.htm

Past Notable Women of Computing

A great resource for information on pioneering women of mathematics and computing.

URL http://www.cs.yale.edu/homes/tap/past-women.html

Personal Computer Museum

This museum in Sweden holds more than 250 different personal computers.

URL http://www.hogia.se/pcmuseum/index.html

Virtual Museum of Computing

View the exhibitions at this online museum.

URL http://www.comlab.ox.ac.uk/archive/other/museums/computing.html

World Wide Web Consortium

The people who started the World Wide Web are working to develop common standards as it grows and evolves.

URL http://www.w3.org/pub/WWW

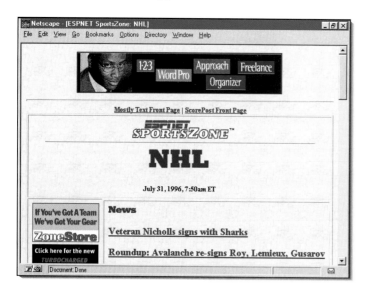

Take a shot at our hockey sites.

HOCKEY

ESPNET SportsZone: NHL

Up-to-the-minute scores, interviews, statistics and news on the National Hockey League.

URL http://espnet.sportszone.com/nhl

FOX NHL Scoreboard and Stats

The FOX Network brings you this collection of NHL information: teams, statistics, newsroom stuff and FOX T.V. game coverage.

URL http://www.fyionline.com/mci-news/newsroom/NHL

Hockey Frequently Asked Questions

This list covers such things as "What is the puck made of?" and "How thick is the ice?"

URL http://janis.nashville.org/hockey_faq.html

Hockey Hall of Fame

Find out how to get to the Hockey Hall of Fame and what you can do there.

URL http://www.hype.com/hhof

Hockey News

Browse through the current online version of this well-known hockey magazine or look through the back issues.

URL http://transc.com/hockey/home.htm

Hockey Server

Score with this top-notch collection of hockey information.

URL http://www2.nando.net/
SportServer/hockey

LCS: Guide to Hockey

Le Coq Sportif is an online magazine that features the best in all kinds of hockey information. A must-see for any hockey fan.

URL http://www.canadas.net/sports/sportif

National Hockey League

From The Sports Network, this site covers the latest NHL news.

URL http://www.sportsnetwork.com:80/
filter/filter.cgi/nhl/index.html

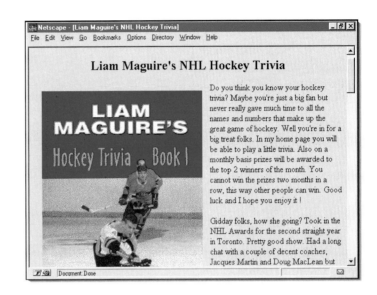

NHL Hockey Trivia

A hockey fanatic and trivia expert by the name of Liam Maguire brings you this monthly trivia contest.

URL http://infoweb.magi.com/~liam/
hockey.html

NHL Open Net

Schedules, news, scores, teams, superstars and more from the National Hockey League's official Web site.

URL http://www.nhl.com

NHL Players' Association

The official Web site for the NHLPA has trivia as well as up-close and personal information on your favorite players.

URL http://www.nhlpa.com

TSN Online

Canada's national sports channel features lots of NHL action in an attractive site.

URL http://www.tsn.ca

HOCKEY *continued*

USA Today NHL

Daily updates on the latest National Hockey League news and a team index with the results of all the games from the past season.

URL http://www.usatoday.com/sports/hockey/shn/shn.htm

World Electronic Hockey League

A game that simulates managing a hockey team. Create a team, exchange press releases, trade players, pick a strategy and take your team to the championship.

URL http://alphasim.abacom.com/wehl/wehl.htm

HOME FURNISHINGS

Aardwolf's RestorationNet

Lists of companies specializing in home and building restoration, offering everything from antique lights to graffiti removal.

URL http://www.wp.com/OLDHOUSE

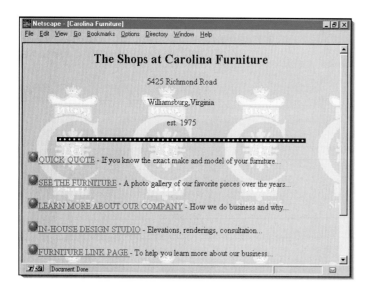

Advanced Furniture Outfitters

A site full of ready-to-assemble furniture that can be shipped anywhere in the U.S.

URL http://www.afo.com

Americh Whirlpool Bath Tubs

Find the right whirlpool for your house.

URL http://americh.com

Bean Bag City

There's nothing like collapsing into a big bag of mush at the end of a hard day.

URL http://www.beanbag.com

BUILDER Online

Learn professional trade secrets or search through more than 300 popular house plans at the site of *BUILDER* magazine.

URL http://www.builderonline.com

Carolina Furniture

This fine furniture store offers specials, quotations and a design team to help you make the right selection.

URL http://www.wmbg.com/furnish

Carpeteria

Get help deciding on carpet, hardwood and laminate flooring or choose from a selection of rugs.

URL http://carpeteria.com

Domain Home Fashions

Take a test to find your decorating personality profile and then look at some displays of furnished rooms.

URL http://www.domain-home.com

Dulux Paint Assistant

With the paint selection program, paint calculator and painting tips, your paint problems will be solved!

URL http://www.dulux.com/dulux.htm

Four Seasons Solar Products Corp.

Find the perfect sunroom or skylight for your house.

URL http://www.four-seasons-sunrooms.com

Full Upright Position

An online catalog of modern furniture by designers that include Wright, Eames and Le Corbusier.

URL http://www.teleport.com/~fup

Home Furnishing Netquarters

Links to Web retailers along with helpful furniture buying guides and decorating, cleaning and repair tips.

URL http://www.homefurnish.com

inter.Light

Light up your life with these listings of lighting design professionals, companies and lights. See the newest products online!

URL http://www.light-link.com

Jeremiah Kitchens

Check out different cabinet styles and get an online quotation.

URL http://www.jeremiah.com/jerindex.html

KraftMaid Cabinetry

Planning a kitchen? Check out samples of KraftMaid's many styles and finishes.

URL http://www.kraftmaid.com

Ladybug's Solid Cedar Design

Outdoor furniture in solid cedar. Order online for shipment throughout the United States and around the world.

URL http://www.eden.com/~bgg/scd.html

National Wood Flooring Association

Choose the right wood for your floor and follow the tips on finishes, maintenance and repairs offered by this non-profit trade association.

URL http://www.woodfloors.org

Old World Gazebos

Beautiful gazebos available in kit form.

URL http://www.gazebos.com

Pella Windows and Doors

Take the Crash Course and learn all about windows before you buy or renovate.

URL http://www.pella.com

Solco Plumbing Supply, Inc.

An online catalog featuring the full line of Kohler products.

URL http://www.solcoplumbing.com

Traditional Building

A searchable resource for suppliers of products for home restoration and decoration.

URL http://www.traditional-building.com

Velux Roof Windows and Skylights

Where there is light, there is life. See what a difference a skylight can make to a dark loft.

URL http://www.velux.com

HORROR

Cabinet of Dr. Casey

A huge horror resource for movies, literature, comics and more.

URL http://www.cat.pdx.edu/~caseyh/horror/index.html

Carrion Dreams

Some very frightening and disturbing fiction and poetry.

URL http://www.geocities.com/Hollywood/4143

Clocktower

Music, artwork and writing can all be found at this dark site.

URL http://www-scf.usc.edu/~kneedy/index.html

Commotion Strange

Anne Rice's personal newsletter to her fans as well as interviews and information about the famous horror author.

URL http://ecosys.drdr.virginia.edu/~jsm8f/commotion.html

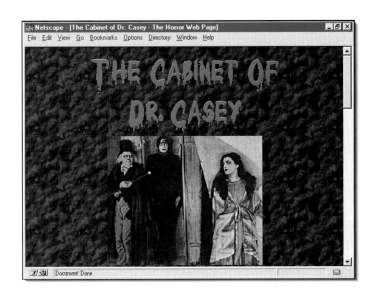

Our horror sites are a scream!

Dark Side of the Web

Your source for all that goes bump in the night on the Web.

URL http://www.cascade.net/darkweb.html

DarkEcho's Web

Horror writers will find lots of useful information here.

URL http://w3.gwis.com/~prlg

Dean Koontz

This fan-run site has many articles, reviews, interviews and a poll.

URL http://www.hway.net/zebster/koontz

Ellison Webderland

The official home page of Harlan Ellison, the writer who lives his life in a state of moral outrage.

URL http://www.menagerie.net/ellison

HORROR *continued*

Frankenstein

A comprehensive list of resources for the study of Mary Shelley's *Frankenstein*.

URL http://www.georgetown.edu/irvinemj/
english016/franken/franken.html

Fright Site

Read a tale that will disturb and appall you.

URL http://www.fright.com

Haunted House

Games, recipes and scary tales to make the kids' Halloween party a spooky affair.

URL http://www.islandnet.com/~bedford/
hallow.html

Horror Author's Address List

Send an e-mail message to your favorite horror writer.

URL http://darkwing.uoregon.edu/
~mikea/email.html

Horror Haven Movie Archive

One fan of horror movies has put his horror movie picks at the disposal of everyone on the Web.

URL http://www.magicnet.net/
~tkearns/horror.html

House of Usher

Find many of Edgar Allan Poe's writings and other fascinating information.

URL http://infoweb.magi.com/
~forrest/index.html

H.P. Lovecraft

A great deal of biographical information about the author of some of the most frightening stories of all time.

URL http://www.primenet.com/~dloucks/
hplpage.html

Pandora Station

Dedicated to three contemporary gothic horror writers: Poppy Z. Brite, Caitlin R. Kiernan and Christa Faust.

URL http://www.negia.net/~pandora

Stephen King

Information about the king of popular horror.

URL http://wwwcsif.cs.ucdavis.edu/~pace/king.html

Theatre des Vampires

A great place to go to learn more about the intriguing undead.

URL http://users.aol.com/mishian/nosferatu/TdV.html

Vincent Price Tribute

A biography, filmography, picture collection and movie posters of one of the greatest horror film actors there ever was.

URL http://www.leba.net/~ghlong

HOTELS

Bed & Breakfast Canada Online!

An online database complete with color photos of more than 800 B&Bs across Canada.

URL http://www.bbcanada.com

Bed & Breakfast Innkeepers Association of New Jersey

Information about B&Bs in New Jersey.

URL http://www.bbianj.com

Best Western International

At this site you can view hotel information, pictures and make confirmed online reservations at Best Western International hotels around the world.

URL http://www.bestwestern.com/best.html

Canadian Pacific Hotels

Pick a Canadian Pacific hotel and you will find information on dining, shopping, weather, entertainment and much more.

URL http://www.cphotels.ca

Choice Hotels International

Find a room at any of the hotels operated by Choice Hotels International, including Quality Inn, Comfort Inn and five other chains.

URL http://www.hotelchoice.com

HOTELS *continued*

Delta Hotels & Resorts

Delta has 34 hotels across Canada, the U.S. and Asia. Check out the personal guide to travel safety and security at this site.

URL http://www.deltahotels.com

Embassy Suites

Check room rates and availability or make a reservation at any of the locations across the U.S. or around the world.

URL http://www.embassy-suites.com

Go Native's Guide to Bed and Breakfast Inns

A directory of more than 8,000 inns across the U.S.

URL http://www.go-native.com

Holiday Inn

Find out what Holiday Inn has to offer and take an interactive hotel tour.

URL http://www.holiday-inn.com

Check into our hotel sites.

Internet Guide to Bed & Breakfast Inns

A searchable database of more than 3,000 B&Bs in the U.S., with complete descriptions and colorful photos.

URL http://www.traveldata.com/biz/inns

Pariscope

A guide to hotels in the City of Light. Look under Practical Paris to find phone numbers, prices and a brief description of each hotel.

URL http://pariscope.fr/Pariscope/Welcome.E.html

Sheraton Worldwide Directory

You will find Sheraton hotels on every continent except Antarctica.

URL http://www.sheraton.com

HTML (HYPERTEXT MARKUP LANGUAGE)

Accent Multilingual Publisher

Publish Web documents in more than 30 languages with this program.

URL http://www.accentsoft.com

Background Generator

A valuable site that lets you edit the colors of a ready-made background and then save it.

URL http://east.isx.com/~dprust/Bax/index.html

Background Sampler

Looking to add some spice to your Web page? Try a colorful background from Netscape's collection.

URL http://home.netscape.com/assist/net_sites/bg/backgrounds.html

Bare Bones Software, Inc.

Get a free demo version of BBEdit, the critically acclaimed text editor for the Macintosh.

URL http://www.barebones.com

Barry's Clip Art Server

A popular and thorough index of clip art resources on the Web.

URL http://www.barrysclipart.com

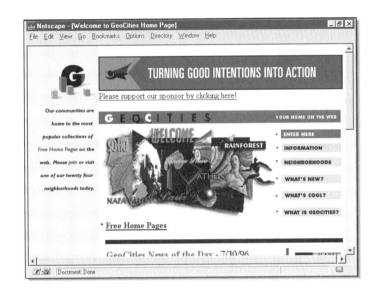

Beginner's Guide to HTML

A great general introduction to the language used to make Web pages.

URL http://www.ncsa.uiuc.edu/General/Internet/WWW/HTMLPrimer.html

Bullets

Bullets add visual interest to your Web pages. Grab some from this site.

URL http://www.eng.nus.sg/civil/Gif/Bullet/index.html

Color Manipulation Device

A handy utility for Windows that lets you customize the background, text and link colors for HTML documents.

URL http://www.meat.com/software/cmd.html

GeoCities

Want to create a personal home page on the Web for free? It's possible with this site!

URL http://www.geocities.com

HoTMetaL

SoftQuad's well-known HTML editor for Windows, Macintosh and Unix.

URL http://www.sq.com/products/hotmetal/hm-ftp.htm

Randy's Icon and Image Bazaar

Pick up arrows, backgrounds, buttons and icons for your Web pages.

URL http://www.infi.net/~rdralph/icons

WebMania!

Create Web pages incorporating forms, frames, JavaScript and more with this HTML assistant from Q&D Software.

URL http://www.q-d.com/wm.htm

World Yellow Pages Network

Don't pay to have a Web page made for you! Create your business page here by following the simple steps.

URL http://wyp.net

HUMAN RIGHTS

ACLU Freedom Network

The home page of the American Civil Liberties Union presents information on the death penalty, free speech, voting rights and more.

URL http://www.aclu.org

Amnesty International

Updates and information on worldwide efforts to protect human rights.

URL http://www.amnesty.org

Banned Books Online

A collection of books that have faced censorship or censorship attempts throughout history.

URL http://www.cs.cmu.edu/Web/People/spok/banned-books.html

Carter Center

This organization was founded by former United States President Jimmy Carter and his wife Rosalynn to fight hunger, disease, poverty, conflict and oppression.

URL http://www.emory.edu/ CARTER_CENTER/homepage.htm

Electronic Frontier Foundation

A non-profit civil liberties organization dedicated to protecting privacy, freedom of speech and access to information in the online world.

URL http://www.eff.org

Human Rights Resources

Updates on recent events and links to many other resources and organizations.

URL http://www.igc.apc.org/hr

Human Rights Web

This site offers information for new human rights activists as well as documents dealing with international law and other human rights issues.

URL http://www.traveller.com/ ~hrweb/hrweb.html

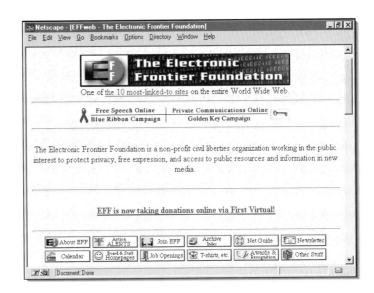

OneWorld Online

Photo exhibits and online articles dealing with human rights issues around the world.

URL http://www.oneworld.org

Project DIANA

A searchable collection of international human rights documents.

URL http://www.law.uc.edu:80/Diana

Red Cross

An excellent page with maps and photos detailing Red Cross efforts around the world.

URL http://www.icrc.ch

RefWorld

The databases of the United Nations High Commissioner for Refugees.

URL http://www.unicc.org/unhcrcdr

*Amuse yourself
at our humor
sites.*

University of Minnesota Human Rights Library

This library contains more than 90 of the most important international human rights treaties and documents.

URL http://www.umn.edu/humanrts

HUMOR

3 Stooges Virtual Museum

Enter the museum to get a complete Stooge episode guide or check out the links to other Stooge sites.

URL http://www.waterloo.net/~vrtiks/
stooge.html

Ask Dr. Science

Scientific proof that scientists have a sense of humor too. Check out Dr. Science's answer to the question of the day, ask him your own question or venture into his store to buy some wacky merchandise.

URL http://www.drscience.com

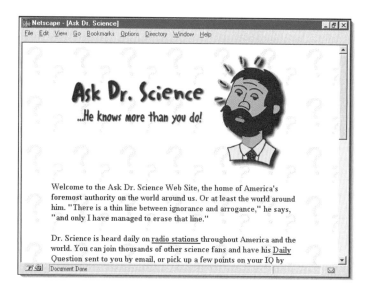

Biggest List of HUMOR SITES On the Web

This monster list of humorous sites on the Web is a comedy fan's dream come true.

URL http://mars.superlink.net/~zorro/
humor.htm

Comedy Central Online

Visit the site of this T.V. comedy channel for a few laughs. Maybe you would like to try some of Dr. Katz's E-Therapy by filling out the hilarious Auto-Diagnosis Form!

URL http://www.comcentral.com

Conspiracy.Net

A tongue-in-cheek look at the conspiracies that may or may not lurk just beyond our awareness.

URL http://www.warwick.ac.uk/~aeram/
conspir.html

Consummate Hitchhiker's Guide

Don't panic! This is a great guide to things dealing with Douglas Adams' *Hitchhiker's Guide to The Galaxy*.

URL http://www.vu.union.edu/~ellinj/42

Courtroom Bloopers

Some of the funniest things ever said or done in front of a judge.

URL http://iquest.com/~fitz/diversions/court.html

Deep Thought of the Day

A daily dose of Jack Handy's warped look at life.

URL http://www.eecs.nwu.edu/cgi-bin/deepthought

Dennis Miller Routine-O-Tron

Do you love Dennis Miller's comedy style? This online program will help you create a stand-up routine just like his.

URL http://www.blairlake.com/dmiller

Fade to Black

A comedy magazine with biting wit and cyber know-how.

URL http://www.fadetoblack.com

George Burns Tribute

Hear what some celebrities said about the passing of this great American comedian at the age of 100.

URL http://www.premrad.com/celeb/burns.html

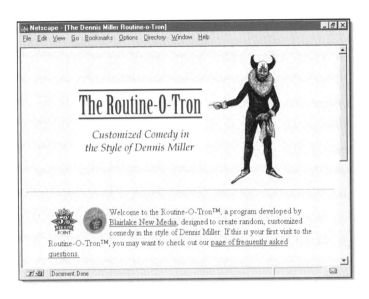

Gotta Love Them Lawyer Jokes!

A great collection of jokes and stories poking fun at the legal profession.

URL http://www.scroom.com/humor/lawyer.html

How to keep an idiot busy for hours

Come here for hours of light-hearted entertainment.

URL http://www-csag.cs.uiuc.edu/individual/pakin/idiot/chapter1.html

I Hate Computers!

A weekly newsletter that takes a humorous look at computer news and issues.

URL http://extlab1.entnem.ufl.edu/IH8PCs/index.html

Instrument Jokes

Musicians will enjoy this extensive list of clever jokes, organized by instrument.

URL http://www.mit.edu:8001/people/jcb/other-instrument-jokes.html

Jim Carrey: A Tribute

Several pictures of Jim Carrey, as well as many bizarre sounds from his movies!

URL http://www.en.com/users/bbulson/jim.html

Keepers of Lists

A new list every day and a collection of past hits such as Top 122 Mailman Gripes.

URL http://www.dtd.com/keepers

Kyle's Joke Lists

Get a random joke or a whole list of jokes from the category of your choice.

URL http://www.calvin.edu/~kvbeek/cgi-bin/thejokes.cgi

Laughter—The World's Common Language

This site finds humor in public speaking, social climbing, hosting a party and more!

URL http://www.laughter.com

Laurel & Hardy

Learn more about these masters of comedy by checking out the filmography, reviews, monthly movie listings and more.

URL http://www.sirius.com/~sramsey/TheBoys/LandH.html

Marx Brothers

Lots of pictures, sounds and facts about this very funny comedy team.

URL http://www.internetland.net/~gsumner

Monty Python's Flying Circus

Scripts, sketches, song lyrics, sound files, pictures and more make this a must-see site for fans of this popular British comedy troupe.

URL http://203.0.168.99/wwwsites/python/index.htm

Murphy's Laws

Anything that can go wrong, will go wrong! Check out many more of Murphy's Laws at this site.

URL http://www.pol.pl/humor/murphye.htm

Penn & Teller

Bizarre humor with a magical twist. Be entertained by reading the Guest rant or find out where Penn & Teller will be appearing next.

URL http://www.sincity.com

Pranksta's Paradise

Want to play a joke on someone but need some ideas? Look no further than this site's creative list of pranks.

URL http://www.voicenet.com/~mika

Rec.humor.funny Home Page

Thousands of jokes and humorous stories make this site a popular hangout for cyber-comedians.

URL http://comedy.clari.net/rhf

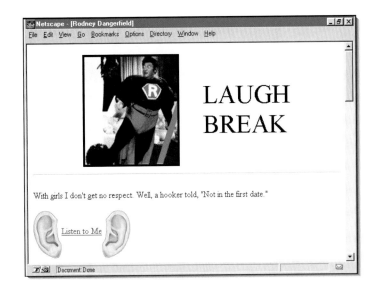

Rodney Dangerfield

Even on the Internet, he gets no respect!

URL http://www.rodney.com/rodney/
joke.of.the.day/joke.html

Stand-Up Comedy Bingo

This site makes fun of predictable comedy routines.

URL http://www.fadetoblack.com/bingo.htm

Top Ten Lists from the Late Show with David Letterman

You don't have to stay up late to hear the Top Ten List! Search all of Dave's famous nightly lists or read the favorite lists of the show's writers.

URL http://www.cbs.com/lateshow/ttlist.html

Universal Problem Solver

Put your tongue in your cheek, answer the questions and get a kick out of the results.

URL http://www.svsu.edu/~blc/solv/
index.html

HI

HUMOR *continued*

W.C. Fields

This fantastic site takes an in-depth look at the life and work of this late, great comic. Don't miss the witty W.C. Fields Quote of the Week or the unusual Fieldsian Dictionary.

URL http://www.louisville.edu/~kprayb01/WC.html

Websurfer's Handbook

Humorous definitions of slang used on the Web.

URL http://asylum.cid.com/handbook/handbook.html

I

NSURANCE

AccuQuote

Calculate how much life insurance you need and find information about the types of policies available.

URL http://www.accuquote.com

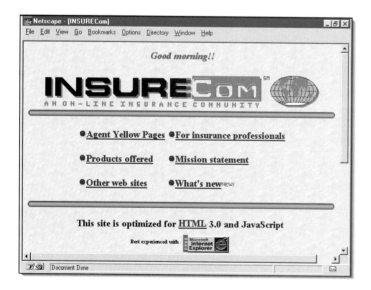

Aetna

Up-to-date information on life and health coverage.

URL http://www.aetna.com

Blue Cross

Blue Cross and Blue Shield provide health care coverage for one in four Americans.

URL http://www.bluecares.com

Chubb Corporation

This company has been protecting people, homes and businesses for more than 110 years.

URL http://www.chubb.com

INSURECom

Insurance resources including an agent directory, tips and more.

URL http://www.insurecom.com

ITT Hartford Group, Inc.

Check out the insurance and financial services company that had Abraham Lincoln as a client!

URL http://www.itthartford.com

Locy Insurance Company of California

Online auto, home and life insurance rates for California residents.

URL http://pages.prodigy.com/insurance.ca

MetLife

Get advice on everything from credit to preparing for a tornado. You can also check out insurance information and locations of MetLife representatives across the country.

URL http://www.metlife.com

Prudential

It is a lot more than insurance. Meet seven households and learn how The Prudential is helping them secure their financial futures.

URL http://www.prudential.com

Royal Insurance

A guide for people who need insurance across the U.S. and around the globe.

URL http://www.royal-usa.com

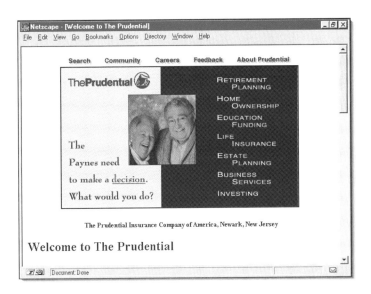

State Farm Insurance

Interesting information on home and auto insurance.

URL http://www.statefarm.com

Travelers Property and Casualty

Games, tips and information on personal and business insurance.

URL http://www.travelers.com

INTERNATIONAL

Carter Center

This institute fights world hunger, poverty, disease, conflict and oppression.

URL http://www.emory.edu/
CARTER_CENTER/homepage.htm

International Affairs Network

This site maintains a collection of links to international affairs resources on the Internet.

URL http://www.pitt.edu/~ian/ianres.html

Break into our insurance sites.

International Agencies and Information on the Web

A large and detailed list of sites where you can find information on international organizations and agencies.

URL http://www.lib.umich.edu/libhome/
Documents.center/intl.html

International Monetary Fund

Learn about the place where countries go when they need a loan.

URL gopher://imfaix3s.imf.org

NATO (North Atlantic Treaty Organization)

The home page of NATO, the alliance that links 14 European nations to Canada and the U.S.

URL http://www.nato.int

Organization of American States

Learn all about the organization to which the countries of North, South and Central America belong.

URL http://www.oas.org

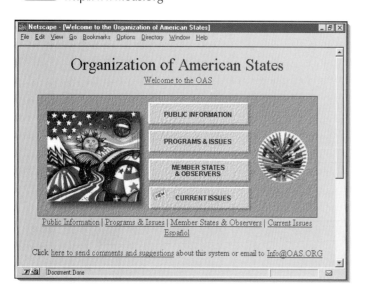

Policy Instruments Database (PIDB)

Search this database for the full text, summaries and status of international treaties and agreements involving global environmental change.

URL http://sedac.ciesin.org/pidb/
pidb-home.html

Red Cross

An excellent site with maps and photos detailing Red Cross efforts around the world.

URL http://www.icrc.ch

Rulers

Wondering who the current prime minister of Denmark is? Look through these lists of heads of state and government to find out.

URL http://www.geocities.com/Athens/1058/
rulers.html

Treaties and International Law

A comprehensive collection of laws and treaties dealing with international trade, human rights and war.

URL http://www.pls.com:8001/his/89.htm

United Nations

Find out about this international body and keep up-to-date on world affairs.

URL http://www.un.org

University of Michigan Model United Nations

An annual event where high school students experience what it is like to be UN members.

URL http://www.umich.edu/~michmun

U.S. State Department Travel Warnings

Important information about things to watch out for when visiting other countries.

URL http://www.stolaf.edu/network/travel-advisories.html

World Bank

General information on this institution as well as an archive of publications and descriptions of current events.

URL http://www.worldbank.org

World Health Organization

Check up on the World Health Report and find out more about global health issues.

URL http://www.who.ch

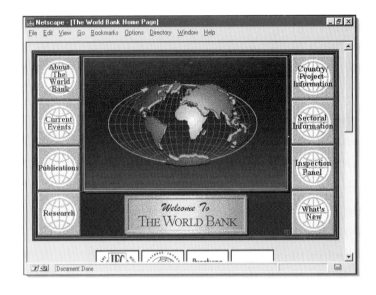

INTERNET SOFTWARE

Plug-ins are special programs that enable your Web browser to display or play certain types of graphics, sound and video on the Web.

Amber

A plug-in for viewing Adobe Portable Document Format (PDF) files in your Netscape window.

URL http://www.adobe.com/Amber

Astound Web Player

GoldDisk brings you an application for Netscape that can play Astound and Studio M sound, animation and graphics.

URL http://www.golddisk.com/awp/index.html

Carbon Copy

Remotely control another PC with this program from Microcom—run applications, view or transfer files.

URL http://www.microcom.com/cc/ccdnload.htm

Crescendo PLUS

This Netscape plug-in lets you hear background music on Web pages that use MIDI sound files.

URL http://www.liveupdate.com/cplus.html

CuteFTP

A free program that enables the transfer of files between remote computers.

URL http://papa.indstate.edu:8888/CuteFTP/index.html

EarthTime

Wondering what time it is in Seoul? EarthTime for Windows covers hundreds of world locations.

URL http://www.starfishsoftware.com/getearth.html

Eudora

The most popular e-mail program around, featuring a spell checker and the ability to attach files.

URL http://www.qualcomm.com/quest

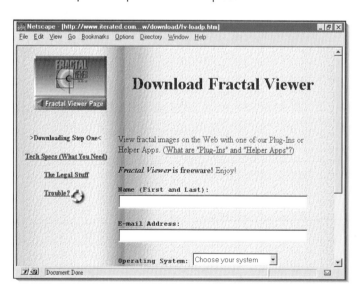

Navigate through our Internet software sites.

Fractal Viewer

View Fractal Image Format (FIF) files with this Netscape plug-in from Iterated Systems.

URL http://www.iterated.com/fracview/download/fv-loadp.htm

Internet Phone

With a microphone, sound card, speakers and the Internet Phone program, you can say good-bye to long distance telephone charges.

URL http://www.vocaltec.com

Microsoft Internet Explorer

This lean, mean Web browser is Netscape's main opponent in the battle of the browsers.

URL http://www.microsoft.com/ie

NCSA Mosaic for Microsoft Windows

The original graphical Web browser, NCSA has kept up with the times and released a new version for Windows 95.

URL http://www.ncsa.uiuc.edu/SDG/Software/WinMosaic/HomePage.html

Netscape Navigator Software

This is the place to get the world's most popular Web browser.

URL http://home.netscape.com/comprod/
mirror/client_download.html

Pegasus Mail

A popular, free e-mail program for both networks and home computers, Pegasus offers a few cool and innovative features.

URL http://www.cuslm.ca/pegasus

RealAudio

RealAudio plays certain types of sound files without a long delay.

URL http://www.realaudio.com

Shockwave

Multimedia presentations made in Macromedia's popular program are available through the Web with this Netscape plug-in.

URL http://www.macromedia.com/Tools/
Shockwave/index.html

SlipKnot

SlipKnot is a graphical Web browser that does not require the typical SLIP or PPP access that other browsers like Netscape and Mosaic need. It can run with Unix and shell accounts.

URL http://plaza.interport.net/
slipknot/slipknot.html

ToolVox

A cool Netscape plug-in designed to add speech to Web pages.

URL http://www.voxware.com

TUCOWS

The Ultimate Collection Of Windows Software that helps PCs use the Internet.

URL http://www.tucows.com

VDOnet

Find out about VDOLive, an innovative Netscape plug-in that lets you add video to Web pages.

URL http://www.vdolive.com

I

Webodex Organizer

Webodex works with your browser to organize favorite Web sites and e-mail addresses.

URL http://nova.novaweb.ca:80/webodex

Word Viewer

A free plug-in that allows you to preview any Microsoft Word 6.0 or 7.0 document within Netscape 2.0.

URL http://www.inso.com

Worlds

The programs offered here let you enter virtual chat rooms to socialize with others.

URL http://www.worlds.net

INVESTMENTS & STOCKS

American Stock Exchange

Check today's market summary or look back through the archives for the past year.

URL http://www.amex.com

Invest some time in our investment and stock sites.

Citizens Trust

Formerly known as Working Assets, this is a socially and environmentally responsible investment alternative.

URL http://www.efund.com

CNNfn the financial network

Up-to-date financial news and stock market quotes online.

URL http://www.cnnfn.com/index.html

Consumer Information Center

A wealth of financial and investment information all online.

URL http://www.pueblo.gsa.gov

E*TRADE

Trade stocks over the Internet, get stock quotes or play the Stock Market Game.

URL http://www.etrade.com

Fidelity Investments

Search more than 800 pages of investment and financial planning information in the Online Investor Center.

URL http://www.fid-inv.com

Gold Funds Page

Find out about investing in gold and other precious metals.

URL http://www.eaglewing.com

Mutual Funds Home Page

Get advice from the experts before you part with your hard-earned cash.

URL http://www.brill.com

NASDAQ

Up-to-date stock market information for companies such as Microsoft and HBO.

URL http://www.nasdaq.com

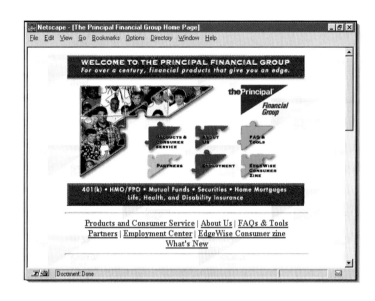

Principal Financial Group

The place to look for information on retirement plans, mutual funds, life insurance and many other investment ideas.

URL http://www.principal.com

Schwab Online

Invest in stocks, bonds or mutual funds online.

URL http://www.schwab.com

Security APL Quote Server

Find current quotes for stocks on the NYSE, ASE, NASDAQ and all the Canadian stock exchanges.

URL http://www.secapl.com/cgi-bin/qs

Universal Currency Converter

Find the exchange rate between any of more than 50 different currencies at this easy-to-use site.

URL http://www.xe.net/currency

IJ

VISA Expo

Special information and offers for VISA cardholders around the world.

URL http://www.visa.com

Brewing Java: A Tutorial

From the maintainer of the Java FAQ, this is a tutorial on programming in Java.

URL http://sunsite.unc.edu/javafaq/ javatutorial.html

Caffeine Connection

This site features a Java applet index, Java news, product reviews and more.

URL http://www.online-magazine.com/ cafeconn.htm

Get interactive with our Java sites.

ClipApps

Ready-to-use Java applets that you can incorporate into your Web pages. Grab some free samples from this site.

URL http://www.clipapps.com

Gamelan Java Directory

A well-organized collection of Java information and clever applets.

URL http://www.gamelan.com

JARS

The Java Applet Rating Service features various ratings for applets plus an applet bank.

URL http://www.jars.com

Java Applets

What exactly is Java? Netscape explains it all, provides links to some Java resources and lets you sample some applets.

URL http://home.netscape.com/comprod/ products/navigator/version_2.0/ java_applets/index.html

Java Boutique

A resource for users who would like to add Java applets to their own Web sites.

URL http://weber.u.washington.edu/~jgurney/java

Java FAQ

Frequently asked questions about Java, from novice to expert.

URL http://sunsite.unc.edu/javafaq/javafaq.html

Java Games from MagnaStar

Try out Java versions of Space Invaders, Breakout and Gobbler.

URL http://www.magnastar.com/games

JavaSoft

Sun Microsystems, the creators of Java, bring you the latest official Java information.

URL http://www.javasoft.com

JavaWorld

IDG's monthly magazine for the Java community.

URL http://www.javaworld.com

Jerry's Java Page

A listing of the best Java applications.

URL http://www.flinet.com/~rummy/javahtml/java1.html

Presenting Java: Information Sources

Get the latest news about the Java programming language and related technologies from this site.

URL http://www.december.com/works/java/info.html

The Impressionist—Painting with Java

The Impressionist is a cool Java program that lets you paint an Impressionist-style picture or photograph.

URL http://reality.sgi.com/employees/paul_asd/impression/index.html

JEWELRY

Associate Jewelers Tradeshop

One of the best jewelry sites on the Web. Be sure to check out the Hall of Shame.

URL http://www.tradeshop.com

Diamonds

Presented by the publishers of The Rapaport Diamond Report, here you will find a fortune in diamond information.

URL http://www.diamonds.com

Gemological Institute of America

Since 1931, the GIA has offered a host of education and technical services.

URL http://www.gia.org

Goldmine.Com

Choose from more than a thousand pieces of jewelry in the online catalog.

URL http://www.goldmine.com

James & Williams Jewelers

Dress and sport watches from an Illinois jewelry company that has been in business since 1962.

URL http://www.jwjewelers.com

Jewelers Internet: Gold and Diamond Warehouse

Order from a large online selection of gold, platinum and diamond jewelry or get a membership and buy at cost.

URL http://www.dataimages.com/jewelersinternet

JewelryNet

Check out a wide variety of jewelry from retailers and designers across the U.S.

URL http://www.jewelrynet.com

Jud Industries

Choose from an assortment of pre-owned Rolex watches, all with one-year warranties.

URL http://www.planetc.com/jud

Millennium Jewelry Collection

An online catalog of pearl and semi-precious stone jewelry.

URL http://www.rust.net/~janken/index.html

PC-Jewel

Gold bracelets, necklaces and earrings you can order online.

URL http://www.iu.net/pcjewel

S.A. Peck & Co./Vanity Fair Diamonds

This Chicago-based company has been selling diamonds directly to the public since 1921.

URL http://www.microserve.net/sapeck/index.html

Silver & Gems

Online ordering from a catalog of hundreds of pieces of sterling silver jewelry with gems such as amethyst, topaz and garnet.

URL http://www.tucson.com/silver/index.html

Swatch Shop

Order a funky Swatch watch online for delivery around the world.

URL http://www.vol.it/swatchshop

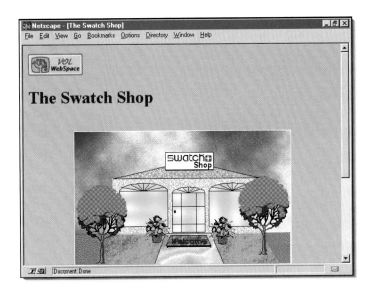

Swatch Site

Collectors can join The Club and art lovers can check out the gallery.

URL http://www.swatch-art.com

Time & Time Again Watches Online

Order from more than a dozen quality watch lines.

URL http://www.timepiece.com

Timex

Find out about the Sunlight Roaster, Sweat Box, Power Plunger and other Torture Tests that measure the durability of Timex watches.

URL http://www.timex.com

Traders of Babylon Fine Jewelers

A huge selection of diamonds, colored gemstones, ancient coins and finished jewelry.

URL http://www.diamonds.net/babylon

J

Tyler-Adam Corp.

Order gold and silver jewelry or check out the comprehensive diamond information.

URL http://www.tyler-adam.com

Watch World

Men's and women's watches at discount prices.

URL http://www.ntr.net/~watches

wristwatch.com

Purchase watches priced from less than $30 to more than $100,000.

URL http://www.wristwatch.com

JOBS

Move up in the world at our job sites.

America's Job Bank

Search for jobs by key word, job code, location and more. You will also find links to job postings on state, private agency and employer Web sites.

URL http://www.ajb.dni.us

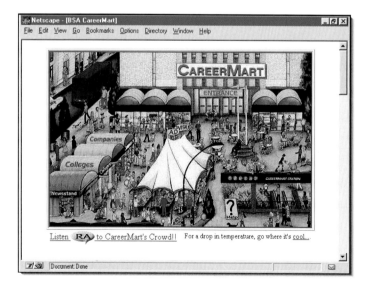

CareerMart

Jobs, jobs and more jobs from around the world.

URL http://www.careermart.com

CareerMosaic

Many of the world's largest corporations post their open positions at this site.

URL http://www.careermosaic.com

CareerNet

Find thousands of links to jobs and employers as well as many career-related resources.

URL http://www.careers.org

CareerPath.com

Find a new career by looking through more than 40,000 job ads from newspapers across the U.S. Search by newspaper, job category or key word.

URL http://www.careerpath.com

CareerWEB

Find jobs from around the world, evaluate yourself with the Career Inventory or cruise the bookstore for job-related titles.

URL http://www.cweb.com

E-Span

Search the database of employment ads or submit your résumé confidentially.

URL http://www.espan.com

helpwanted.com

Browse through available jobs listed by company or check out the job of the week.

URL http://www.helpwanted.com

IntelliMatch

Job seekers can use Watson to build online résumés and employers can use Holmes to find candidates who match the available positions.

URL http://www.intellimatch.com

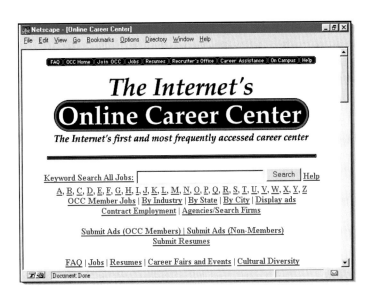

Monster Board

Listing more than 55,000 jobs from companies around the world, the Monster Board helps you tame the otherwise scary job market.

URL http://www.monster.com

NationJob Network

Search for a job or company that meets your criteria or have P.J. Scout find jobs for you.

URL http://www.nationjob.com

Olsten Corporation

Submit your résumé online to Olsten offices across the U.S.

URL http://www.worknow.com

Online Career Center

Search through thousands of jobs by key word, industry, state or city or check out jobs in the medical and academic fields.

URL http://www.occ.com

L

LANGUAGES

Basic ASL Aid

This site will help you speak and understand American Sign Language.

URL http://home.earthlink.net/~masterstek/ASLDict.html

BritSpeak

An American-British dictionary to help you learn the Queen's English.

URL http://pages.prodigy.com/NY/NYC/britspk/main.html

Foreign Languages for Travelers

An online language tutor that includes text and sound for the world traveler.

URL http://www.travlang.com/languages

History of the English Language (HEL)

Explore the history of English, from its earliest forms to modern usage.

URL http://ebbs.english.vt.edu/hel/hel.html

Human-Languages Page

Learn a language online with this site's links to lessons, dictionaries and helpful programs.

URL http://www.willamette.edu/~tjones/Language-Page.html

Language Identifier

This site will identify the language of the word, phrase or sentence you provide.

URL http://www.cs.cmu.edu/~dougb/ident.html

List of Dictionaries

A listing of the dictionaries available on the Web.

URL http://math-www.uni-paderborn.de/HTML/Dictionaries.html

Old English Pages

Texts, images and sound recordings of Old English.

URL http://www.georgetown.edu/cball/oe/old_english.html

Smiley Dictionary

Ever wonder what those little faces such as **:-)** and **:-(** mean? This site has the answers.

URL http://www.eff.org/papers/eegtti/ eeg_286.html

Totally Unofficial Rap Dictionary

A collection of words and their meanings from the world of rap music.

URL http://www.sci.kun.nl/thalia/rapdict

LEGAL & ACCOUNTING

American Incorporators Ltd.

With the help of this company, you can incorporate your business for just $99.

URL http://www.village.com/inc

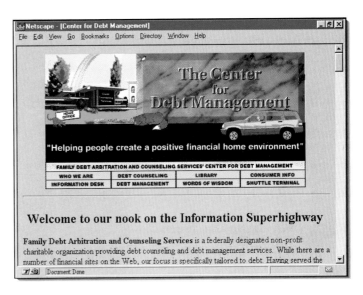

AttorneyNet

Need legal information? Ask a question in the Law Forum or check out some of the legal links.

URL http://www.attorneynet.com

BDO Accountants and Consultants

Part of the seventh largest accounting and consulting organization in the world. Find the nearest office and see what they can do for you.

URL http://www.bdo.com

Business Incorporating Guide

Use the online form to incorporate your business in any state in as little as 24 to 48 hours.

URL http://www.corporate.com

Center for Debt Management

This center has extensive consumer information and provides help to those in debt.

URL http://members.aol.com/DebtRelief/ index.html

Cyberjury

Read about a current court case and then help decide the outcome.

URL http://www.cyberjury.com

Ernst & Young LLP

Find information on accounting, tax services and much more.

URL http://www.ey.com

H&R Block Tax Services

Look for tax tips and other information from the company that completed more than 17 million tax returns last year.

URL http://www.handrblock.com/tax/
index.html

Home Office Association of America

Find legal advice and 50 ideas for starting up a home-based business.

URL http://www.hoaa.com

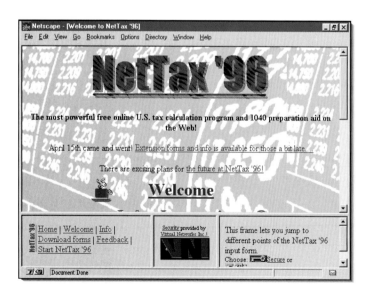

Internet Arbitrator

This online dispute resolution service is free and available to U.S. residents for claims up to $5,000.

URL http://www.angelfire.com/free/
arbitrate.html

KPMG International

Information and news from this accounting and consulting firm.

URL http://www.kpmg.com

Law Journal EXTRA!

Top legal stories and directories of appraisers, consultants, court reporters and more.

URL http://www.ljextra.com

LegalBits

The home page of this lawyer offers many links to legal resources on the Internet.

URL http://www.legalbits.com/pub/cthornto/
home.html

NetTax '96

Get online help with this U.S. tax calculation program and print out a tax form.

URL http://www.vni.net/~nettax

Nolo Press

This leading publisher of law-related titles has a self-help book to cover almost every aspect of the law.

URL http://www.nolo.com

PEACEMAKERS

A group that hopes to resolve legal conflicts through education and co-operation.

URL http://spider.lloyd.com/~fdelmer

QPAT-US

Search this online database for information on U.S. patents issued since 1974.

URL http://www.qpat.com

TRW Information Systems & Services

This leading provider of consumer and business credit information offers answers to common credit questions online.

URL http://www.trw.com/iss/iss.html

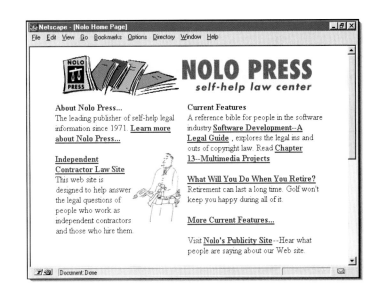

U.S. Supreme Court on the Web

View a different classic court case decision each week or search Supreme Court decisions from 1967 to the present by subject matter, word or phrase.

URL http://www.usscplus.com

LIFE SCIENCES

3-D Undersea Life

This gallery contains small images and descriptions of some undersea creatures.

URL http://oberon.educ.sfu.ca/splash/
3dlib/thumb.htm

A Brief Tour of the Brain

Take a tour of the brain! This site includes illustrations and explanations of the brain's components.

URL http://altair.syr.edu:2024/MM/Biology/
biology.html

Figure things out with these legal and accounting sites.

Electronic Zoo

Click on one of the animals on the home page to access pages of scientific information.

URL http://netvet.wustl.edu/e-zoo.htm

Mann Library

This library has a huge collection of science-related resources.

URL http://www.mannlib.cornell.edu

Natural History Museum

The Natural History Museum aims to further our understanding of the natural world.

URL http://www.nhm.ac.uk

Nonnative Fish

This site examines the effects of introducing foreign fish species into the coastal and inland waterways of the U.S.

URL http://www.nfrcg.gov/noni.fish

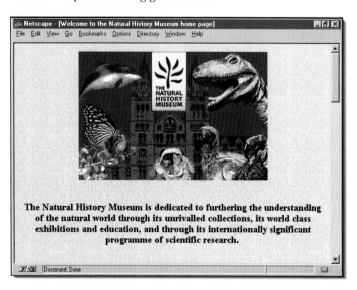

The Natural History Museum is dedicated to furthering the understanding of the natural world through its unrivalled collections, its world class exhibitions and education, and through its internationally significant programme of scientific research.

Our Living Oceans Annual Report

A report on the condition of various types of American marine resources.

URL http://kingfish.ssp.nmfs.gov/olo.html

Science Online

For news and information in every field of science, browse through the online version of this well-known magazine.

URL http://science-mag.aaas.org/science

The Heart: An Online Exploration

All kinds of valuable information about the heart and how to keep it healthy.

URL http://sln2.fi.edu/biosci/heart.html

Trilobite Home Page

This site will peak your interest in this class of extinct marine organisms.

URL http://www.ualberta.ca/~kbrett/Trilobites.html

Visible Human Project

This project of the United States National Library of Medicine is an attempt to create a detailed 3-D representation of the male and female human bodies.

URL http://www.nlm.nih.gov/research/
visible/visible_human.html

LITERATURE

221B Baker Street

The adventures of Sherlock Holmes can be found here, complete with pictures and sounds.

URL http://www.cs.cmu.edu/afs/
andrew.cmu.edu/usr18/mset/
www/holmes.html

American Literary Classics—A Chapter A Day

Read a chapter a day from great works of literature.

URL http://www.mindport.net/~arezis

Author, Author!

A source of links to literature resources on the Web, including the home pages of authors, libraries and more.

URL http://www.li.net/~scharf/author.html

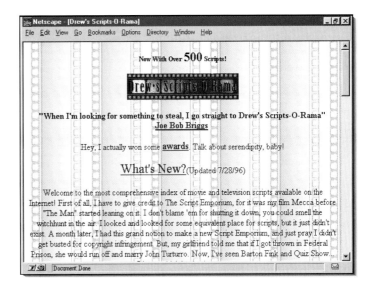

You will enjoy reading about our literature sites.

Bartlett's Familiar Quotations

The famous collection of quotations is now offered online.

URL http://www.cc.columbia.edu/acis/
bartleby/bartlett

Center for Electronic Texts in the Humanities (CETH)

A listing of electronic text resources of interest to those in the humanities.

URL http://www.ceth.rutgers.edu

Cool Word of the Day

Learn a new word and its meaning every day.

URL http://www.dsu.edu/projects/
word_of_day/word.html

Drew's Scripts-O-Rama

Movie and T.V. scripts can be found here.

URL http://home.cdsnet.net/~nikko11/
scripts.htm

L

LITERATURE *continued*

Homonym/Homophone Page

A listing of words that sound the same but have different spellings and meanings.

URL http://www-usacs.rutgers.edu/~finifter/homonym.html

Hypertext Webster Interface

Webster's Dictionary online.

URL http://gs213.sp.cs.cmu.edu/prog/webster

Internet Anagram Server

Type a word or phrase and this site switches the letters around to create new words or phrases.

URL http://www.wordsmith.org/awad-cgibin/anagram

Internet Book Information Center, Inc.

A great site for people who love books, with links to numerous other literary sites.

URL http://sunsite.unc.edu/ibic/IBIC-homepage.html

Internet Top 100 SF/Fantasy List

Science fiction and fantasy book enthusiasts vote on their favorite works.

URL http://www.clark.net/pub/iz/Books/Top100/top100.html

On Beauty and Love...

Prose and poetry on themes of beauty, love, romance and life.

URL http://www.cc.gatech.edu/grads/b/Gary.N.Boone/beauty_and_love.html

Online Books Page

An index of hundreds of online books and documents.

URL http://www.cs.cmu.edu/Web/books.html

Online Children's Stories

A great place to visit when it's your child's bedtime.

URL http://www.ucalgary.ca/~dkbrown/stories.html

Personalized Shakespearean Insult Service

Do you enjoy being insulted? If so, you will love this site.

URL http://kite.preferred.com/insults

Phrase Finder

Enter a word and Phrase Finder will supply a list of phrases related to that word.

URL http://www.shu.ac.uk/web-admin/
phrases

POETS Library

Books, journals, reference works, technical documents and more.

URL http://www.notredame.ac.jp/POETS/
Library/index.html

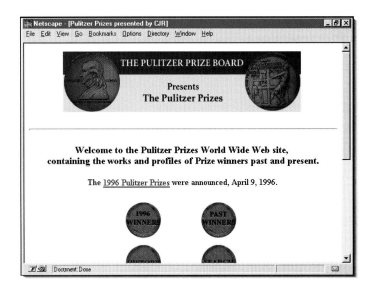

Pulitzer Prizes

This site contains the works and profiles of past and present winners.

URL http://www.pulitzer.org

Shakespeare

Read the complete works of William Shakespeare online.

URL http://the-tech.mit.edu/
Shakespeare/works.html

Stories From Downtown Anywhere

Participate in an ongoing electronic novel by making decisions on where the story will go next and adding your own ideas.

URL http://www.awa.com/stories

Strunk's Elements of Style

The classic composition guide goes online.

URL http://www.columbia.edu/acis/
bartleby/strunk

Tech Classics Archive

Looking for classical Greek and Roman texts in English translation? This searchable collection has almost 400 works.

URL http://the-tech.mit.edu/Classics

LITERATURE *continued*

Web del Sol

Some of the best contemporary prose and poetry on the Web can be found here.

URL http://www.cais.net/aesir/fiction/fiction.htm

"Byte" into our Macintosh and PowerPC sites.

MACINTOSH & POWERPC

adobe.mag

This monthly magazine for Adobe software users covers issues relating to digital and online design and publishing.

URL http://www.adobemag.com

Alien Skin Software

Looking for filters for Adobe Photoshop? Try here first.

URL http://www.eskimo.com/~bpentium/skin.html

Ambrosia

The site of this Macintosh software company features games, utilities and more.

URL http://www.AmbrosiaSW.com/Ambrosia.html

Apple Computer

The Macintosh home page informs users about the latest news at Apple.

URL http://www.apple.com

Apple User Groups

Questions about your Mac? Apple's list of online user groups will guide you to the answers.

URL http://www2.apple.com/documents/usergroups.html

Bare Bones Software, Inc.

Have a look at the latest products from the company that brought you BBEdit, the famous text editor.

URL http://www.barebones.com

Bungie

Cool Mac games including the Marathon series and Abuse.

URL http://www.bungie.com

Cyan

Need some information or hints for playing the Macintosh game Myst? Then follow the links at this site.

URL http://www.cyan.com

Cyberdog

Apple has put a bunch of Internet tools into one program. Try out the latest version.

URL http://cyberdog.apple.com

Evolution of Apple

Trace the development of Apple from its humble beginnings in the '70s to its current success in the '90s.

URL http://support.info.apple.com/aboutapple/timeline.html

eWorld Off World Tour

Orphans of eWorld, the short-lived Apple community, can now meet here.

URL http://www.axon.net.au/eworld

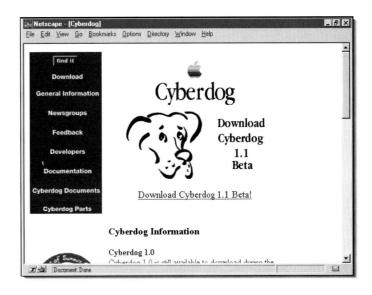

Fractal Design Corporation

Find out about FDC graphics products and don't miss the Digital Art Gallery.

URL http://www.fractal.com

Guy Kawasaki's Home Page

This well-known Macintosh personality has his own site featuring information about his books, software and magazine articles.

URL http://www.umsl.edu/~sbmeade/macway

Image Soup

An online journal about digital graphic design on the Macintosh.

URL http://home.dti.net/shadow/imagesoup

Intuit

A collection of financial programs for the Macintosh, including Quicken.

URL http://www.qfn.com

Power Macintosh
7100/66CD

Mac FAQs

Lists of frequently asked questions, covering topics such as software, hardware, buying and selling Mac products and more.

URL http://www.macfaq.com/faqs.html

Mac Net Journal

This independent monthly Mac journal covers news and features from a personal point of view.

URL http://www.blol.com/web_mnj

Mac OS

Information about the Macintosh Operating System, including an introduction to Copland OS.

URL http://www.macos.apple.com

Mac Software Catalog

Search this extensive catalog of Mac Software for everything from games to utilities.

URL http://pubweb.nexor.co.uk/public/mac/
archive/welcome.html

Macintosh Educator's Site

Resources for educators who use Macs in the classroom.

URL http://www.hampton-dumont.k12.ia.us/
web/mac

Macintosh Utilities from Jumbo

Jumbo brings you this huge collection of utilities, including compression, hypercard and more.

URL http://jumbo.com/util/mac

MacPlay

MacPlay provides high-quality entertainment and educational software for the Macintosh.

URL http://www.macplay.com

MacUser Web

Find out all the latest news and information on Apple products and software.

URL http://www.zdnet.com/macuser

Microsoft Office for Macintosh

The popular suite of office applications for the PC has come to the Mac.

URL http://www.microsoft.com/macoffice

More Mac FAQs

Still have questions? Here are more lists of frequently asked questions, taken from various Usenet newsgroups.

URL http://www.cis.ohio-state.edu/hypertext/faq/usenet/macintosh/top.html

NCSA Software

Get some interesting Mac software at this site.

URL http://www.ncsa.uiuc.edu/Indices/Software/Platform.html

PageSpinner

Need some help creating a Web page? Check out PageSpinner shareware for the Mac.

URL http://www.algonet.se/~optima/pagespinner.html

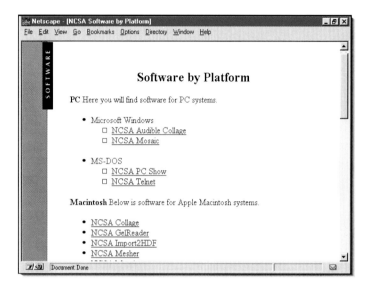

Power Computing Corporation

Find out about the company that made the first fully featured Macintosh-compatible computer.

URL http://www.powercc.com/index.html

PowerPC News

A free electronic magazine covering everything of interest to the PowerPC community.

URL http://apt.usa.globalnews.com/powerpc

Save the World! Buy a Macintosh!

Myths and facts about the Macintosh family of computers.

URL http://www.geeksrus.com/copland/copland.html

TidBITS

Check out TidBITS for up-to-date information on products and events in the world of the Mac.

URL http://www.dartmouth.edu/pages/TidBITS/TidBITS.html

MN

Try our mall sites on for size!

utexas mac archive

This huge software archive covers everything from anti-virus software to utilities.

URL http://wwwhost.ots.utexas.edu/ mac/main.html

MALLS

60s Trading Post for the 90s

The '60s did not die, they moved to the Web! Incense, crystals, black lights and lava lamps can be purchased here.

URL http://artitude.com

Alaskan Center Shopping Mall

Art, food, real estate, tours, vacations and more from the 49th state.

URL http://alaskan.com/mall.html

Branch Mall

Dozens of retailers present almost every item under the sun.

URL http://branch.com

Classic England Shopping Mall

Manufacturers and distributors from all over the U.K. offer clothing, food, collectibles and much more.

URL http://www.classicengland.co.uk

Cybershop

Wander through this online mall and take care of all your shopping without leaving your computer. There is even a gift registry for cyber-brides.

URL http://www.cybershop.com

DigiMall

This mall goes beyond the regular shopping experience by providing an online art gallery and film reviews.

URL http://digimall.com

DreamShop

Check out the shopping section of the Pathfinder site to find The Bombay Company, Eddie Bauer, Williams-Sonoma and more.

URL http://pathfinder.com

Evansville Electronic Mall

Gazebos, safes and ties are just a few of the diverse items you can find at this mall.

URL http://www.evvmall.com

Fashionmall.com

You don't have to shop 'til you drop! Browse through more than a dozen stores without leaving your desk.

URL http://www.fashionmall.com

Free Forum

Get free film, magazines, software and catalogs from many different stores at this site.

URL http://www.ven.com

Gallery Mall

Cruise through more than a dozen online shops that sell everything from auto parts to watches.

URL http://www.thegallery.com/main.html

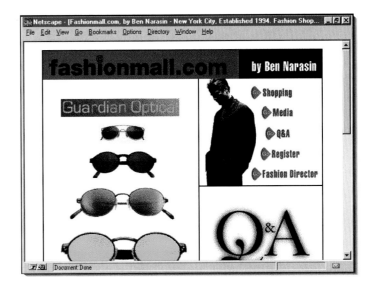

Gui 'n da Hood

Variety really is the spice of life. Check out this mall that carries everything from garlic and chili braids to rollerblades and suspenders.

URL http://www.dnai.com/~gui

iMALL

You name it, they've got it—electronics, clothing and even art are available at this site.

URL http://www.imall.com

Industry.Net

This online mall is geared toward the needs of the manufacturing industry.

URL http://www.industry.net

InterMall

Many merchants display almost everything you need, from automotive products to travel services.

URL http://iaswww.com/mall.html

Internet Shopping Network

With thousands of products available online, this is a great place to find computers and home office equipment—plus a few surprises.

URL http://www.internet.net

Mall of America

The unofficial home page for America's biggest mall, this site offers a calendar of mall events, a directory and more.

URL http://www.winternet.com/~julie

marketplaceMCI

Find great stores such as Borders Books and Music, L'eggs and The X-Files Store.

URL http://www2.pcy.mci.net/marketplace

Oakland Mall

Check out the events, information, mall directory and floor plan for this Detroit area mall.

URL http://OaklandMall.com

OutletBound

This guide to more than 12,000 factory outlets throughout the U.S. is a bargain hunter's paradise.

URL http://www.outletbound.com

Potomac Mills Mall

This outlet mall with more than 200 stores is located just south of Washington, D.C.

URL http://www.potomac-mills.com

Roosevelt Field Mall

Use the mall directory and layout to find your way around the seventh largest mall in the U.S.

URL http://www.roosevelt-field.com

Saint Louis Galleria

More than 150 stores, 18 restaurants and more in a spectacular space of marble, wood and polished brass.

URL http://www.saintlouisgalleria.com

Shopping Europe

If you appreciate fine English and European products from designers like Christian Dior and Laura Ashley, this shopping site is for you.

URL http://www.virtualeurope.nl

Shoppingmart

Browse through this site to find out about placing your mall on the Web.

URL http://www.shoppingmart.com

UTC Online Shopping Center

Don't miss out on the cyber-savings! Grab the coupons and save at this Southern California mall.

URL http://www.shoputc.com

West Edmonton Mall

More than 800 stores and services, the world's largest indoor amusement park and much more.

URL http://www.westedmall.com

World Mall

Choose from stores that sell everything from radio controlled planes to posters.

URL http://worldmall.com

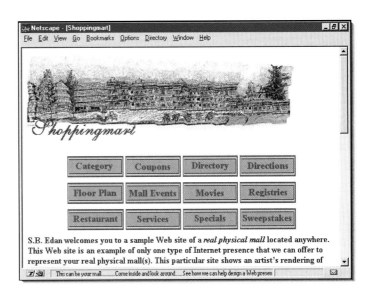

MN

MATHEMATICS

ACM SIGACT

The Association for Computing Machinery Special Interest Group on Algorithms and Computation Theory will be of interest to those who enjoy mathematics.

URL http://hercule.csci.unt.edu:80/sigact

Aircraft Aerodynamics and Design Group

Practical applications of mathematics to aerodynamic analysis and aircraft design.

URL http://aero.stanford.edu

Fractal Frequently Asked Questions and Answers

Find answers to your questions about fractals and learn how to generate a few fractals on your own.

URL http://www.cis.ohio-state.edu/ hypertext/faq/usenet/ fractal-faq/faq.html

Gallery of Interactive Geometry

Create and explore mathematical shapes and concepts, such as rainbows or conics.

URL http://www.geom.umn.edu/apps/gallery.html

Geometry Center Graphics Archive

Here you can view digital art, fractals and various geometric shapes.

URL http://www.geom.umn.edu/graphics

History of Mathematics

Read biographies of 17th and 18th century mathematicians and check out the links to other sites on the history of mathematics.

URL http://www.maths.tcd.ie/pub/HistMath/HistMath.html

Kali

Kali is an interactive program that allows you to draw tilings, infinite knots and other neat-o patterns.

URL http://www.geom.umn.edu/apps/kali/about.html

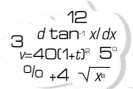

Figure our mathematics sites into your busy schedule.

Kids Web—Mathematics

This student resource contains links to many different mathematics Web sites.

URL http://www.npac.syr.edu/textbook/kidsweb/math.html

MacTutor History of Mathematics

Along with the biographies of famous mathematicians, this site contains indexes for math topics, famous curves and more.

URL http://www-groups.dcs.st-and.ac.uk:80/~history

Mathematical Association of America

Visit this site to find books, news, articles and links to math sites on the Web.

URL http://www.maa.org

Mathematical Quotations Server

This server offers quotes from many famous people on the topic of math.

URL http://math.furman.edu/~mwoodard/mquot.html

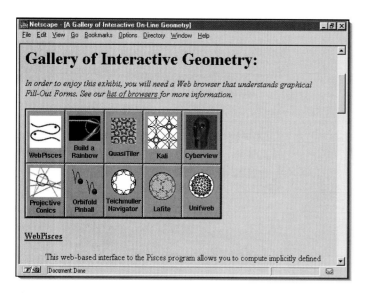

Mathematics Archives WWW Server

This site of mathematical resources is especially handy for teachers.

URL http://archives.math.utk.edu

Pavilion of Polyhedreality

Peek into this page and perceive the perplexing polyhedra.

URL http://www.li.net/~george/pavilion.html

QuasiTiler

Find out what Penrose tilings are and how to modify them, and read a mathematical explanation of how they work.

URL http://www.geom.umn.edu/apps/
quasitiler/start.html

Sprott's Fractal Gallery

Attractive and fascinating fractals can be accessed from this large collection.

URL http://sprott.physics.wisc.edu/
fractals.htm

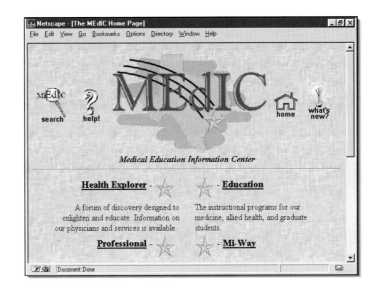

MEDICINE

MN

American Medical Association

Journals, current medical news, product catalogs and much more.

URL http://www.ama-assn.org

FDA Approved Animal Drug Data Base

This is a searchable database of animal drugs that have been approved by the Food and Drug Administration.

URL http://scholar.lib.vt.edu/ejournals/
vetfda.html

Global Emergency Medicine Archives

Interesting articles for physicians involved with emergency medicine.

URL http://gema.library.ucsf.edu:8081

Medical Education Information Center

If you are thinking of becoming a nurse or doctor, you might want to examine this site.

URL http://medic.med.uth.tmc.edu

MGH Department of Emergency Medicine

The Massachusetts General Hospital features case studies where you can guess a diagnosis.

URL http://emergency.mgh.harvard.edu

National Library of Medicine

Access medical and scientific information from this huge library.

URL http://www.nlm.nih.gov

Nursing Network Forum

If you are a nurse, you will want to check out this site for its e-mail groups, newsgroups and information on continuing education programs.

URL http://www.access.digex.net/~nurse/
nursnet3.htm

MOVIES

Academy of Motion Picture Arts and Sciences

Learn about the famous motion picture organization and the Academy Awards.

URL http://www.ampas.org

All-Movie Guide

Find out more about your favorite movies and actors at this searchable database.

URL http://allmovie.com/amg/movie_Root.html

Drew's Scripts-O-Rama

You can look at more than 300 complete movie and T.V. scripts at this site.

URL http://home.cdsnet.net/~nikko11/
scripts.htm

Film Zone

A great magazine with lots of informative articles on independent, foreign, animated and Hollywood films.

URL http://www.filmzone.com

Hitchcock Page

This page is dedicated to the all-time master of cinematic suspense, Alfred Hitchcock.

URL http://www1.primenet.com/~mwc

Hollywood Online

A full Hollywood multimedia experience, complete with movie clips, celebrity interviews and a photo gallery.

URL http://www.hollywood.com

Internet Movie Database

This free source of movie information is the largest of its kind on the Internet.

URL http://us.imdb.com

M.O.V.I.E. Monthly Trivia Contest

A games gallery and trivia contest where you can win prizes for your film knowledge. You can also buy M.O.V.I.E. merchandise to help support the making of independent movies.

URL http://www.moviefund.com/trivia.html

Movielink

Find out what's playing at a theater near you.

URL http://www.movielink.com

MovieWEB

Previews of upcoming movies, movie merchandise and more.

URL http://movieweb.com/movie/movie.html

Mr. Showbiz

Articles, reviews, the latest news from the entertainment world and much more.

URL http://web3.starwave.com/showbiz

Screen Shots

Movie reviews, celebrity interviews and movie trivia—all in one site.

URL http://www.screenshots.com

www.filmmusic.com

A site for composers and fans of film music.

URL http://www.filmmusic.com

M

MOVIES—REVIEWS

Best Video Guide

This site features information about new and upcoming videos, including blockbusters and B movies.

URL http://rampages.onramp.net/~jbeckley

CyberCritic

Be a critic—rate videos and movies at this site.

URL http://www.starguideweb.com/rateform.html

Film at The Gate

Reviews from the critics at the *San Francisco Chronicle*.

URL http://www.sfgate.com/ea/film

Film.com

Whether you are a film critic, writer or just a movie buff, you will find something here to interest you.

URL http://www.film.com

From the Snack Bar...Movie Reviews with David Ramsey

This professional reviewer gives short and sweet assessments of the latest releases.

URL http://amdream.com/Dream/snackbar.htm

Hype! Movie World

You can be the critic at this site and rate films you love or hate.

URL http://www.hype.com/movies/home.htm

Interactive Movie Reviews

More detailed than most do-it-yourself reviews, this site lets you know whether a movie is worth your money.

URL http://batech.com/cgi-bin/showmovie

Movie Critic

Rate movies you have already seen and find out which movies are worth seeing.

URL http://www.moviecritic.com

Movie Emporium

Check out the latest movie reviews and celebrity interviews.

URL http://www.filmcritic.com

Movie Review Query Engine

Just type in the name of the movie you are interested in and this site will find a review for it somewhere on the Internet.

URL http://www.cinema.pgh.pa.us/movie/reviews

Pilot Online—Movies

This longtime movie critic for the *Virginian-Pilot* offers reviews, celebrity interviews and behind-the-scenes information on today's hottest films.

URL http://www.infi.net/pilot/movies

Roger Ebert at the Movies

Search for this famous reviewer's opinions on films from 1985 to the present or check out the One Minute Movie Reviews of the latest releases.

URL http://www.suntimes.com/ebert/ebert.html

You will applaud our movie review sites.

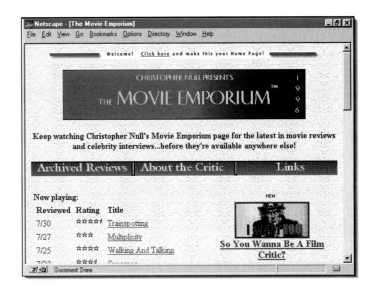

Teen Movie Critic

This reviewer may only be in his teens, but he is already a celebrity on the Internet.

URL http://www.dreamagic.com/roger/teencritic.html

MOVIES—STUDIOS

Metro Goldwyn Mayer—United Artists

MGM proudly displays its recent and upcoming films and video collection.

URL http://www.mgmua.com

Miramax

A contest, movie news and video images of new and classic Miramax movies.

URL http://www.miramax.com

New Line Cinema

The company behind movies like *Ace Ventura* and *Teenage Mutant Ninja Turtles*.

URL http://www.newline.com

Paramount Pictures

An entertaining look at the new releases from Paramount Studios.

URL http://www.paramount.com

Sony Pictures Entertainment

Neat sneak previews of upcoming movies along with a look backstage.

URL http://www.spe.sony.com/Pictures/index.html

Trimark

Visit the Trimark Village to see work in production and preview films coming out soon.

URL http://www.trimarkpictures.com

Troma

Maker of such films as *The Toxic Avenger* and *Class of Nuke 'Em High*, Troma is in a class by itself. So is its site!

URL http://www.troma.com

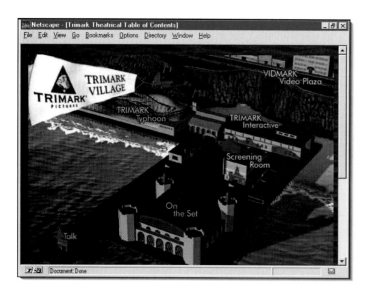

Twentieth Century Fox

At this site you have a private invitation to view special screenings, get the latest news, chat about movies and even take a stroll on the studio lot.

URL http://www.fox.com

Universal Pictures

A truly interactive look at recent productions and a sneak peek at upcoming releases.

URL http://www.mca.com/universal_pictures

Walt Disney Pictures

Find out more about your animated favorites and Disney's new releases.

URL http://www.disney.com/DisneyPictures

Warner Brothers

A neat, interactive look at the studio's recent releases, along with production news.

URL http://www.movies.warnerbros.com

MUSEUMS

African Primates At Home

Come see and hear what primates do when they monkey around.

URL http://www.indiana.edu/~primate/primates.html

Alexander Palace Time Machine

Step into this site for a virtual tour of the Tsar's Palace near St. Petersburg, Russia.

URL http://www.travelogix.com/emp/batchison

Blue Dot

A truly interesting and interactive art gallery.

URL http://www.razorfish.com/bluedot

Computer Museum

A museum dedicated to computers and the Information Age.

URL http://www.net.org

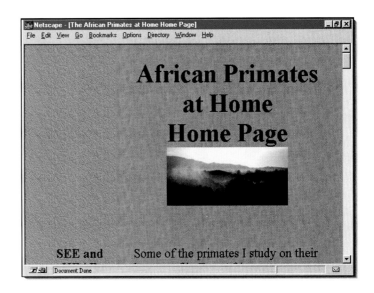

Exploratorium

This site features many great science and history exhibits.

URL http://www.exploratorium.edu

Franklin Institute Science Museum

Visit this science museum without leaving your desk.

URL http://sln.fi.edu

Gallery Walk

Sample what some of the world's finest art galleries have to offer.

URL http://www.ECNet.Net/users/mfjfg/galwalk.html

Internet Arts Museum for free

A collection of contemporary art, photography, literature and music.

URL http://www.rahul.net/iamfree

MN

JackØvacs—People's Gallery

An art exhibit that lets you contribute your own artwork for the whole world to see.

URL http://www.netm.com/art

Leonardo da Vinci Museum

This site is dedicated to the great Renaissance artist and engineer.

URL http://www.leonardo.net/main.html

Metropolitan Museum of Art

This famous New York museum displays works of art from its impressive collection.

URL http://www.metmuseum.org/htmlfile/
gallery/gallery.html

Ocean Planet

Immerse yourself in this site dedicated to the Earth's oceans.

URL http://seawifs.gsfc.nasa.gov/
ocean_planet.html

Discover the treasures in our museum sites.

Ontario Science Center

Canada's Ontario Science Center is famous for its exhibits and now offers a virtual tour online.

URL http://www.osc.on.ca/Default.html

Rock & Roll Hall of Fame and Museum

Read all about the Legends of Rock & Roll and listen to their hits when you visit this site.

URL http://www.rockhall.com

Sistine Chapel

This site offers 325 images of the art found in the great church in Rome.

URL http://www.christusrex.org/www1/
sistine/0-Tour.html

Smithsonian Institution Home Page

The famous Smithsonian Institution is online!

URL http://www.si.edu/start.htm

Vatican Museums

View works of art from the Vatican museums.

URL http://www.christusrex.org/
www1/vaticano/0-Musei.html

Virtual Museum

See some great art at this site.

URL http://www.initiative.com/virtual.html

WebMuseum

Find great works of art in the Famous Paintings collection and check out the special exhibitions on display here.

URL http://www.emf.net/louvre

World Art Treasures

Several guided tours of art images are offered in both English and French.

URL http://sgwww.epfl.ch/BERGER

MUSIC—ARCHIVES

Eyeneer Music Archives

New releases, sound and video samples and more for such musical styles as jazz and classical.

URL http://www.eyeneer.com

Grendel's Lyric Archive

A huge collection of song lyrics from yesterday's legends and today's hottest artists.

URL http://www.seas.upenn.edu/~avernon/
lyrics.html

Internet Albums Top 100

Vote for your favorites on this weekly chart and see what others in cyber-space are listening to.

URL http://www.xs4all.nl/~jojo/cma.html

Internet Underground Music Archive

The place to go for all kinds of music information.

URL http://www.iuma.com

Love Songs

The lyrics to more than 300 of the best love songs.

URL http://www.st.nepean.uws.edu.au/users/
mbuena/songwords.html

Lyrics Server

A searchable database containing the lyrics of
thousands of songs.

URL http://archive.uwp.edu/pub/music/lyrics

Muppet Songs

The collected lyrics of Jim Henson's creations,
including *It's Not Easy Bein' Green.*

URL http://www.cs.unc.edu/~arthur/
muppet-songs.html

OLGA

The Online Guitar Archive is a collection of chords
for thousands of songs, information on building
guitars, links to other guitar-related sites and
more.

URL http://www.olga.net

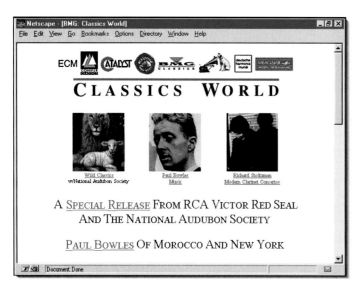

Rockmine

This massive collection of music publications,
videos, audio material and memorabilia is a
prime example of how one man's obsession
can benefit the entire world.

URL http://www.rockmine.music.co.uk

T.V. Theme Songs & More

A great collection of sound recordings for a
huge number of T.V. theme songs.

URL http://wso.williams.edu/~mgarland/
sounds

MUSIC—CLASSICAL

@concertatore

This site's nicely explained links and Discussion
Board will benefit classical musicians and fans
alike.

URL http://www.concertatore.com/concertatore

BMG: Classics World

Performers and composers galore, with CDs
that you can order online. Check out the news,
concert listings and audio clips.

URL http://www.classicalmus.com

CD Scout

The Web edition of this classical CD review magazine covers both new and old releases.

URL http://www.cdscout.com/cdscout

Classical Net

This site includes everything from a composer index to a beginner's guide to collecting CDs.

URL http://www.classical.net

Contemporary Classical Music Archive

An educational site that provides biographies, pictures and discographies for many 20th century classical music composers.

URL http://www.eyeneer.com/
CCM/index.html

Handel & Haydn Society

This professional chorus and orchestra performs baroque, classical and early romantic music using period instruments and techniques.

URL http://www.arts-online.com/hh.htm

J.S. Bach

Browse through a picture-filled biography of Johann Sebastian Bach or check out his complete works and a huge bibliography.

URL http://www.tile.net/tile/bach

Ludwig van Beethoven

Devoted to every aspect of Beethoven's life and work, this site includes images and audio files.

URL http://magic.hofstra.edu:7003/immortal/
index.html

Midori

Sony Music's Midori site offers sound clips and information on the young Japanese violinist.

URL http://www.music.sony.com/Music/
ArtistInfo/Midori.html

Mozart Among Us

Information on contemporary art music and the people who write it.

URL http://www.io.com/~glenford/
Mozart_Among_Us_TOP.html

Mozart Project

The life, times and music of Wolfgang Amadeus Mozart.

URL http://www.vivanet.com/~sboerner

Music Hall

This site features the papal choir of the Sistine Chapel and the Chigi codex as well as images and descriptions of historical music manuscripts.

URL http://www.ncsa.uiuc.edu/SDG/Experimental/vatican.exhibit/exhibit/e-music/Music.html

New York Philharmonic

Information on Philharmonic members, upcoming concerts and education programs.

URL http://www.nyphilharmon.org

Symphonix

Symphony music fans will enjoy the Los Angeles Philharmonic's home on the Internet.

URL http://www.laphil.org

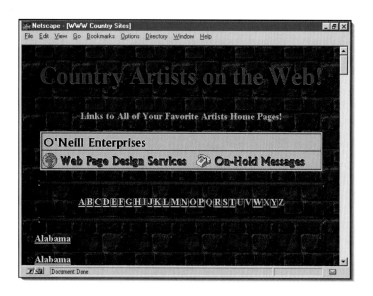

Mosey on over to our country music sites.

MUSIC—COUNTRY

Country Artists on the Web

Tons of links to the home pages of your favorite country artists, from Garth Brooks to Shania Twain.

URL http://members.gnn.com/Demon/cmalist1.htm

Country Connection

Everything for the country music fan—links, photos, tour dates and more.

URL http://digiserve.com/country

Country Page

Pictures, discographies, links and a searchable database of country artist tour information.

URL http://infoweb.magi.com/~jamesb/country/country.html

Country Standard Times

A Web magazine that brings you the latest country music news, CD and concert reviews and more.

URL http://www1.usa1.com/~cst/CST.html

Information Super Dance Floor

Going to a hoedown? This is a great resource for those who want to learn some country music dance steps.

URL http://www.apci.net/~drdeyne

MCA Nashville Cafe

From the cafe menu you can play the jukebox, get the latest country news or find the e-mail addresses of your favorite country artists.

URL http://www.mca-nashville.com

Roughstock's History of Country Music

A great presentation of country music history from the 1930s to the present. Be sure to check out the images, sounds and digital movies.

URL http://www.roughstock.com/history

Virtual Nashville

An online game where you take a virtual tour of Nashville, U.S.A., in an effort to secure a recording contract.

URL http://virtualnashville.com

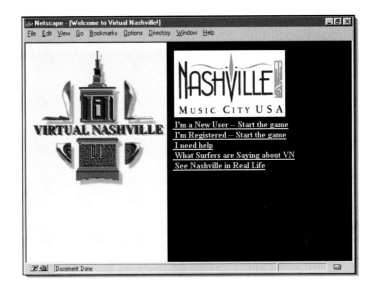

MUSIC—INDUSTRIAL

Cleopatra Records Online

New releases and difficult-to-find re-releases.

URL http://www.hallucinet.com/cleopatra

Fragface's Page of Industrial Band Pictures

Visit this site for digital pinups and album covers of Front Line Assembly, Nine Inch Nails, Ministry, Tool and other industrial heroes.

URL http://www.cris.com/%7Efragface/band.shtml

Front 242

The band's complete discography, selected lyrics, reviews, interviews and sound samples.

URL http://www.waste.org/~terje/front242

Industrial Page

A collection of information on industrial music, complete with extensive links to industrial bands, record labels, clubs and more.

URL http://bird.taponline.com/industrial

Ministry: The Unofficial Home Page

Articles, lyrics, lists of bootleg recordings as well as sound clips dealing with these industrial kings.

URL http://pulsar.cs.wku.edu/~gizzard/ ministry.html

NettWEB

The home of Nettwerk Productions, which represents artists such as Skinny Puppy.

URL http://www.nettwerk.com

Nine Inch Nails: The Unofficial Home Page

One of the many unofficial home pages devoted to Trent Reznor and his industrial band.

URL http://nothing.nin.net/%7Epatters/nin.html

Sister Machine Gun

A clever site for Sister Machine Gun, featuring writings by band member Chris Randall.

URL http://www.smg.org

Waxtrax! Records

Waxtrax! Records created the contemporary industrial sound and continues to bring you the latest from Die Warzau, KMFDM and others via the Internet.

URL http://www.waxtrax.com/waxtrax.html

MUSIC—JAZZ

American Jazz Symposium

Jazz heritage and performance are promoted and preserved through the efforts of the AJS, whose Web site includes record reviews, monthly featured artists and more.

URL http://members.aol.com/AJSExec/ajs.htm

Blue Highway

A great source of information on legendary blues artists, with links to other sites that deal with the blues.

URL http://www.vivanet.com/~blues

Contemporary Jazz Online

Experience the exciting world of contemporary jazz by checking out the artists, jazz publications, jazz clubs and other features of this site.

URL http://www.cjazz.com/default.htm

Epistrophy: The Jazz Literature Archive

This online resource explores the influence of jazz music on 20th century literature.

URL http://ie.uwindsor.ca/jazz

great day in harlem

In 1958, 57 jazz greats came together in Harlem to have their group portrait taken. Explore that moment and the artists with this cyber-documentary.

URL http://www.beatthief.com/greatday

InterJazz

Information on jazz clubs, artists and agencies along with a chat line where you can talk with artists online.

URL http://interjazz.com

Jazclass

A free online course on how to play jazz and the blues!

URL http://www.ozemail.com.au/~jazclass

Jazz Central Station

This must-see site for jazz fans includes featured artists, CD reviews, sound clips and cool graphics.

URL http://www.jazzcentralstation.com/jcs/station/index.html

JAZZ Online

A beautiful and informative monthly magazine with more than 200 image-and-sound-packed pages.

URL http://www.jazzonln.com

John Coltrane—A Love Supreme

A chronology of Coltrane's life, recommendations for new listeners and more.

URL http://www.inetworld.net/~keith/coltrane.john

Miles Davis Discography

This site covers Davis' recordings from 1945 to 1991.

URL http://www.wam.umd.edu/~losinp/music/md-list.html

Jazz things up with these sites.

New Orleans Jazz Festival

Everything from live chats to a photo and poster gallery.

URL http://www.nojazzfest.com

MUSIC—LABELS

A&M Records

A behind-the-scenes look at A&M artists.

URL http://www.amrecords.com

Atlantic Records

Some of the hippest artists, such as Hootie & The Blowfish, are featured here.

URL http://www.atlantic-records.com

Capitol Records at Hollywood and Vine

Grab a tour schedule at Leaning Tower Travel Center, tour the stars' rooms at Starland Motel and more at this entertaining site.

URL http://www.hollywoodandvine.com

Columbia House

Check out Columbia House's Music Club and read articles from *SPIN* magazine.

URL http://www.columbiahouse.com

Def Jam

This innovative rap label, launched over a decade ago, has sound clips and artist information online.

URL http://spider.media.philips.com/defjam/defhome.html

Elektra

AC/DC, Colin James and Natalie Merchant are just a few of the many talented artists on the Elektra label.

URL http://www.elektra.com

EMI Music Canada

Take the musical hitchhiker's guide through this cleverly designed site.

URL http://www.EMImusic.ca

EMI Records

This colorful site is crammed with video and sound clips and has interesting information about EMI's artists.

URL http://www.emirec.com

Geffen/DGC

Artists such as Peter Gabriel and the Cowboy Junkies are part of this family. From this page you can visit the artists' self-produced sites.

URL http://www.geffen.com

Giant Step

Specialists in acid jazz, smooth jazz and other up-and-coming styles of music.

URL http://www.giantstp.com

Heyday Records

The Web site of an independent label specializing in San Francisco artists.

URL http://www.iuma.com/heyday

One of the 10 most adventurous small labels in the world"
- *Rolling Stone magazine's 'Independents Daze' survey.*

Indie Labels on the Web

A great resource for connecting to the many independent labels that are making music history on the Web.

URL http://kathoderay.org/music/labels.html

Island Records

This U.K. label has featured musical legends such as Bob Marley and the B-52's.

URL http://www.island.co.uk

MCA

Lots of pictures and sound recordings as well as tips on how to be a "cool dude."

URL http://www.mcamei.com

Mercury Records

Check out featured artists, tour dates, interviews and interactive press kits.

URL http://www.mercuryrecords.com/mercury

MUSIC—LABELS *continued*

These music sites really rock!

PolyGram Records

This site features sound and video clips as well as a diverse collection of artists such as Def Leppard and ABBA.

URL http://www.polygram.com/polygram/Music.html

RCA Victor

See why *Billboard Magazine* named this label the #1 distributor of world music.

URL http://www.rcavictor.com

Reprise Records

View artists' sites and find out about new releases.

URL http://www.RepriseRec.com

Rhino Records

This label releases albums from Paul Anka, the Stray Cats and other artists from the '50s right up to the '90s.

URL http://cybertimes.com/Rhino/Welcome.html

Sony Music

Artist information, tour dates and a collection of sound and video recordings of your favorites can be found here.

URL http://www.music.sony.com/Music/MusicIndex.html

Virgin Records

Sample new music online, contact Virgin Records' representatives and find out about Virgin's recording artists.

URL http://www.vmg.co.uk

Warner Bros. Records

Madonna, R.E.M., The Red Hot Chili Peppers and k.d. lang are just a few of the artists who call Warner home.

URL http://www.wbr.com

MUSIC—METAL

Black Sabbath Home Page

Links to mountains of information on the well-known band.

URL http://www4.ncsu.edu/eos/users/j/jbmyers/www/BlackSabbath.html

Christian Heavy Metal and Alternative Home Page

Sound samples, guitar chords and plenty of links to other Christian metal sites.

URL http://www.wp.cc.nc.us/%7Ejwood

Earache Records

Click on the blue door and enter the Earache Club for information about some of the loudest metal bands in existence.

URL http://www.earache.com

Heavy Metal

One fan's extensive tribute to the music he loves, from Anathema to White Zombie.

URL http://www.eecs.nwu.edu/~autopsy/metal

Impaled Existence

An online magazine that provides interviews, news and reviews of all forms of extreme music, including metal, industrial and thrash.

URL http://www.cybergate.com/~azari/
impaled.html

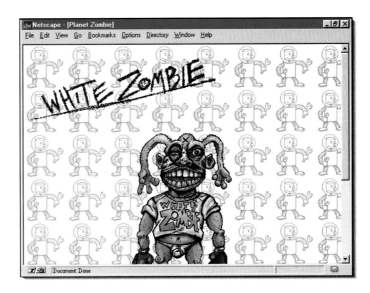

Metallica Club

Information on the Official Metallica Fan Club.

URL http://www.dorsai.org/%7Ejkeis/
metallica/metclub.html

Planet Zombie: The White Zombie Home Page

Maneuver your way around the band's colorful and darkly humorous home page.

URL http://www.geffen.com/planetzombie

Tracks of Creation: The Hard Music Pages

This online magazine profiles CDs, bands, recent concerts and Web sites.

URL http://www.ratw.com/creation

MUSIC—ROCK

ArtRock ONLINE

Use the search tool to find art rock posters and memorabilia.

URL http://www.artrock.com

Internet Music Shop

Search the Internet Music Shop's online catalogs of more than 20,000 music-related items.

URL http://www.musicsales.co.uk

L.A. Rock & Roll Road Map

Find everything from concert sites to rock artists' final resting spots on this road map.

URL http://www.net101.com/rocknroll/index.html

LIFE Rock & Roll Gallery

One of the best rock sites on the Web, this gallery offers information and images of rock & roll subjects from *LIFE* magazine.

URL http://pathfinder.com

Rock & Roll Hall of Fame and Museum

When you can't visit the Rock & Roll Hall of Fame in person, this site is the next best thing.

URL http://www.rockhall.com

Rock Online Home Page

Rock Online is a one-stop site for information and links to rock artists, record labels, indie bands and more.

URL http://www.rockonline.com

Rock&Roll

This fabulous site is filled with backstage interviews, contests and information on rock & roll radio and T.V. shows from PBS.

URL http://www.pbs.org/RocknRoll/rr.html

RockNet

RockNet offers reviews, interviews and a rock hotline for up-to-date rock news.

URL http://www.rocknet.com

Rockweb Interactive

Rockweb Interactive has it all—links to rock Web sites, hip chat, interviews with rock artists and more.

URL http://www.rockweb.com

MUSIC—STORES

1-800 Music Now

Choose from thousands of CDs online and listen to album samples.

URL http://www.1800musicnow.mci.com

Anthem Entertainment Network

An online entertainment superstore offering more than 100,000 CDs, including imports from Europe, Japan and Australia, as well as more than 7,000 laser discs and lots of CD-ROMs.

URL http://www.AnthemEnt.com

BackTrac Records

Do you miss the 45 single? Browse through this catalog of 45s and extended plays. There are special sections for Beatles and Elvis recordings.

URL http://users.aol.com/backtrac45/private/page1.htm

Bargain Finder

Looking for a rock or pop recording? This innovative service compares prices at online stores.

URL http://bf.cstar.ac.com/bf

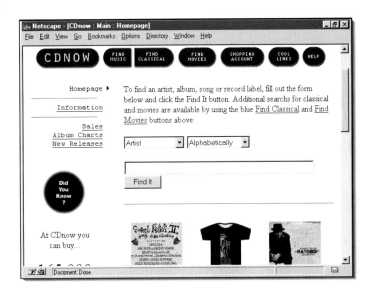

Camsco Music

Hard-to-find and independently produced folk music by more than 120 artists.

URL http://www.camsco.com

CD Land

Search by artist or title, look at brand new releases or find out who the staff's favorite artists are.

URL http://www.persimmon.com/CDLand

CDnow

Look for new titles or the top hot albums in this collection of 165,000 CDs, with shipping available to almost anywhere in the world.

URL http://www.cdnow.com

CDworld

More than 100,000 CDs and cassettes that you can search by artist, title or label, as well as music videos, CD-ROMs and accessories.

URL http://cdworld.com

*Check out our
noteworthy
music sites!*

Classic Records

Get classical, jazz and popular recordings on good old vinyl LPs.

URL http://www.classicrecs.com

elektra.com

Look at artists' pages, photos, biographies and more, and then listen to their hit songs with RealAudio.

URL http://www.elektra.com

EMusic

More than 100,000 titles online, with lots of album cover photos.

URL http://www.emusic.com

GEMM

This comprehensive site lists more than 600,000 new and used CDs, LPs and other music memorabilia from around the world.

URL http://gemm.com

H&B Recordings Direct

For collectors of classical music CDs. Members save 10% off the regular prices.

URL http://www.hbdirect.com

i? music/media

Find lots of independent labels, unsigned and underground artists and mainstream releases.

URL http://eve.icw.com/cd/imm1.html

Music Boulevard

Take a walk down the Boulevard to find a large selection of music titles, as well as contests, music news and more.

URL http://www.musicblvd.com

Music Connection

A catalog of more than 75,000 CD titles, a 20-day return policy and free shipping in the U.S. if you order nine or more CDs.

URL http://www.inetbiz.com/music

Reprise Records

Lots of cool information on artists from Alanis Morissette to Neil Young, plus contests and news of the day.

URL http://www.RepriseRec.com

Rhino Records

The king of re-issues. Search the catalog and order anything from disco to Nancy Sinatra.

URL http://cybertimes.com/Rhino

Sound Spectrum

The 30,000 classical choices are just part of the 120,000 titles available here. Worldwide concert information and other music news are also offered.

URL http://www.soundspectrum.com

NETWORKS

Advanced Micronet Solutions

This company offers complete networking services, including design and planning.

URL http://www.advmicronet.com

American Research Group

ARG provides extensive training on networking topics, including ISDN and Unix.

URL http://arg.catalogue.com

Asanté

Get Macintosh network acceleration software and check out what is new from this Ethernet specialist.

URL http://www.asante.com

Ascend Communications

Winner of many awards for wide area network hardware.

URL http://www.ascend.com

Cisco Connection Online

A leading global supplier of internetworking products, including local area network switches and dial-up access servers.

URL http://www.cisco.com

Compaq

Visit the online outpost of a worldwide leader in networking technology and design.

URL http://www.compaq.com

Digital Equipment Corporation

An international supplier of networked computer systems, software and services.

URL http://www.digital.com

Farallon

In addition to providing local area network products, Farallon is known for its Netopia family of high-speed Internet access products.

URL http://www.farallon.com

FORE Systems

This company is at the forefront of increasing network speed and capacity through the use of asynchronous transfer mode technology.

URL http://www.fore.com

Introduction to ISDN

A well-written introduction to Integrated Services Digital Network—a very fast connection to the Internet.

URL http://www.zdnet.com/cobb/ibusines/
9506/isdn.html

Introduction to Network Management

An introduction, written by a beginner for beginners, to the Simple Network Management Protocol (SNMP) used on Unix networks.

URL http://www.undergrad.math.uwaterloo.ca/
~tkvallil/snmp.html

Introduction to Networking

A site covering the history of networking, TCP/IP networks, Ethernet and more.

URL http://linuxwww.db.erau.edu/NAG/
node3.html

Introduction to the Internet

This simple presentation explains how local area networks connect to wide area networks, ultimately resulting in the Internet.

URL http://www.onshore.com/
inet-presentation/lanvwan.html

Legato

This company is a leading supplier of network-wide data storage management software.

URL http://www.legato.com

Networking from IBM

IBM's site features interviews with prominent networking experts and allows you to copy IBM LAN Client to your computer for free.

URL http://www.raleigh.ibm.com/nethome.html

Novell

Novell's well-known local area network and wide area network products include NetWare and LAN WorkPlace.

URL http://www.novell.com

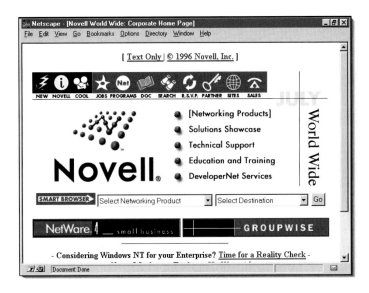

Proteon

This company provides products for internetworking systems and client/server connections.

URL http://www.proteon.com

Quick Reference Guide to the Ethernet System

Wondering what Ethernet is? This informative site offers a concise description.

URL http://wwwhost.ots.utexas.edu/
ethernet/10quickref/ch1qr_1.html

Rockwell Network Systems

RNS produces top-quality hardware for networking—take a look at some of the latest products.

URL http://www.rns.com

Shiva

The remote access specialists, Shiva provides products and services for telecommuters, large enterprise networks and small branch offices.

URL http://www.shiva.com

NETWORKS *continued*

Standard Microsystems Corporation

SMC supplies products for connecting personal computers over local area networks.
URL http://www.smc.com

U.S. Robotics

This networking company covers business, home and office networks.
URL http://www.usr.com

NEWS

ABC News Updates Archive

Several months of ABC news updates are kept here for quick reference.
URL http://www.prognet.com/contentp/abc/
updates.html

ABC RadioNet

Listen to the latest weather, news and sports from ABC.
URL http://www.abcradionet.com

Read all about our news sites.

Air Force Radio News

Listen to the Air Force's daily five-minute news broadcast or watch a short news report on your computer.
URL http://www.brooks.af.mil/realaudio/
newsbyte.html

ALLSPORTS

Cyber-visitors can check out sports news, contests, a live chat area and more.
URL http://www.allsports.com

Atlantic Monthly

This magazine has been covering politics, society and the arts for more than a century.
URL http://www.theatlantic.com

Boston Globe

Not just news! The Globe's Web site has a variety of interactive games and polls.
URL http://www.globe.com

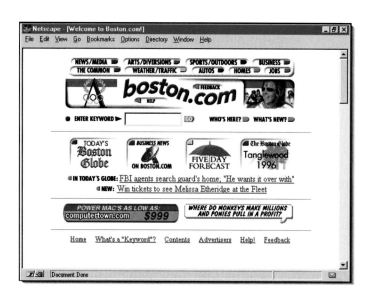

Capitol Watch Online

Want to find the latest political news and learn how the American government works? This is the place to go!

URL http://www.capitolwatch.com

CBC Newsworld

The home page of the Canadian Broadcasting Corporation's news and information network.

URL http://www.cbc.ca/nw

CBC Radio News

Headlines, program scheduling and sound recordings from the Canadian Broadcasting Corporation's daily radio shows.

URL http://radioworks.cbc.ca

CBS News: UTTMlink

CBS News Up to the Minute provides you with all the latest news items.

URL http://uttm.com

CBS RADIO NETWORKS

An excellent source of information on the latest baseball and football news and more.

URL http://www.cbsradio.com

CFRA Radio

This major Canadian radio station is the first in the world to transmit live on the Internet!

URL http://www.cfra.com

Chicago Sun-Times Online

News and more from one of the Windy City's leading papers.

URL http://www.suntimes.com

ClariNet e.News on the Web

This online service provides news and information to newsgroups on the Internet.

URL http://www.clarinet.com/newstree.html

CNET radio

Take an audio tour of this popular radio show or find out what's new in the world of computers.

URL http://www.cnet.com/Content/Radio

CNET: The Computer Network

Find out what's coming up on this acclaimed cable computer news show next week or review the transcript from a previous episode.

URL http://www.cnet.com/Content/Tv

CNN Financial

Catch news from the financial industry as it breaks!

URL http://www.cnnfn.com

CNN Interactive

Read the latest headlines, try today's quiz or visit the Video Vault to watch video clips of recent news.

URL http://www.cnn.com

Colin Soloway's Article Archive

This reporter's personal archive contains stories he wrote for U.S. newspapers and magazines on his experiences in the former Yugoslavia.

URL http://www.vmedia.com/colin/index.htm

Comic Strip

Why not turn to the funny pages for a break from the hard news of the day?

URL http://www.unitedmedia.com/comics

ComputerWise

Check out the latest computer news and software releases.

URL http://cs7bbs.com/compwise.html

Corporate Financials Online

This site provides links to corporate news as well as general business news.

URL http://www.cfonews.com

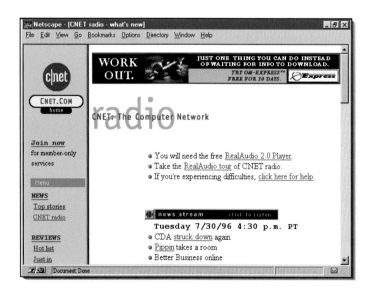

CRAYON

Create your own newspaper that includes only the information of interest to you.

URL http://crayon.net

Deja News

This site lets you search through all the Usenet newsgroups to find what you are looking for.

URL http://www.dejanews.com

Detroit News

The site of one of Detroit's largest newspapers is updated daily.

URL http://detnews.com

Electric Library

Browse through thousands of articles from newspapers and magazines.

URL http://www.elibrary.com

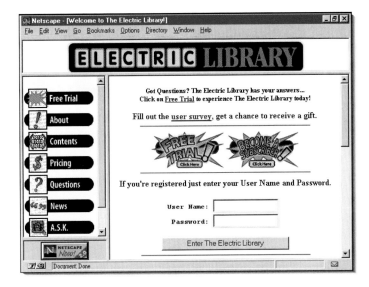

Electronic Newsstand

Check out many popular magazines and even subscribe to your favorites online.

URL http://www.enews.com

Electronic Telegraph

An impressive online version of the United Kingdom's *Daily Telegraph*.

URL http://www.telegraph.co.uk

ENN Radio

Entertainment Network News offers a great collection of links to radio stations on the Web.

URL http://www.slip.net/~scmetro/radio.htm

ESPNET SportsZone

All the latest scores and stories from ESPN.

URL http://ESPNET.SportsZone.com

NEWS *continued*

Financial Times

This site makes it easy for you to follow the world's business, economic and political news.

URL http://www.usa.ft.com

Financial Times Television

Get the latest updates on European business and economics.

URL http://www.ftvision.com

Fox Television

Fox offers up-to-date information and statistics for all your favorite sports.

URL http://www.fox.com/foxtv.htm

Globe and Mail

Canada's national newspaper is online at this site.

URL http://www.globeandmail.ca

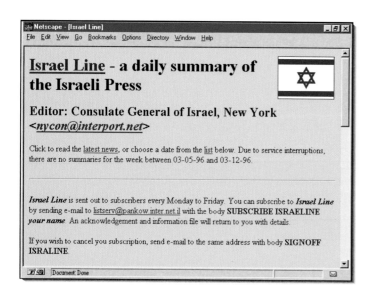

Grassroots

This is an international environmental magazine that also offers a version specifically for today's young people.

URL http://www.bendtech.com/library/grassroots

HotWired

The online version of the magazine that offers an offbeat look at cyber-space and cyber-culture.

URL http://www.hotwired.com

Infoseek Personal

Choose the news topics of interest to you and have a personalized online newspaper prepared for you daily.

URL http://personal.infoseek.com

Israel Line

Daily news summaries of the Israeli press from 1994 to the present.

URL http://gauss.technion.ac.il/israeline

Kansas City Star

You will find much more than news, weather and sports in this online newspaper.

URL http://www.kcstar.com

Kidz in the Newz

Profiles of young people who are making a difference.

URL http://www.azc.com/client/enn2/kidsnews.htm

Los Angeles Times

Headlines, information about L.A. and, of course, entertainment news.

URL http://www.latimes.com/HOME

Maclean's

This weekly news magazine covers current Canadian events.

URL http://www.canoe.ca/Macleans

Tune in to our news sites.

Maps in the News

Find out more about the geography of all the places you keep hearing about on the six o'clock news.

URL http://www-map.lib.umn.edu/news.html

Mercury Center News Library

Free access to the headlines and first paragraphs of almost one million articles published in the *San Jose Mercury News* since 1985.

URL http://spyglass.sjmercury.com/library

MoJo Wire

This site offers political exposés from the people behind *Mother Jones* magazine.

URL http://www.mojones.com

Montreal Gazette Online

Find out what's happening in this historic Canadian city.

URL http://www.montrealgazette.com

Movietone News Online

The famous newsreel producers have created an entertaining archive where you can view the films.

URL http://www.iguide.com/movies/movitone

My Virtual Newspaper

An excellent collection of links to American and international papers.

URL http://www.refdesk.com/paper.html

Nando Times

Check out this useful source of U.S. and international news.

URL http://www.nando.net/nt/nando.cgi

National Public Radio

Listen to the latest newscast or read transcripts of earlier shows.

URL http://www.npr.org

Nature

Weekly news from the scientific community is offered online by this international journal.

URL http://www.nature.com

NBC News

Information on NBC's news shows, such as Dateline and the Nightly News, as well as recent headlines and weather forecasts.

URL http://www.nbc.com/news/index.html

Netly News

There are more than 35 million stories in cyber-space and this site investigates a new one every day.

URL http://pathfinder.com/Netly

New York Times

The site for this famous newspaper includes the daily crossword puzzle.

URL http://www.nytimesfax.com

News Resource

A collection of links to newspapers and other news sources around the world.

URL http://newo.com/news

newsday.com

An exciting look at news and issues from New York.

URL http://www.newsday.com

Newsgroups Archives

This page allows you to search the current month's newsgroup archives for the latest computer and Internet gossip.

URL http://awebs.com/news_archive

Newsletter Library

Choose topics from this extensive list and free copies of the appropriate newsletters will be mailed to you.

URL http://pub.savvy.com

Uncover the truth at our news sites.

NewsPage

Get up-to-date information on every industry from computers to health care.

URL http://www.newspage.com

NewStocks Daily

Every business day brings news for investors as well as a regular commentary on how to survive in today's workplace.

URL http://www.dma.net/dom

Online DailyNews

The news at this site is updated 24 hours a day.

URL http://www.dailynews.net

Online Newspapers

A huge online collection of American and international newspapers.

URL http://www.ucc.uconn.edu/~jpa94001/papers.html

Pathfinder

Find excerpts from many of your favorite magazines such as *TIME*, *Life* and *People*.

URL http://www.pathfinder.com

PBS Online NewsHour

Transcripts, letters to the editor and current stories can be found here.

URL http://www.pbs.org/newshour

Pointcast Network

At this site you can get a free program that will search the Web for you and send personalized news, stock quotes and more directly to your computer screen!

URL http://www.pointcast.com

Popular Mechanics Zone

The popular technology magazine now maintains a site on the Web.

URL http://popularmechanics.com

Radio on the Internet

Search the directory of sound files or check out the links to other news radio sites.

URL http://town.hall.org/radio

San Diego Source

The online version of the *San Diego Daily Transcript* covers much more than just news.

URL http://www.sddt.com

San Jose Mercury News

Visit the site of one of the first papers to go online.

URL http://www.sjmercury.com

Sports Byline USA

Find out about America's most popular sports talk show here.

URL http://www.sportsline.com/u/ronbarr/
index.html

Sports Illustrated Online

This site offers sports stories and a sampling of the famous Swimsuit Issue.

URL http://www.pathfinder.com/si

SportsLine USA

Sports news and updates, contests and more can be found here.

URL http://www.sportsline.com

Television News Archive

Vanderbilt University has been collecting and indexing television newscasts for almost 30 years. Check out the collection at this site.

URL http://tvnews.vanderbilt.edu

The Gate

Two of San Francisco's top newspapers—*The Chronicle* and *The Examiner*—provide lots of information daily.

URL http://www.sfgate.com

The Nation

The online version of America's oldest weekly magazine is dedicated to providing intelligent and honest reporting.

URL http://www.thenation.com

The Times

Browse through today's edition of *The Times* from London or check out past issues.

URL http://www.the-times.co.uk

This is True

A collection of bizarre, but true, stories collected from news services around the world.

URL http://www.freecom.com/true/index.html

TIME

Articles from current and past issues of this widely read weekly news magazine are available here.

URL http://www.pathfinder.com/time/
magazine/magazine.html

NO

NEWS *continued*

TIME Archives

This site contains covers, tables of contents and articles from *TIME* magazine's past issues.

URL http://pathfinder.com/time/magazine/1995timeline.graphics.html

Top 100 Newspapers

Links to the top 100 newspapers in the U.S.

URL http://www.interest.com/top100.html

Toronto Star

Canada's largest newspaper offers all the essentials, and then some.

URL http://www.thestar.com

U.S. News Online

This site delivers everything you would expect from a news magazine—and more.

URL http://www.usnews.com

USA Today

The online version of one of the most popular American national newspapers.

URL http://www.usatoday.com

Vancouver Province

In addition to news, weather and sports, this Canadian newspaper provides its online readers with a guide to the Internet.

URL http://www.southam.com:80/vancouverprovince

Virtual News/Talk Radio

If you're looking for news, this site has all the links you'll need.

URL http://www.speakeasy.org/~radiospy

Voice of America

A radio service that brings the news as America sees it to countries around the world.

URL http://www.voa.gov

Wall Street Journal

This continually updated site is the business person's best friend.

URL http://update.wsj.com

Washington Times Weekly

A look at the news and politics of the U.S. capital.

URL http://www.washtimes-weekly.com

WEB 500 Current Events

This site provides links to sites that deal with the week's hottest topics.

URL http://www.web500.com/categories/Current_Events/current.htm

What's New in the World of Science

The latest discoveries and a look at current issues, with links to related Web sites.

URL http://www.exploratorium.edu/learning_studio/news

Yahoo Headlines

This is a quick way to check out daily headlines on a variety of topics.

URL http://www.yahoo.com/headlines

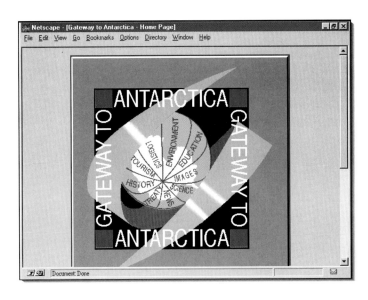

ZEN Electronic News Summaries

This weekly summary focuses on the biggest news in electronics and information technology.

URL http://www.eecg.toronto.edu/~zahir

OCEANIA & AUSTRALIA

Australian Government

Information on the government of the Land Down Under.

URL http://gov.info.au

Gateway to Antarctica

Find out about Antarctica's history and environment or plan a trip to the continent.

URL http://icair.iac.org.nz

OCEANIA & AUSTRALIA *continued*

Indonesian Government

Check out links to many Indonesian government Web pages here.

URL http://www.ece.iit.edu/~mmarwali/government.html

New Zealand Government

This site contains information about the government and constitution of New Zealand.

URL http://www.govt.nz

Pacific Islands

If you dream of escaping to a South Pacific island paradise, check out this site.

URL http://coombs.anu.edu.au/WWWVL-PacificStudies.html

Papua New Guinea Online

At this site you can learn about one of the most exotic places in the world.

URL http://www.niugini.com/~pngcom/profile.htm

Philippines Government and Laws

An extensive collection of information on the laws and government of the Philippines.

URL http://pdx.rpnet.com/rpnet/homepage/govlaw.htm

Singapore Government

Find out about the government of this fascinating nation.

URL http://www.gov.sg

OFFICE SUPPLIES

Boise Cascade Office Products

One of the largest manufacturers and distributors of office products in North America provides a fun site with lots of information.

URL http://www.bcop.com

Business Resource Center

A great guide for anyone starting a business, this site covers business planning, marketing, management and financing.

URL http://www.kciLink.com:80/brc

Canon

Find the copier that suits your needs, from small machines for the home to high-speed color copiers.

URL http://www.usa.canon.com/copiers/index.html

Esselte Online

Check out the complete range of products or get free fonts from one of the top office product suppliers in the world.

URL http://www.esselte.com

Kinko's

Find out about Kinko's products, services and locations around the world.

URL http://www.kinkos.com

Laser-Tone International

Looking for recycled laser printer cartridges, drums and developer units? This company offers free pickup and delivery in the U.S.

URL http://www.laser-tone.com

Stock up with our office supply sites.

LithoQuoter

Get hot printing tips and free online quotes from top-quality printers across the U.S.

URL http://www.lithoquoter.com

OfficeMax Online

Order office supplies, computers, furniture and more online and have them delivered to your door.

URL http://www2.pcy.mci.net/marketplace/ofcmax

Rubbermaid Online!

Not just containers—this site provides ordering information for all your office supplies.

URL http://home.rubbermaid.com

Sir Speedy

Need a project designed, printed or copied? With more than 800 locations worldwide, there is sure to be a Sir Speedy center near you.

URL http://www.sirspeedy.com

OP

OFFICE SUPPLIES *continued*

Stacey's Professional Bookstore

A huge selection of business books and more. Read sample chapters or order books online.

URL http://www.staceys.com

Steelcase

A whole family of office furniture available around the world.

URL http://www.steelcase.com

OPERA

Cyberspace Opera

You can help create this comic opera about five lonely souls in cyber-space.

URL http://www.en.utexas.edu/~slatin/opera

Fat Lady Sing Off

Your coast-to-coast guide to opera schedules in North America.

URL http://www.toyota.com/hub/livingarts/opera

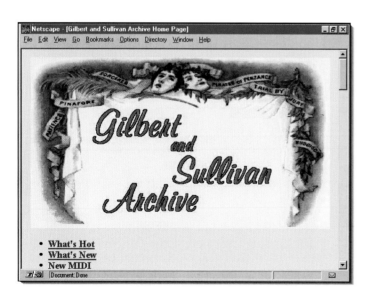

Gilbert and Sullivan Archive

Lots of information about Gilbert and Sullivan operas, including the lyrics, music and pictures of the original performers.

URL http://math.idbsu.edu/gas/GaS.html

Lied and Song Texts Page

A large collection of poems and lyrics of German art songs used by classical operatic composers.

URL http://www.recmusic.org/lieder

Making of Rigoletto

Experience Verdi from the viewpoint of college students who put on their own production of this famous opera.

URL http://gray.music.rhodes.edu/Musichtmls/RigolettoProj.html

OperaGlass

This site is a good starting point for anyone who wants to explore opera on the Web. Check out the home pages of opera professionals and fans.

URL http://rick.stanford.edu/opera/main.html

OperaWeb

Reviews, opera sing-alongs and an interactive quiz with prizes are just some of the things that await you here.

URL http://www.doit.it/OperaWeb/English/ OperaWeb.html

Virtual Opera House

A light-hearted, entertaining look at the world of opera that still provides some pretty solid information.

URL http://www.lia.co.za/users/dlever

OS/2

Ever Onward OS/2 Campaign

OS/2 users unite! If you favor OS/2, e-mail this group and share your opinion.

URL http://www.aescon.com/innoval/everos2

FAQ: Should I Buy OS/2 Warp 3.0?

These frequently asked questions about the OS/2 operating system present the facts without playing favorites.

URL http://psych.colorado.edu/~rsmith/ buy-os2.html

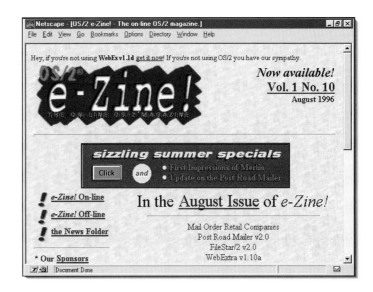

Inside OS/2

Check out some tips and techniques for using OS/2.

URL http://www.cobb.com/ios/index.htm

LEO-OS/2 Archive

A searchable collection of OS/2 software, including applications and multimedia.

URL http://www.leo.org/archiv/os2/ index_grouped.html

OS/2 Compatibility Chart

Wondering if your hardware will work with OS/2? This site covers everything from motherboards to keyboards.

URL http://www.austin.ibm.com/pspinfo/ os2hw.html

OS/2 e-Zine!

This online magazine covers issues of interest to OS/2 users.

URL http://www.haligonian.com/os2

OS/2 Games

Interested in developing new games for OS/2? Want to play DOS and Windows games on OS/2? Check out this site first.

URL http://www.austin.ibm.com/os2games

OS/2 Must-Have Utilities

A great collection of free OS/2 utilities.

URL http://www.os2.hammer.org/OS2

OS/2 Software

A small but useful collection of OS/2 utilities, including Internet and multimedia applications.

URL http://www.state.ky.us/software/os2.html

OS/2 Warp

Visit IBM's official page for OS/2 Warp and find out all about this operating system.

URL http://www.austin.ibm.com/pspinfo/os2.html

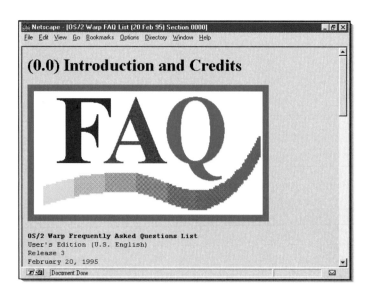

OS/2 Warp Frequently Asked Questions List

This document will answer almost any question you might have about OS/2 Warp, whether you are a beginner or an advanced user.

URL http://www.mit.edu:8001/activities/os2/faq/os2faq0000.html

OS/2 Warp Hot-Links

A comprehensive list of OS/2 links in a simple, easy-to-use format.

URL http://www.engr.iupui.edu/~gdamlova/os2.html

OS/2 Warp Migration Assistant

Planning a move from OS/2 2.x to OS/2 Warp? Check out this stylish site for assistance.

URL http://pscc.dfw.ibm.com/warpmi

Ports Applications & WisheS

PAWS is dedicated to OS/2 software development and porting.

URL http://www.teamos2.org/paws

TeamOS/2 Online

TeamOS/2 is an international group of volunteers dedicated to promoting the OS/2 operating system.

URL http://www.teamos2.org

The OS/2 Internet Apps Page

Everything you need to go online with OS/2, including dialers, Web browsers, e-mail, news, ftp, telnet and irc programs.

URL http://www.phoenix.net/~vccubed/ os2apps.html

Toma's OS/2 Game Page

Information on many games for OS/2.

URL http://exo.com/~toma/os2games/ index.html

Warp Online

This guide to OS/2 Warp computing contains features, tips, software previews and more.

URL http://in.net/~mcdonajp

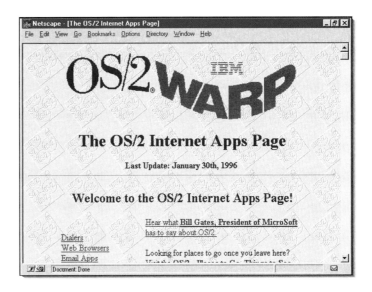

Warp Pharmacy

Troubleshooting and tips for OS/2 problems.

URL http://www.zeta.org.au/~jon/ WarpPharmacy.html

WebExtra

Add Netscape-like bookmarks and other features to the OS/2 WebExplorer browser.

URL http://www.aescon.com/innoval/ webextra/index.htm

PARANORMAL

Aquarian Age

An online school of astrology and New Age studies.

URL http://www.aquarianage.org/index.html

AwareNET

This site will show you how to predict your future using numerology and astrology.

URL http://www.awarenet.com

P

Contact Project

Can you help decipher a message from Tau Ceti, a fictional alien civilization?

URL http://sunsite.unc.edu/lunar/alien.html

Crop Circle Connector

A great resource for information and pictures of the latest crop circles.

URL http://www.hub.co.uk/intercafe/cropcircle/connector.html

Dream Archive

Read accounts of other people's dreamlives or submit one of your own dreams.

URL http://www.tbyte.com/people/joe/dreams/welcome.htm

Facade

Have your Tarot cards or your runes read and check out your biorhythm here.

URL http://www.facade.com

Have a close encounter with our paranormal sites.

Frontier—The Fortean Times Online

An online version of the monthly magazine that deals with all manner of bizarre and strange phenomena.

URL http://www.forteantimes.com/frontier

Ghost Stories R Us

Add your own ghostly encounter and read the stories of others.

URL http://www.azc.com/client/page/fright.html

Independent Research Center for Unexplained Phenomena

Articles and research dealing with UFOs, crop circles, parapsychology and more.

URL http://rainbow.medberry.com/enigma/index.html

Isis Unveiled

A comprehensive guide to occult resources on the Web.

URL http://malkuth.sephiroth.org/occult.html

ParaScope

This site is dedicated to uncovering information on conspiracies, UFOs and other paranormal phenomena.

URL http://www.parascope.com/index.htm

Prophetic Insights

A detailed look at the prophecies of Nostradamus.

URL http://www.concentric.net/~adachi/prophecy/prophecy.html

Reincarnation—The Way of Soul Evolution

Many articles and personal accounts dealing with the reincarnation of the soul.

URL http://www.spiritweb.org/Spirit/reincarnation.html

Shadowlands Bigfoot Page

Lots of pictures, accounts and the latest research on this elusive creature.

URL http://www.serve.com/shadows/bf.htm

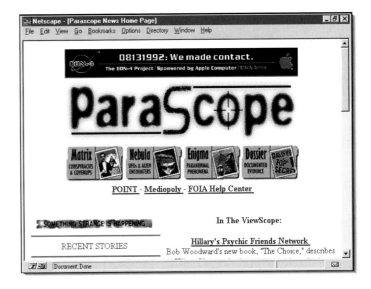

Shadowlands Ghosts Page

Links to spooky sites and ghostly pictures.

URL http://users.aol.com/shadoland2/ghost.html

Skeptics Society

Using logic, reason and scientific methods, these people investigate the claims of those who have had paranormal experiences.

URL http://www.skeptic.com

Strange Magazine

The magazine that approaches strange phenomena in an objective manner.

URL http://www.cais.com/strangemag/home.html

Strange Universe

Ghosts, UFOs, angels and other paranormal activities.

URL http://www.europa.com/~itm/strange.htm

P

PARANORMAL *continued*

UFONEWS World Report

The latest news and views on UFOs.

URL http://www.ufonews.com

Uri Geller's Interactive Psychic City

You are invited by one of the world's top psychics to test your own psychic ability by trying to bend a spoon across the Internet in order to win $1,000,000.

URL http://www.urigeller.com

Voodoo Information Pages

Everything you ever wanted to know about voodoo but were afraid to ask.

URL http://www.vmedia.com/shannon/
voodoo/voodoo.html

Weekly Horoscope

Come here to find out what the week has in store for you.

URL http://www.cam.org/~fishon1/
horo.html

World Wide Web Ouija

An online Ouija board.

URL http://www.math.unh.edu/~black/
cgi-bin/ouija.cgi

X-Files

The official site for the popular T.V. show that deals with the paranormal.

URL http://www.thex-files.com

PERSONAL CARE

Aveda

Hair care and skin care products available around the world.

URL http://www.aveda.com

Avon

Avon is now wired! U.S. residents can submit an online catalog request or arrange to have an Avon sales representative contact them.

URL http://www.avon.com

BeautiControl Cosmetics

Skin care and cosmetic products for men and women available throughout the U.S., Canada, Puerto Rico and the United Kingdom.

URL http://www.beauticontrol.com

Clinique

Find out about this popular line of makeup and skin care products and take advantage of the online personal consultation.

URL http://www.clinique.com

Colgate

Learn how you should really be brushing and flossing your teeth—then choose the right toothbrush and toothpaste!

URL http://www.colgate.com

Rembrandt Oral Care

Find answers to frequently asked questions about dentistry, dental health, toothpaste and mouthwash.

URL http://www.rembrandt.com

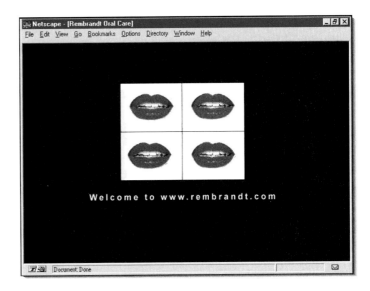

Revlon Report

Learn about fleshtone colors. If you are in the U.S. or Canada you can get a free copy of the Revlon Report.

URL http://oscars.guide.com/revlon

Schick

Welcome to a land of high-tech razors, basketball players and pictures of a woman shaving her face.

URL http://www.schick.com

Shiseido

Visit Cyber Island and get a look at Les Salons du Palais Royal Shiseido in Paris.

URL http://www.shiseido.co.jp/e/home_e.html

The Body Shop

See what this innovative cosmetics and body care company has done since 1976 when it started with a single shop in Brighton, England.

URL http://www.the-body-shop.com

P

PERSONAL CARE *continued*

Urban Decay Cosmetics

This hip site offers an online color sampler and helps you find the nearest retailer.

URL http://www.urbandecay.com

Warner-Lambert

A host of brands you will recognize from a company you may not be familiar with.

URL http://www.warner-lambert.com

PHYSICS

Discover our physics sites.

Advanced Light Source (ALS)

The ALS produces the brightest ultraviolet light in the world.

URL http://beanie.lbl.gov:8001/als/
als_homepage.html

Applied Optics Group

People who play with mirrors and prisms.

URL http://prism.ph.ed.ac.uk/welcome.html

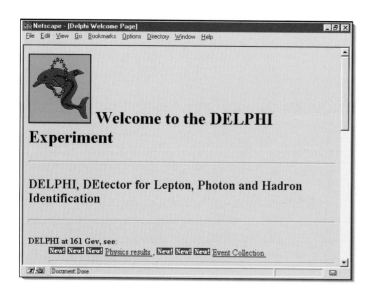

DELPHI—Detector for Lepton, Photon and Hadron Identification

Detecting the tiniest particles in the world is a really big job.

URL http://www1.cern.ch/Delphi

Dynamic Structure of Space

Explore this site if you want to know more about space-time and the structure of space.

URL http://www.execpc.com/~skaufman/
book.html

Particle Data Group (PDG)

This organization compiles and analyses data from particle physics studies and makes the data available to researchers, teachers and others.

URL http://www-pdg.lbl.gov

Physics 150 Home Page

Get a feel for university physics by doing the readings, homework and tests for this introductory physics course.

URL http://seidel.ncsa.uiuc.edu/Phys150

Physics at Cal State Fullerton

Learn some physics at this site with the Virtual Physics Tutorial.

URL http://chaos.fullerton.edu/physics.html

University of Oregon Department of Physics

This attractive multimedia site has movies, sounds, an animation gallery and more—don't miss it!

URL http://zebu.uoregon.edu

xxx.lanl.gov e-Print archive

Page after page of physics information.

URL http://xxx.lanl.gov

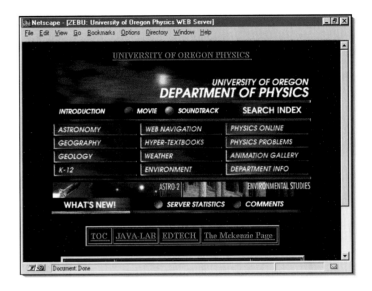

PROGRAMMING

All Basic Code Home Page

A collection of BASIC code snippets written by users for users.

URL http://charlie.simplenet.com/abc/
abchome.html

Allegro Common Lisp for Windows

Get a free version of Allegro CL for Windows.

URL http://www.franz.com/weblisp.html

BASIC Archives

Covers frequently asked questions, compilers and interpreters, along with the history of BASIC.

URL http://www.fys.ruu.nl/~bergmann/
basic.html

Beginners BASIC Home Page

Online tutorials, source code and more.

URL http://intermid.com/basic/basic.htm

Borland C++

A promotional site for Borland's Windows and DOS C++ environment.

URL http://www.borland.com/Product/
Lang/cpp5/index.html

OP

P

C Programmer's Pages

Includes the history of C, programming tips and tricks, source code and more.

URL http://pitel-lnx.ibk.fnt.hvu.nl/~rbergen/cmain.html

C++ Virtual Library

A well-organized library site that includes links to virtual courses and tutorials on the C++ language.

URL http://info.desy.de/user/projects/C++.html

Carl & Gary's Visual Basic Home Page

A great resource for the Visual Basic community, including technical information, programming tips, product opinions and more.

URL http://www.apexsc.com/vb

Common Lisp the Language, 2nd Edition

An online edition of the standard reference book for Lisp programmers.

URL http://www.cs.cmu.edu/Web/Groups/AI/html/cltl/cltl2.html

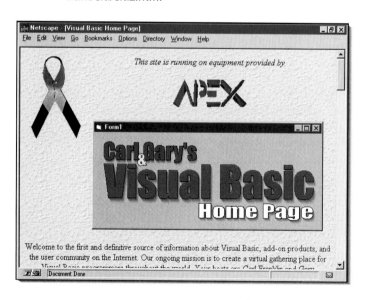

Forth Page

All about the Forth language, including an introduction, information about conferences and commercial vendors, and a bibliography.

URL http://chaos100.paisley.ac.uk/%7Ecis/forth

Fortran 90 Software Repository

A large public collection of Fortran 90 code.

URL http://www.nag.co.uk:70/1h/nagware/Examples

Fortran FAQ

Answers to frequently asked questions about Fortran.

URL http://www.cis.ohio-state.edu/hypertext/faq/usenet/fortran-faq/faq.html

Fortran Market

The place to find outstanding products, services and general information related to the Fortran programming language.

URL http://www.fortran.com/fortran/market.html

Introduction to Common Lisp

Common Lisp is a popular artificial intelligence language. This document covers issues for both beginners and more advanced users.

URL http://www.apl.jhu.edu/~hall/lisp.html

Introduction to Object-Oriented Programming Using C++

Provides a general introduction to Object-Oriented Programming (OOP).

URL http://www.gnacademy.org:8001/uu-gna/text/cc/index.html

Microsoft Visual Basic

Information about Visual Basic from the people who created it.

URL http://www.microsoft.com/vbasic

Programming in C

A great tutorial on in-depth C programming.

URL http://www.cm.cf.ac.uk/Dave/C/CE.html

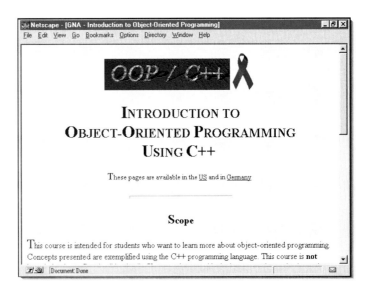

Get answers to your programming questions at these sites.

Prolog Frequently Asked Questions

Questions and answers about the Prolog programming language can be found here.

URL http://www.cis.ohio-state.edu/hypertext/faq/usenet/prolog/faq/faq.html

Understanding C++: An Accelerated Introduction

A thorough introduction to C++ in eight tutorials.

URL http://www.iftech.com/classes/cpp/cpp0.htm

Watcom C/C++

The latest information on Watcom's popular C/C++ programming environment.

URL http://www.powersoft.com/products/languages/watccpl.html

PSYCHOLOGY

Altered States of Consciousness

Parapsychology, dreams, out-of-body experiences, hypnosis, drugs and more.

URL http://www.utu.fi/~jounsmed/asc/asc.html

PR

PSYCHOLOGY *continued*

CyberPsychologist

A self-help center to help you reduce depression and stress, improve relationships, overcome addictive habits and more.

URL http://www.onramp.net/cyberpsych

Hypnosis

Learn how to hypnotize yourself and others.

URL http://www.utu.fi/~jounsmed/
asc/hyp.html

Keirsey Temperament Sorter

Take the personality test at this Web site to find out more about yourself.

URL http://sunsite.unc.edu/jembin/mb.pl

Mind Tools

A resource designed to help you optimize the performance of your mind and achieve your dreams and ambitions.

URL http://www.mindtools.com

Psych Web

Numerous tips for psychology students on how to write research papers and lab reports and apply to graduate school.

URL http://www.gasou.edu/psychweb/
psychweb.htm

Psycoloquy, Behavioral & Brain Sciences

Here you will find psychology journals and other related publications.

URL http://www.princeton.edu/~harnad

The Ascent of Mind

This book on the evolution of intelligence can be read online.

URL http://weber.u.washington.edu/
~wcalvin/bk5.html

RACQUET SPORTS

AARA Racquetball Rules

This site details the rules of racquetball as written by the American Amateur Racquetball Association.

URL http://www.pacifier.com/~wogman/aara

ATP Tour Online

The site of one of the most exciting and competitive series of tournaments for men's professional tennis.

URL http://atptour.com

Badminton Pictures

Pictures of badminton action shots, players, art and more.

URL http://mid1.external.hp.com/
stanb/pictures.html

Ed's Racquetball Page

An informative site about racquetball that includes basic rules, equipment suggestions and court diagrams.

URL http://www-video.eecs.berkeley.edu:/
~changed/Rball/rballpage.html

FOX Tennis

Daily tennis news from the FOX Network.

URL http://www.iguide.com/sports/wire/
sptteno.sml

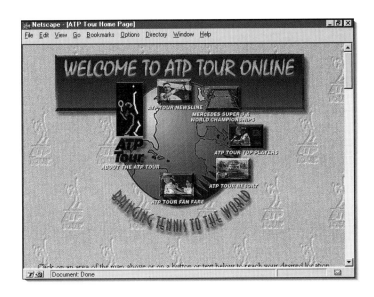

Men's Tennis

The Sports Network brings you the latest in men's tennis news.

URL http://www.sportsnetwork.com/filter/
filter.cgi/tennis/tennis-m.html

Racquetball Frequently Asked Questions

Find answers to many of your questions about racquetball at this site.

URL http://www.mcs.com/~toma/www/
files/rqb.faq.html

Tennis Frequently Asked Questions

Answers to questions about tennis, covering tournaments, rankings, players, equipment and more.

URL http://www.mindspring.com/~csmith/
TennisFAQ.html

Tennis Server

Visit this site to see why it was voted the 1996 Awesome Sports Site of the Year.

URL http://www.tennisserver.com

OP

RS

R

RACQUET SPORTS *continued*

We serve up great racquet sport sites.

TennisONE

Anyone who plays tennis, beginner or expert, will find the information at this site useful.

URL http://www.tennisone.com

U.S. Professional Racquetball Association

At this racquetball site you can ask a certified referee umpiring questions or get information on official rules, rankings, tournaments and more.

URL http://www.uspra.com

U.S. Professional Tennis Association

The USPTA offers news, rules, league information and more about tennis.

URL http://www.uspta.org

Women's Tennis

Follow the latest developments in women's tennis at the USA Today sports site.

URL http://www.usatoday.com/sports/other/
sotnw.htm

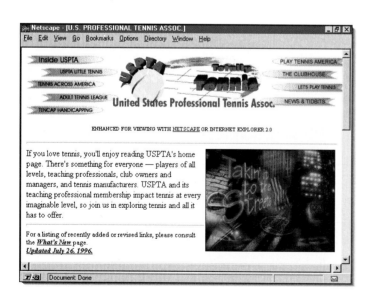

WomenSports Tennis

A spotlight on women in tennis.

URL http://www.womensports.com/tennis

Yahoo! Scoreboard—Tennis

This source for tennis information is updated frequently.

URL http://sports.yahoo.com/ten

RADIO

Amateur Radio

This guide to amateur radio includes links to callbooks, newsgroups and related Web sites of interest to amateurs.

URL http://www.mcc.ac.uk/Radio

cartalk.com

The Web site of this talk show, heard on National Public Radio, has plenty of automotive information and even allows you to send a digital postcard to a friend.

URL http://www-dev.cartalk.com/Working/
calendar.html

Columbia Records Radio Hour

Upcoming shows, playlists from previous weeks, photos of featured artists and more.

URL http://www.sony.com/Music/ArtistInfo/CRRadioHour

Earth & Sky

Visit the Web version of this popular natural science talk show, heard on hundreds of radio stations across North America.

URL http://www.earthsky.com

Grateful Dead Hour

Check out the station list to find out where you can hear the radio show devoted to America's most popular touring band.

URL http://www.well.com/user/tnf/gdhour.html

Guide to Talk Radio Programming

Browse through this directory of talk, news and sports radio programming and find out what is on the airwaves.

URL http://www.talkradioguide.com

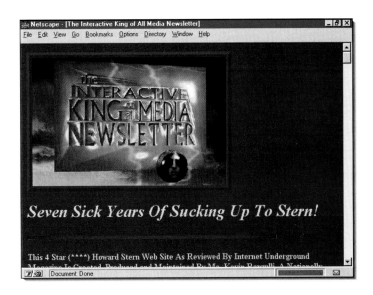

Interactive King of All Media Newsletter

This fan-run site is dedicated to talk radio's master shock jock, Howard Stern.

URL http://haven.ios.com/~koam

Mancow

Whether you leave your mark on this site by making your own Web page or just marvel at the photos, you're sure to be entertained.

URL http://www.mancow.com

MIT List of Radio Stations on the Internet

Wondering if your favorite station is on the Internet? Find out by browsing through this collection of links to radio stations worldwide.

URL http://wmbr.mit.edu/stations/list.html

Oliver North

Send e-mail to former Colonel North and he might reply on his talk show, heard on more than 150 stations across America.

URL http://www.northamerican.com

RS

R

RADIO *continued*

Radio Online

Links to radio databases, show information, job opportunities and more.

URL http://www.radio-online.com

Reagan Information Exchange

Son of a former president, Michael Reagan has moved part of his successful radio talk show into cyber-space.

URL http://www.reagan.com

Rick Dees

Send a digital postcard, examine Rick's inner child and read the Weekly Top 40 chart.

URL http://rick.com

Right Side of the Web

Rush Limbaugh's politics and philosophy, as well as summaries of his radio broadcasts.

URL http://www.rtside.com/rtside/
      rushpage.html

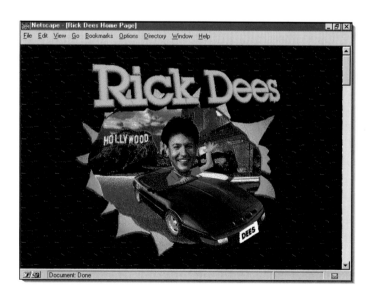

Rock Around the World

Hear sound recordings before they hit the streets or enter some excellent contests at this show's home on the Web.

URL http://www.ratw.com

Small Planet Radio

Radio shows heard across the U.S., such as *The Amazin' 80s* and *The Lost 45s*, call this site home.

URL http://www.planetradio.com

Sports Byline USA

Respond to the commentaries, send messages to the hosts or catch up on the features of America's most popular sports talk show.

URL http://www.sportsline.com/u/ronbarr/
      index.html

Tribute to Wolfman Jack

An informative and touching look at the world's most famous rock & roll DJ.

URL http://www.stinky.com/wolfman

REAL ESTATE

Alpine Mortgage Services Inc.

This site provides information on mortgages and current loan rates. Use the online calculator to find out how much you can afford to pay on a house.

URL http://www.alpinemtg.com

Century 21

This large real estate corporation has one Web site for the U.S. and one for Canada.

URL http://www.century21pro.com

URL http://www.century21.ca

Cybertimes' Property Net

Find properties for sale or rent across the United States.

URL http://cybertimes.com/propnet/home

Douglas Elliman Online

A selection of real estate in New York and around the world.

URL http://www.nytimes.com/de

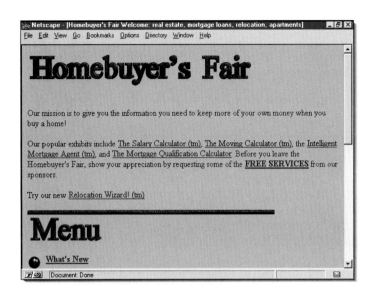

Home Pages

This site specializes in property listings for the eastern U.S.

URL http://www.thehomepages.com

Homebuyer's Fair

This site offers many resources to help make finding and moving to a new home as painless as possible.

URL http://www.homefair.com

Homes & Land

Search through a database of more than 200,000 properties for sale and rent in the United States.

URL http://www.homes.com/Welcome.html

ListingLink

Here you can search for properties by state, county and price.

URL http://openhouses.com

RS

REAL ESTATE *continued*

Marcus & Millichap

Commercial real estate on the Web from a company with offices in more than 20 cities across the U.S.

URL http://www.mmreibc.com

Matchpoint

Enter your housing requirements for an online search or leave your e-mail address and you'll be notified when a suitable property turns up.

URL http://www.nji.com/mp

National Association of Realtors Home Search

More than 230,000 listings in more than 20 states from coast to coast.

URL http://www.realtor.net

Planners Mortgage

Find information on mortgage rates, request a quote or get a loan application at this site.

URL http://www.plannersmortgage.com

Real Estate Junction

Look for residential, farm, commercial or resort property for sale at this site.

URL http://www.valleynet.com/~webcity

Real Estate Online

Find residential, retail and commercial property in Connecticut, New Jersey and New York.

URL http://greenthal.nyrealty.com

Real Estate Xtra!

Listings of houses and condominiums for sale across the United States and Canada.

URL http://www.rextra.com

RealtyWeb

Look at property listings across the U.S. and contact the brokers by e-mail.

URL http://www.c2m.com/usa/index.html

RE/MAX International

Get hints on buying and selling property and find RE/MAX offices around the world.

URL http://www.remax.com

Rent Net

An easy-to-use database of thousands of rental units in 500 cities across the U.S. and Canada.

URL http://www.rent.net

Stribling & Associates

A great place to look for luxury Manhattan real estate.

URL http://www.adsearch.com/stribling.html

Strider's Ranches & Estates

Find information on ranches and estates for sale in the U.S. and Canada.

URL http://www.iway101.com/strider/strider.htm

Who's Who in Luxury Real Estate

This online magazine helps you find luxury real estate for sale in the U.S. and around the world.

URL http://www.luxury-realestate.com/jbl

WorldWide Real Estate Network

Find real estate for sale in Canada, Mexico and the United States.

URL http://www.america-homes.com/newindx.shtml

WRENet—World Real Estate Network

Search for property anywhere in the U.S.

URL http://www.wren.com

RESTAURANTS

Ben and Jerry's

This company is famous for its bizarre ice cream names like Wavy Gravy and Cherry Garcia. Discover more about this flavorful company here.

URL http://www.benjerry.com/indexg.html

RS

R

RESTAURANTS *continued*

Diners' Grapevine

Information on nearly 7,000 restaurants worldwide.

URL http://www.dinersgrapevine.com

DineSite

A guide to restaurants with reviews from people who have eaten there.

URL http://www.dinesite.com

Food Finderz

You can order gift certificates for any of the restaurants listed in this database.

URL http://food.finderz.com

Hooters

At this site you can locate a Hooters near you, take a look at the online menu or even take a peek at the *Hooters* magazine.

URL http://www.hooters.com

Sink your teeth into our restaurant sites.

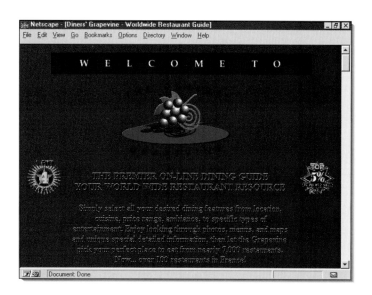

Kentucky Fried Chicken

Site for the Colonel and his secret recipe.

URL http://www.kentuckyfriedchicken.com

Little Caesars Pizza

Build your very own virtual pizza, take a look at a menu and find the location nearest you.

URL http://www.onthego.com/little_caesars

McDonald's

The restaurant that has served up billions of burgers. This colorful site has sections for both adults and kids.

URL http://www.mcdonalds.com

Subway

A restaurant chain with more than 11,000 locations. At this site you can use the Subway locator, take a look at a menu or check out Extreme Subway.

URL http://www.subway.com

Taco Bell Net

An excellent unofficial page dedicated to Taco Bell.

URL http://www.csh.rit.edu/~gentry/tbnet.html

ROLE PLAYING GAMES

Chaosium

Get information about the latest releases from the makers of the popular Call of Cthulhu game.

URL http://www.sirius.com/~chaosium/chaosium.html

d8 Annex

This online magazine of role playing culture offers a list of gaming resources, photos of other-worldly fashions, contests and more.

URL http://www.voicenet.com/~d8mag

FASA

Find out what's new from the company that publishes role playing games like Shadowrun and BattleTech.

URL http://www.fasa.com

Fractal Worldmap Generator

Create your own maps for use with role playing games.

URL http://www.edu.isy.liu.se/~d91johol/fwmg.html

Illusia

This multi-player graphical game with 3-D areas to explore and hundreds of characters is played online.

URL http://www.illusia.com

Iron Crown Enterprises, Inc.

Find out what products are available from the creators of the role playing games based on J.R.R. Tolkien's writings.

URL http://www.ironcrown.com

Irony Games' Dice Server

Forget where your dice are? Don't worry, you can roll some virtual dice at this site.

URL http://www.servtech.com/public/irony/igroll.html

RS

RS

ROLE PLAYING GAMES *continued*

Live Role Playing FAQ

Answers to frequently asked questions about Live Role Playing games.

URL http://www.cs.wisc.edu/~desmet/live-action.html

Steve Jackson Games

Visit the site of this British role playing game manufacturer to get information about new releases or browse through the catalog.

URL http://www.io.com/sjgames

Tower Fiend

All you need is a pair of dice to play this online adventure.

URL http://www.omnigroup.com/People/beska/towerfiend/intro.html

TSR

Information about Dungeons & Dragons, a product list, important e-mail addresses and more.

URL http://members.aol.com/tsrinc

Usenet Complete Role Playing Games List

Every role playing game ever published is listed at this site, even if it's out of print!

URL http://www.cqs.washington.edu/~surge/gaming/rpgs.html

S CIENCE FICTION & FANTASY

Alix of Dreams

This is an illustrated novel published in its entirety right on the Web.

URL http://www.primenet.com/~ciaran

Cosmo's Fantasy's

Check out this large collection of fantasy art.

URL http://www.premier1.net/~milham

Creative Archive

X-Files fans try their hand at writing episodes for this popular sci-fi show.

URL http://www.exit109.com/~fazia/DDEBCreative.html

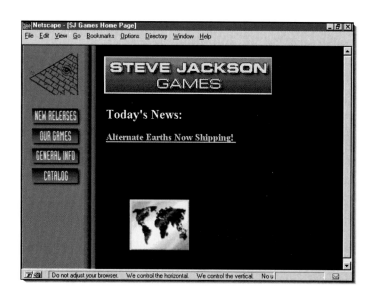

Dark Carnival Online

The Dark Carnival Bookstore in Berkeley, California, brings you articles, book reviews, interviews and more.

URL http://www.darkcarnival.com

Fandom Domain

Links of interest to fans of science fiction, fantasy, horror and anime.

URL http://www.greyware.com/sfrt3/sflinks.htm

Green Cross

This site provides a means for aspiring authors to publish their original short stories, poetry, magazine articles and reviews online.

URL http://www.grncross.com

Internet Top 100 SF/Fantasy List

Stuck for which book to read next? Take a look at this weekly updated list of top 100 science fiction and fantasy books as voted by cyber-fans.

URL http://www.clark.net/pub/iz/Books/Top100/top100.html

Our science fiction and fantasy sites are a dream come true.

Isaac Asimov

Reviews, bibliographical information and links related to this master of science fiction.

URL http://www.clark.net/pub/wmcbrine/html/Asimov.html

J.R.R. Tolkien Information Page

Follow the links at this site to find numerous Web resources dedicated to the Tolkien culture.

URL http://www.csclub.uwaterloo.ca/u/relipper/tolkien/rootpage.html

Linköping Science Fiction & Fantasy Archive

This site offers bibliographies on writers of science fiction and fantasy along with book and movie reviews, an art gallery and more.

URL http://sf.www.lysator.liu.se/sf_archive

Science Fiction and Fantasy Writers of America (SFWA)

This site includes articles on how to become a writer.

URL http://www.sfwa.org/sfwa

Science Fiction Gallery

A look at the development of science fiction from the earliest silent films to modern works, including monster movies, anime and T.V. shows.

URL http://www4.onestep.com/scifi

Science Fiction Review Archives

If you are thinking about getting a new book, check here first to find a review of it.

URL http://julmara.ce.chalmers.se/stefan/WWW/saifai_search.html

Science Fiction Weekly

A great online magazine on science fiction authors, games, movies and more.

URL http://www.scifi.com/sfw

Unio-Mystica Fantasy

A variety of links to fantasy sites on the Web.

URL http://www.best.com/~wooldri/awooldri/fantasy.html

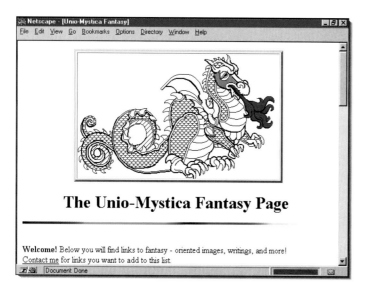

SEARCH TOOLS

A2Z

An offbeat alphabetical guide to the Web, featuring descriptions of the sites written by A2Z staff.

URL http://a2z.lycos.com

AltaVista

Quickly search millions of Web pages and thousands of newsgroups.

URL http://altavista.digital.com

ArchiePlex

Archie is a tool for finding files on public ftp sites on the Internet. ArchiePlex lets you search for files at ftp sites using the Web.

URL http://www.lerc.nasa.gov/archieplex

Deja News

Calling itself the premier Usenet search utility, Deja News lets you perform simple or detailed searches of all newsgroups.

URL http://www.dejanews.com

Electric Library

Search through hundreds of newspapers, magazines and journals, as well as books, maps and pictures.

URL http://www.elibrary.com

Excite

Excite lets you search for information using a phrase of key words.

URL http://www.excite.com

Four11

Looking for someone on the Internet? Visit Four11 and access more than 6.5 million e-mail addresses.

URL http://www.four11.com

GNN Select

An up-to-the-minute catalog of Web sites, listed by category.

URL http://gnn.com/gnn/wic/wics/index.html

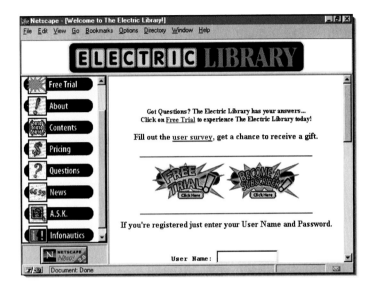

Infoseek

A diverse search tool covering the Web, newsgroups and e-mail addresses.

URL http://www.infoseek.com

Lycos

Search the Web or check out the directory service from Carnegie Mellon University.

URL http://www.lycos.com

Magellan

The McKinley Group presents this well-indexed guide to the Web.

URL http://www.mckinley.com

MetaCrawler

MetaCrawler has nine different tools perform your search all at once.

URL http://metacrawler.cs.washington.edu:8080/index.html

RS

Open Text Index

A well-established search tool for the Web that allows for complicated searches, such as "ketchup and mustard but not relish."

URL http://www.opentext.com/
omw/f-omw.html

Point

Point rates and reviews the best sites on the World Wide Web.

URL http://www.pointcom.com

SEARCH.COM

This site combines more than 250 search tools to help you find anything and everything you need.

URL http://www.search.com

Shareware.com

This service lets you browse through a huge collection of shareware on the Internet.

URL http://www.shareware.com

WebCrawler

A combination search tool and directory of Web sites, presented by Global Network Navigator, Inc.

URL http://www.webcrawler.com

WhoWhere?

Need to know someone's e-mail address? Check out this useful site.

URL http://www.whowhere.com

WWWW—World Wide Web Worm

A well-established Web search tool.

URL http://wwww.cs.colorado.edu/wwww

Yahoo!

The first popular search tool, Yahoo provides a colorful guide to the online world.

URL http://www.yahoo.com

SECURITY & ENCRYPTION

A–Z Antivirus

Learn what computer viruses are and how to protect your computer from them.

URL http://isteonline.uoregon.edu/istehome/
edtechnews/antivirus/Viruses.html

Dr Solomon's Computer Virus Information

The doctor provides an introduction to viruses, a searchable virus encyclopedia and more.

URL http://www.drsolomon.com

Electronic Frontier Foundation

This organization works to protect privacy, free expression and access to online information.

URL http://www.eff.org

Electronic Privacy Information Center

Read about the hot debate over encryption and free speech on the Internet.

URL http://epic.org

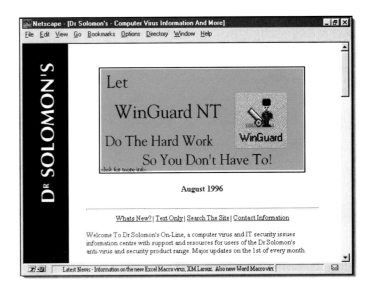

Feel free to go through our security and encryption sites.

Internet Privacy Coalition

This group exists to promote privacy and security on the Internet.

URL http://www.privacy.org/ipc

National Computer Security Association

Learn about security, computer ethics and more at this site.

URL http://www.ncsa.com/ncsamain.html

Noah's Anonymous E-mail

You can send an anonymous e-mail message through this Web site.

URL http://noah.pair.com/anon.html

PGP and what it does

A good introduction to Pretty Good Privacy (PGP).

URL http://www.arc.unm.edu/
~drosoff/pgp/pgp.html

RS

PGP for Eudora

This utility lets you use Pretty Good Privacy (PGP) with Eudora, the popular e-mail program.

URL http://www.xs4all.nl/~comerwel/manual.html

PGP Frequently Asked Questions

Information on Pretty Good Privacy (PGP), the program that lets you securely transfer text files over the Internet.

URL http://www.cis.ohio-state.edu/hypertext/faq/usenet/pgp-faq/top.html

Private Idaho

A popular privacy utility for Windows.

URL http://www.eskimo.com/~joelm/pi.html

Wired Privacy Archive

The publishers of *Wired* magazine and the Hotwired Web site bring you a collection of information about privacy on the Internet.

URL http://www.hotwired.com/clipper

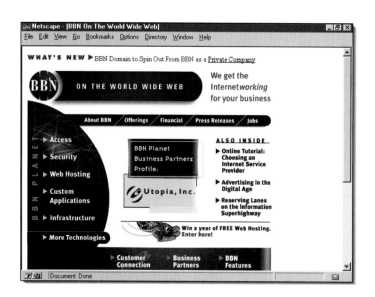

SERVICE PROVIDERS

America Online

You can get software to try out the services provided by America Online.

URL http://www.aol.com

AT&T WorldNet

AT&T WorldNet offers Internet access to over 200 cities across the United States. WorldNet will soon be available internationally.

URL http://www.att.com/worldnet/wis

BBN

Expert corporate Internet services from the company that helped build the Internet.

URL http://www.barrnet.net

CompuServe

Pay a visit to one of the oldest online services and see what it has to offer.

URL http://www.compuserve.com

EarthLink Network

A popular service provider that covers all of the United States.

URL http://www.earthlink.net

Global Enterprise Services, Inc.

This company services corporate America and was the first to have a T1 connection to the Internet.

URL http://www.ges.com

Internet Service Providers Directory

Thinking of moving abroad? You can look for a service provider in this international list, brought to you by CommerceNet.

URL http://www.commerce.net:8000/directories/products/isp/isp.html

Juno—Free Internet E-mail Service

Juno is a free e-mail service that allows you to send and receive e-mail even if you do not have Internet access.

URL http://www.juno.com

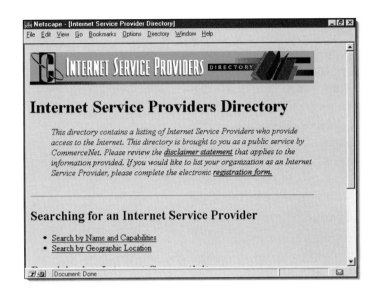

NETCOM

An international service provider that features its own Web browser called NetCruiser.

URL http://www.netcom.com

On Ramps: Internet Access Options

A well-referenced document intended for schools considering making the leap to the Internet.

URL http://www.state.wi.us/agencies/dpi/www/on_back.html

POBoxes.com

This company provides free, permanent e-mail addresses so that if you change your service provider your e-mail address will stay the same.

URL http://www.poboxes.com

Prodigy

This well-known service provider offers a trial membership complete with software.

URL http://www.prodigy.com

RS

The List

This directory of service providers is a popular site for people looking for a good buy.

URL http://www.thelist.com

thedirectory

A large list of Internet Service Providers (ISPs) and Bulletin Board Systems (BBSs) from around the world.

URL http://www.vni.net/thedirectory

UUNET Technologies

One of the longest running service providers, UUNET targets mainly the business market.

URL http://www.uu.net

SEX

Adult E-Mall

Toys, videos, CD-ROMs and more, for adults only.

URL http://lao2.power.net

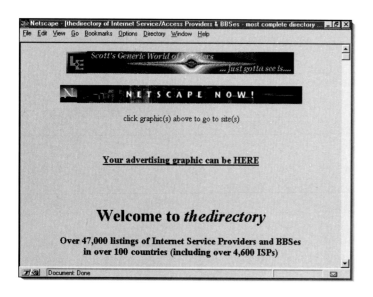

Body Jewelry by Judy

Find out about jewelry for all your secret places.

URL http://www.sexy-jewelry.com

Brandy's Tubetop Site

Animated and revealing pictures of Brandy at college. She'll also sell you some erotic goodies.

URL http://www.tubetop.com

Complete Internet Sex Resource Guide

The title says it all. This site includes links to sex-related newsgroups, mailing lists, Web pages and more.

URL http://sleepingbeauty.com/world/netsex.html

Condoms Express

Order condoms, lubricants and love potions or just get tips and instructions on safe condom use.

URL http://www.webcom.com/condom/express/express.html

Danni's Hard Drive

Danni Ashe, model and dancer, poses for visitors at this site.

URL http://www.danni.com

Fetish.Com

People with fetish fantasies can check out the pictures or order videos.

URL http://www.fetish.com

Garlique

Lots of high-quality images you can copy to your computer.

URL http://www.garlique.com

Genetics & IVF Institute

World's largest provider of infertility treatment and genetics services.

URL http://www.givf.com

Hustler Online

Check out samples from three online magazines and then subscribe to see even more!

URL http://www.hustler.com

Lusty Love Shack

A huge selection of lingerie and erotic fashions for men and women.

URL http://www.loveshack.com

Plainwrapped Chocolates

Chocolates in some rather naughty shapes.

URL http://www.eden.com/~plainwrp/choco

Safer Sex Page

Keep yourself informed and safe with this helpful site.

URL http://www.safersex.org

RS

Sexpedition

A comprehensive list of links to sexually explicit sites—all categorized, summarized and rated.

URL http://www.sexpedition.com

Slightly Sinful

Wet, wild and wicked sexual accessories and toys for adults.

URL http://sinful.com

Steamed Heat of California

Hot, exotic clothing for men and women. This site gives new meaning to the "itty bitty bikini."

URL http://www.steamedheat.com

TROJAN Home Page

A product catalog and essential health information from this condom manufacturer.

URL http://www.linkmag.com:80/trojan

Cuddle up to our sex sites. ♥

Wildchild's Photo Gallery

The namesake for this site is both a model and a photographer. Send her an e-mail message.

URL http://www.wildchild.com

SHIPPING

Airborne Express

This company is the third largest air express carrier, specializing in delivery for corporate America. Check out this site to find out what Airborne Express has to offer.

URL http://www.airborne-express.com

Allied Van Lines

Drop by this site for information on Allied Van Lines, how to prepare for your move and what numbers to call. Don't miss the kids section, where you can learn how to make a lemonade stand or train with your leftover boxes.

URL http://www.alliedvan.net

Atlantic Container Line

Need to get your large cargo across the Atlantic Ocean? This company can help.

URL http://www.ACLcargo.com

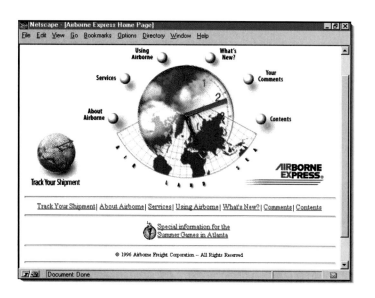

Burlington Air Express

A freight transportation company that can ship a package of any size or weight around the world. At this site you can open an account, request a pickup, track a package and much more.

URL http://www.baxworld.com

CompuTrek, Inc.

Shippers that specialize in handling mainframe computers, printing systems, telecommunications equipment and other delicate high-value products.

URL http://www.computrek-mn.com

DHL Worldwide Express

A company that provides air express transportation to more than 200 countries around the world.

URL http://www.dhl.com

Electronic Shipping Guide

Planning to ship a container? Check this guide with schedules of more than 60 carriers who ship in and out of the U.S. and Canada.

URL http://www.shipguide.com

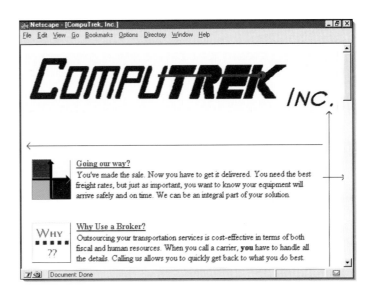

Going our way?
You've made the sale. Now you have to get it delivered. You need the best freight rates, but just as important, you want to know your equipment will arrive safely and on time. We can be an integral part of your solution.

Why Use a Broker?
Outsourcing your transportation services is cost-effective in terms of both fiscal and human resources. When you call a carrier, **you** have to handle all the details. Calling us allows you to quickly get back to what you do best.

Emery Worldwide

This company's Web site provides global shipping tips, seminars on shipping hazardous material and much more.

URL http://www.emeryworld.com

FedEx

Find toll-free numbers for offices around the world, track packages online and obtain shipping software.

URL http://www.fedex.com

URL http://www.fedex.ca

Kitty Hawk Air Charter

The source for same day air freight throughout North America. Kitty Hawk treats each call as an emergency.

URL http://www.onramp.net/kha

Mail Boxes Etc.

This company is not just about mail boxes! Drop by for copies, faxes, office supplies and more.

URL http://www.mbe.com

RS

RYDER

The world's largest provider of transportation solutions. Find information on renting anything from a school bus to a truck.

URL http://www.ryder.inter.net

United States Postal Service

Find postage rates or look up the zip code for any address in the U.S.

URL http://www.usps.gov

UPS

It may have cost only $100 to start United Parcel Service, but now the company spends millions of dollars a year to ensure customer satisfaction!

URL http://www.ups.com

Virtual Mover

A complete resource for anyone planning to move.

URL http://mfginfo.com/mover.htm

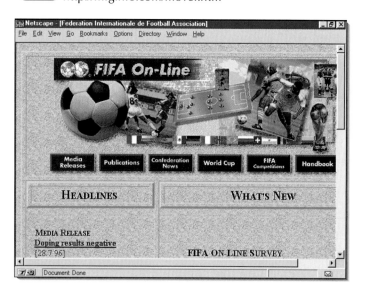

SOCCER

FIFA

This is the official home page of the Fédération Internationale de Football Association, an organization well known in the soccer world.

URL http://www.fifa.com/index.html

net.soccer

The first interactive Internet soccer management game—play fantasy soccer on your computer.

URL http://www.livemedia.co.uk/net.soccer

Rec.Sports.Soccer—The Web Page

This home page of the soccer-related Usenet newsgroup contains soccer terminology, FIFA rules, computer soccer games and more.

URL http://www.atm.ch.cam.ac.uk/sports

Rete! Soccer News

This Italian site offers the latest soccer news and statistics, plus video and team pictures for the serious soccer fan.

URL http://www.vol.it/RETE_/32/00001.html

Soccer NewsNet

A great-looking site which features all kinds of soccer information, including news, equipment, a skills workshop, college watch and a lot more.

URL http://www.soccernews.com

Soccer on U.S. T.V.

Information on television coverage of upcoming soccer matches. You can also chat with other soccer enthusiasts at the Virtual Sports Bar!

URL http://www.best.com/~olivert/soccer/tv.html

SoccerNews Online

Soccer statistics and standings of teams across the world, from the AFC to the CONCACAF.

URL http://www.csn.net/~eid/soccer/sccrindx.html

SportsLine U.S.A.—Soccer

Get the latest soccer news here.

URL http://www.sportsline.com/u/soccer/index.html

Ultimate Soccer

A great resource for soccer-related images, computer games and links.

URL http://www.odyssey.com.au/sports/soccer.html

World Cup 1998

France will host the 1998 World Cup. This site will give you all the information you need.

URL http://www.efrei.fr/~foucher/france98.html

WWW Toto

Place your bets in e-cash on the outcomes of soccer matches and collect your winnings, if you have any, on Mondays.

URL http://www.astro.uva.nl/michielb/toto/toto.html

SOCIOLOGY

American Sociological Association

The ASA is dedicated to advancing sociology as both a scientific discipline and a profession.

URL http://www.asanet.org

RS

Dead Sociologists Index

An excellent resource containing pictures, biographies and overviews of the works of the world's great sociologists.

URL http://diogenes.baylor.edu/WWW
providers/Larry_Ridener/INDEX.HTML

Electronic Journal of Sociology

A free electronic journal that carries its current issue and maintains a library of its back issues.

URL http://olympus.arts.ualberta.ca:8010

Progressive Sociology Network

A worldwide meeting place for sociologists concerned with progressive issues and values, such as civil rights and justice.

URL http://csf.colorado.edu/psn

Sociological Research Online

A journal containing articles and book reviews dealing with current sociological research.

URL http://kennedy.soc.surrey.ac.uk/
socresonline

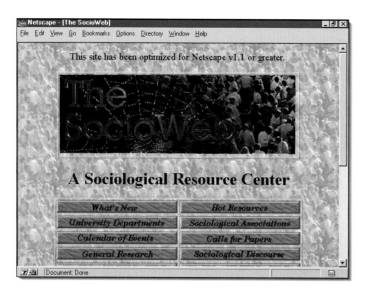

Sociology for Very Short Attention Spans

A humorous look at the world's great sociologists and theories.

URL http://www.webcom.com/dread/
good-soc.html

SocioWeb

A sociological resource center with links to many universities and sociology sites on the Web.

URL http://www.socioweb.com/~markbl/
socioweb

SocNet

A listing of worldwide sociology courses that you can take on the Internet.

URL http://www.mcmaster.ca/socscidocs/
socnet.htm

SOUTH & CENTRAL AMERICA

Argentina

Argentina's Embassy in Washington, D.C., provides you with general information on Argentina.

URL http://athea.ar/cwash

Brazil

The Brazilian Embassy in London offers this impressive site designed to increase knowledge and understanding of Brazil.

URL http://www.demon.co.uk/Itamaraty/welcome.html

BRAZZIL

This monthly English language magazine on Brazilian news and culture offers articles and links to Brazilian publications on the Web.

URL http://www.brazzil.com

Caribbean Week

This Caribbean newspaper summarizes each region's news and business happenings.

URL http://www.sunbeach.net/cweek/home.html

Central American News

News on Central America for businesses, government agencies, educators and students.

URL http://magi.com/crica/news/news.html

Chile

Browse through pages on history and national symbols or check out the government palace.

URL http://www.presidencia.cl/presidencia/webingles

CHIP News

This is the Chile Information Project, an English language news digest about Chile.

URL http://www.chip.cl

CubaWeb

The national Web site for the Republic of Cuba offers the visitor just about everything except a free cigar.

URL http://www.cubaweb.com

Guatemala Weekly

An English language newspaper with articles on events in this Central American nation.

URL http://www.guatered.com/news/gweekly.htm

RS

S

Latin America on the Net

Links to political and constitutional information on Latin America, sorted by country.

URL http://www.latinworld.com/government

Mexican Online News

Many colorful links to Mexican newspapers, magazines and daily news sites.

URL http://www.eng.usf.edu/~palomare/
newspapers.html

Peru

Find out about this country's foreign policy and diplomatic activities at this site.

URL http://www.rree.gob.pe/i-defaul.htm

Uruguay

This site offers information on everything from general facts to why you should spend your retirement in Uruguay.

URL http://www.embassy.org/uruguay

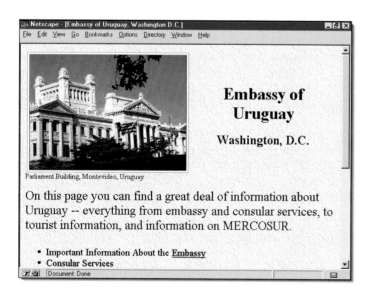

Weekly News Update on the Americas

From the Nicaragua Solidarity Network of Greater New York, this site offers news updates on events in Latin America and the Caribbean.

URL http://homebrew.geo.arizona.edu/
wnuhome.html

SPORTING GOODS

adidas WebZine

This online magazine allows you to see the latest in adidas footwear technology or look back through time in the Sports Shoe Museum.

URL http://www.adidas.com

big deal

An online shop for the boarders who take to the snow or the sidewalk.

URL http://www.bigdeal.com

Bike World

The hottest bicycles, as well as wheels, shocks and lots of other components and accessories for road and mountain bikes.

URL http://www.bikeworld.com

Boreal

Complete online product and dealer information from one of the premier manufacturers of rock climbing shoes.

URL http://www.borealusa.com

CedarWorks

Cedar playsets for all spaces and budgets from this Maine-based company.

URL http://www.midcoast.com/cedarworks

Cycle Path Bicycle Shop

Bicycles, parts and accessories are available for online ordering.

URL http://www.magicnet.net/cyclepath

Endless Pools

Swim for hours in a pool without ever having to turn. How is it possible?

URL http://www.endlesspools.com

Stock up on equipment at our sporting goods sites.

Finish Line

Check out the shoes and athletic wear available at this sporting goods chain.

URL http://www.thefinishline.com

Fish on the Line

Information about introductory, Lunker or Spinner kits, with shipping available to customers across the U.S. and Canada.

URL http://www.primenet.com/~fishone

Holyoke Sporting Goods Co.

Athletic footwear, equipment and apparel for just about every sport you can think of.

URL http://www.empiremall.com/hsgsports/homepage.html

Minor Leagues, Major Dreams

Here you will find apparel from your favorite minor league sports teams.

URL http://www.minorleagues.com/minorleagues

S

Mountain Gear

Check out the hot sheet for current sales on gear for mountaineering, kayaking, backpacking and more.

URL http://www.eznet.com/mgear.html

New Balance Cyberpark

A park filled with athletic shoes and race information from across the United States.

URL http://www.newbalance.com

[no name] Sports

Shop for licensed baseball, basketball, football, hockey and other merchandise online.

URL http://www.sportsmart.com/j2-cat/display

NorCal Swim Shop

An extensive assortment of swimwear that you can order online from Speedo, Nike and other companies.

URL http://www.swimshop.com

Planet Reebok

You'll find training hints here, along with information about some of the people who play in Reeboks.

URL http://www.planetreebok.com

Sports Authority

Check out the wide range of equipment available and then find the Sports Authority store nearest you.

URL http://pwr.com/SportsAuthority/default.html

Sunglasses.com

This company guarantees the lowest prices on sunglasses from Rayban, Serengeti, Revo, Vuarnet and many more.

URL http://www.sunglasses.com/def2.htm

Tennis Warehouse

A huge selection of racquets, bags, shoes, socks, strings and grips. Order online for shipment anywhere.

URL http://www.tennis-warehouse.com

TSI Soccer

Flip through online catalogs filled with the latest in shoes, clothing, gear and accessories, or check out the links to other soccer sites.

URL http://www.tsisoccer.com/tsi

USA Aquatics

Everything for swimmers, from suits and goggles to gear for lifeguards.

URL http://www.sierra.net/usa/index.html

West Enterprises

Order a glove from this manufacturer of custom gloves for baseball and softball.

URL http://www.dreamtek.com/west_ent

Windsurfing Webhouse

The online catalog at this site has a big selection of boards, booms, fins, masts, sails and accessories.

URL http://www.windsurfer.com/Webhouse

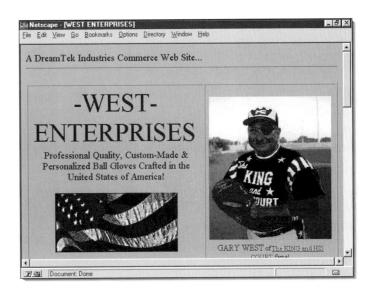

SPORTS NEWS

AudioNet Live Programming

Listen to live sports radio over the Internet.

URL http://www.audionet.com/livelist.htm

CBS Sports

Visit this site to find current sports news and the broadcasting schedule for sports on CBS.

URL http://www.cbs.com/sports

CNN Sports

The Cable News Network hosts this highly informative sports news site.

URL http://www3.cnn.com/SPORTS/index.html

CSC College Sports Network

This site features numerous links to up-to-date information on college sports.

URL http://www.xcscx.com/colsport

ESPNET SportsZone

The latest in sports from ESPN, with feature articles, statistics and scores.

URL http://espnet.sportszone.com

FOX Sports

Scores, news and stats for the NBA, NFL and many other sports.

URL http://www.foxsports.com/sports/
index.html

GNN Sports

Global Network Navigator's site offers a collection of sports links and information.

URL http://gnn.com/gnn/meta/sports/
index.html

LiveSt@ts

Ever wish you had complete statistics at your fingertips while you watch the game? LiveSt@ts gives you all the stats you need.

URL http://www.livestats.com

Nando Sports Server

This site features online sports discussions as well as up-to-the-minute news.

URL http://www.nando.net/SportServer

NBC Sports

NBC brings its quality sports reporting to the Web.

URL http://www.nbc.com/sports/index.html

Online Sports

This site is both a directory and showplace of sports products and services available online and also has a sports career center.

URL http://www.onlinesports.com

Planet Reebok

This commercial site features fitness information, biographies of athletes and more.

URL http://www.planetreebok.com

Sports Summary

A daily-updated sports resource brought to you by internetMCI.

URL http://www.fyionline.com/infoMCI/
update/SPORTS-MCI.html

The Sports Network

Check out TSN's Web site to find coverage of many sports. Click on The Playground to discuss your favorite sport with other fans.

URL http://www.sportsnetwork.com

THE STADIUM

Join The Stadium Club to access discussion rooms, sport chats, insider sports information and much more.

URL http://www.thestadium.com/home.html

USA Today Sports

Find the top sports stories from *USA Today*.

URL http://www.usatoday.com/sports/
sfront.htm

SURFING

Association of Surfing Professionals

Find out what's new in the world of professional surfing.

URL http://www.telepac.pt/surfasp/index.html

Hawaii Weather and Surf

Features hourly weather forecasts and satellite images of current surfing conditions in Hawaii.

URL http://www.hawaii.edu/News/
weather.html

Hey Dude

An online lesson in surfing slang, so you will no longer be a hodad.

URL http://www.malibu-rum.com/dude.htm

Ocean & Snow Surfer

Resources of interest to surfers and would-be surfers, including surf photography, hot new products and *Surfing Life* magazine.

URL http://www.southcoast.com/browse/
scwindan/index.html

RS

SURFING *continued*

Ocean Gear

This site features a bulletin board, equipment sales and surfing tips.

URL http://www.choice1.com/og

Power Surf "JAWS" Video Gallery

Animations of Jaws, the legendary big wave break in Maui, Hawaii.

URL http://www.maui.net/~hookipa/jaws

Surfco

The premier online surf shop features an interactive product catalog.

URL http://alohamall.aloha.com/surfco/surfco.html

SURFERmag.com

Browse through The Surf Shop, check out the surf links, order The Surf Report and more.

URL http://www.surfermag.com

Catch the wave! Visit our surfing sites.

Surfing News

The latest news from the surfing world, including tournament standings, global surf links and more.

URL http://holoholo.org/surfnews

Surfrider Foundation U.S.A.

This nonprofit environmental organization is dedicated to protecting the world's waves and beaches.

URL http://www.sdsc.edu/SDSC/Partners/Surfrider/main.htm

SurfSpot Surf Cameras

View images of the current surf conditions at some of your favorite California beaches.

URL http://www.surfspot.com

Tracks Online

This monthly magazine features surfing animations, weather reports, travel tips and more.

URL http://www.msp.com.au/tracks

TELEPHONE SERVICES

123 Telephones

Order pre-paid phone cards for calls to Asia and Australia.

URL http://www.webplaza.com/Pages/ Communications/123Telephones/ 123PhoneCards.html

AT&T

Find out about a company that offers just about every telephone service possible.

URL http://www.att.com

BellSouth Cellular Corp.

Information on local and cellular service for consumers in the Southeastern United States and California.

URL http://www.com/bscc

CNI Telecom

Check out a long-distance company that gives two percent of its proceeds to charities like Habitat for Humanity and Meals on Wheels.

URL http://www.cnotes.com/telecom/ cnitelpage.html

Ericsson

A multilingual and informative site from this Swedish telecommunications company.

URL http://www.ericsson.se

Fone Saver

Visit this site for long-distance information collected from major U.S. long-distance carriers.

URL http://www.wp.com/Fone_Saver

Frontier Communications

Save your friends and family money by getting your own 1-800 or 1-888 number at home.

URL http://www.spectra.net/mall/frontier

RS

TU

T

Global Cellular Rental

Keep in touch when you are abroad. Rent a cellular telephone!

URL http://plaza.interport.net/cellular

GTE

Information about telephone services from a company known for connecting the world.

URL http://www.gte.com

GTE Mobilnet

Along with service and product information, this Florida-based company offers a helpful All About Cellular section.

URL http://wireless-gte.com

Kallback Home Page

Save money with Kallback by using a U.S. phone line while traveling.

URL http://www.kallback.com

Get connected to our telephone service sites.

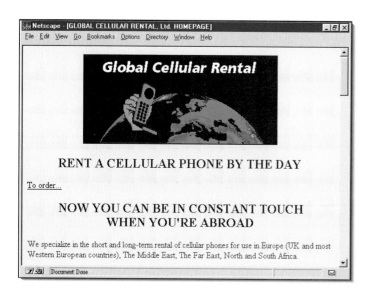

LCI

Find out what this major U.S. long-distance carrier can do for you and your business.

URL http://www.lci.com

LCR Telecommunications

Find out about LCR's phone services, from pagers and calling cards to 1-800 and long-distance service.

URL http://www.lcrtelecom.com

MCI

MCI offers phone and networking services worldwide.

URL http://www.mci.com

Nokia

An extensive forum of information from one of the largest makers of cellular phones in the world.

URL http://www.club.nokia.com

Pacific Bell

If you live in California, look here to find the telephone and Internet services you need.

URL http://www.pacbell.com

Rosenbrewer Communications

Find out how to set up your own 1-900 or 011 service.

URL http://www.CyberNetOne.com/ Rosenbrewer

Schneider Communications

Home of ExpressView, a unique program that will help you analyze and manage your phone bill.

URL http://www.scitele.com

SM Communications and Marketing

Find out how to get guaranteed savings on your long-distance bills or double your money back.

URL http://www.infinet.com/~sm

Sprint

Not just long-distance! This friendly site also offers Cool Stuff, such as the Sports Stop and Rec Room.

URL http://www.sprint.com

Switchboard

Look up any residential or business phone number in the United States. This site lets you search for lost friends or family members.

URL http://www.switchboard.com

Tele-Save Telecommunications

Don't miss the deals on long-distance, phone cards and other services, and check out the helpful hints and telecommunications glossary.

URL http://www.telesave.com/telesave

VTEL

A great place to start if you are interested in videoconferencing.

URL http://www.vtel.com

TU

T

THEATER

Andrew Lloyd Webber

Learn about Sir Andrew himself, read up on his famous musicals like *Cats* and *Phantom of the Opera* or hear recordings online.

URL http://www.reallyuseful.com

Drama

A great collection of dramatic works, screenplays and drama newsgroups.

URL http://english-www.hss.cmu.edu/drama.html

Dramatic Exchange

This site is dedicated to collecting and distributing scripts to help playwrights publish their works and producers find plays.

URL http://www.dramex.org

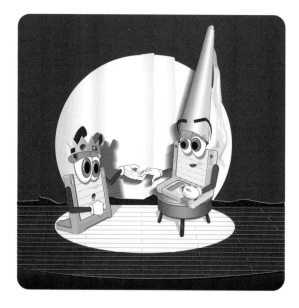

KABUKI for EVERYONE

Learn more about this traditional Japanese form of theater through the pictures, sounds and movies presented here.

URL http://www.fix.co.jp/kabuki/kabuki.html

Musicals Home Page

Song lists, music samples and even pictures of CD covers from your favorite musicals.

URL http://musical.mit.edu/musical

Playbill Online

News, quizzes, general information about current productions and more.

URL http://www.playbill.com

Shakespeare Web

Submit or reply to Shakespeare-related questions, follow links to companies currently producing Shakespeare's plays or find out what happened on this day in Elizabethan history.

URL http://www.shakespeare.com

Theater Central

Your one-stop guide to theater on the Internet, complete with job listings, professional contacts and links to other theater-related sites.

URL http://www.theatre-central.com

TOYS

Bear St.

A huge selection of Gund stuffed animals, from Australian Animals to Whimsical Friends, ready to ship anywhere in the world.

URL http://www.pacificablue.com/bearst

Bungalow Toys

A fine selection of toys from BRIO, Playmobil and more.

URL http://www.toyweb.com

ChildSmile

Storytelling dolls, fabric books and other educational toys via the Internet.

URL http://www.childsmile.com

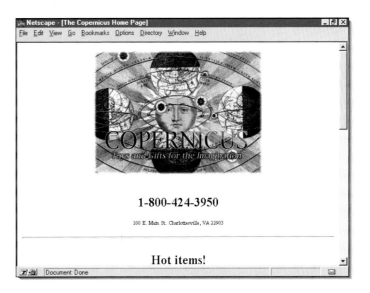

Copernicus: Toys and Gifts for the Imagination

Kits to make a volcano or up to four gallons of root beer, as well as classic toys and lots of gifts to make kids think.

URL http://www.comet.chv.va.us/copernicus

Discount Games Co.

Choose from nearly 15,000 gaming items online.

URL http://www.discountgames.com

FAO Schwarz

Enter the most magical store in toyland—look at toys online or have three different specialty catalogs delivered to your door!

URL http://faoschwarz.com

Games Imported

Limited edition collectible Barbie dolls, along with a big selection of classic games from the United States and abroad.

URL http://www.gamesimported.com/index.html

TU

Infinite Illusions Juggling Supplies

Order juggling supplies, yo-yos and boomerangs online for delivery anywhere in the world.

URL http://pd.net/catalog

Internet Toy Off-White Pages

Visit this site for a color-coded listing of many toy-related links.

URL http://utmdacc.mda.uth.tmc.edu:5014/ eric/rtm/whtepage.html

Kids Universe Toys & Software

Educational toys and software for kids of all ages.

URL http://kidsuniverse.com

Kitty's Collectibles

Visit the home of Barbie and her friends and look through a catalog containing more than 100 pages.

URL http://users.aol.com/kittyscol/kittys.htm

Learning Curve Toys

Fans of Thomas the Tank Engine, Robotix and Woodtown can look through the online catalog and then find a local retailer.

URL http://learningtoys.com

LEGO

The official LEGO site with a complete history detailing the company's early days making wooden toys to its current success making plastic building blocks.

URL http://www.LEGO.com

Lewis Galoob Toys

Star Wars toys, Micro Machines and more from one of the hottest toy manufacturers.

URL http://www.galoob.com

Palo Alto Sport Shop & Toy World

See a selection of rollerblades, swimsuits, shoes and toys, or ask the Toy Guru for advice on gifts.

URL http://www.thirdplanet.com/PASSTW/ pass.html

Texas Toy Store

Lots of collectible toys available online.

URL http://www.tias.com/stores/tx-toys

The Portal

Star Wars, Spawn, Batman and Judge Dredd collectible figures and more.

URL http://www.theportal.com

Toys "R" Us

Tour the virtual store and find photos and descriptions of the top-selling toys, then use the Store Spotter to find locations all over the world.

URL http://www.toysrus.com

Trendmasters

Check out hot new toy lines based on Gumby, Tarzan and more, and see what is on the drawing board.

URL http://www.trendmaster.com

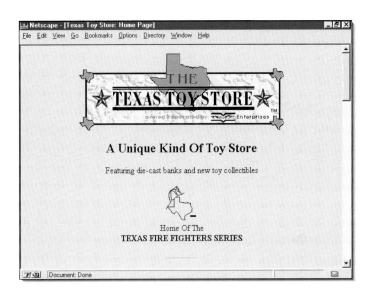

White Rabbit Toys

Online ordering of toys from Gund, BRIO, Ravensburger and more.

URL http://www.toystore.com

TRACK & FIELD

Athletics Home Page

A comprehensive listing of world and country records in track and field events.

URL http://www.hkkk.fi/~niininen/athl.html

Cool Running

This site focuses on marathons and other racing events.

URL http://www.coolrunning.com

Decathlon

Fans of the decathlon can view pictures of events, read news and more.

URL http://dana.ucc.nau.edu/~tms3/dec1.html

Come and play at our toy sites!

TU

Discus Throwers Page

This discus site features world records, links to other discus-throwing information and a frame-by-frame analysis of a discus throw.

URL http://www.uidaho.edu/~carr9432/track.html

Interactive Sports Masters

Order a CD-ROM disc to learn track and field fundamentals at your computer.

URL http://www.zdepth.com/isports

Pole Vault

The U.S.A. Track & Field's Pole Vault site features rankings, news, meets, pictures, records and more.

URL http://www.polevault.org

Runner's World Online

The online version of *Runner's World* magazine features daily headlines and more.

URL http://www.runnersworld.com

Running Frequently Asked Questions

Got a question about running? You will probably find the answer here.

URL http://www.cis.ohio-state.edu/hypertext/faq/usenet/running-faq/top.html

Running with George

A weekly column on running.

URL http://www.YBI.COM/run/index.html

Track & Field Artwork

This site features the sculptures of Bob Sorani, an artist who is inspired by athletes.

URL http://www.sonoma.edu/library/exhibits/sorani

Track & Field Images

Images of famous moments from the world of track and field.

URL http://www.math.ucla.edu/~kscanne/trackpix.html

Ultramarathon World

News, records and more for athletes who run distances beyond the standard marathon.

URL http://Fox.nstn.ca:80/~dblaikie

U.S.A. Track & Field

Read biographies of American track and field stars and learn about upcoming events.

URL http://www.usatf.org

U.S.A. Track & Field Long Distance Running Pages

Long distance running of all kinds with current rankings, world records, events and more.

URL http://www.usaldr.org

TRAVEL

#1 Travel Network

Planning a honeymoon or a rafting vacation? This site has the online reservation services you need.

URL http://www.1travel.com

Above All Travel

Information and reservations on cruises to Antarctica and Tahiti, hiking and biking expeditions in the Alps and more.

URL http://www.aboveall.com

Air Bank

Buy and sell frequent flier miles and other travel awards.

URL http://www.airawards.com

Air Brokers International

Find prices for flights across the Pacific or around the world. Then discover what restaurants are the best at your intended destination.

URL http://www.aimnet.com/~airbrokr

Airline Tickets Wholesale

Buy discounted tickets for flights from American cities to Canada, Mexico, the Caribbean and every state except Alaska.

URL http://www.traveldiscounters.com

American Express Travel

Helpful resources for the vacation planner, with airline ticket ordering, special vacation deals, travel tips and weather forecasts.

URL http://www.americanexpress.com/travel

Avis Galaxy

Get information on renting cars worldwide, view pictures of rental cars, make your reservation online or print out maps.

URL http://www.avis.com

British Airways

Flight schedules and information on everything from aircraft to vaccinations.

URL http://www.british-airways.com

Crowne Plaza

Tour hotels and resorts around the world and check room availability online.

URL http://www.crowneplaza.com

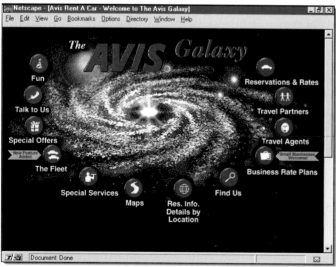

© 1996 Wizard Co., Inc.

EarthWise Journeys

From the Amazon to the Yangtse, this is the place to go if you are looking for a vacation that is out of the ordinary.

URL http://www.teleport.com/~earthwyz

Greyhound

Find out about fares, schedules, ticketing information and more.

URL http://www.greyhound.com

Internet Cruise Travel Network

A great guide for anyone interested in cruises, with information on everything from day cruises to ocean freighters.

URL http://www.cruisetravel.com

Internet Guide to Hostelling

Sure it is not the Park Plaza, but hostels provide a cheap and easy way to travel around the world.

URL http://www.hostels.com/hostels

Kids' Camps

Find a perfect summer camp for your children by using this comprehensive directory with hundreds of entries.

URL http://www.kidscamps.com

Leisureplan Multimedia Travel Decision System

Find accommodation, attractions, car rentals and tours to suit your needs and budget.

URL http://www.leisureplan.com

Mountain Travel Sobek

Choose an adventure based on price, location, level of difficulty or activity.

URL http://www.mtsobek.com

Official Guide to The Islands of The Bahamas

All 700 islands at your fingertips. Get all the facts on swimming, sailing, scuba diving or even getting married on your holidays.

URL http://www.interknowledge.com/bahamas

Take a trip through our travel sites.

mG Cruise Lines

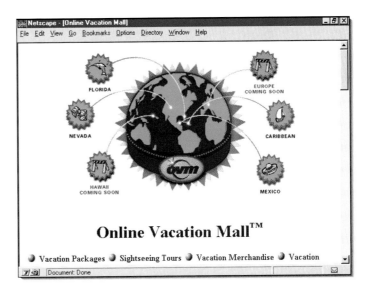

Online Vacation Mall

Find a perfect vacation—you can book and even cancel your reservations online.

URL http://www.onlinevacationmall.com

PC Travel

Check flight availability, compare prices, make a reservation and order tickets—all online!

URL http://www.pctravel.com

Reed Traveler.Net

Use this huge collection of Web resources to plan your vacation or search the hotel index to choose your accommodation based on special promotions, geographic location or personal preferences.

URL http://www.traveler.net

TU

Singapore Airlines

Find out what services will be available on your flight and check out the seating arrangements.

URL http://www.singaporeair.com

Southwest Airlines

Use Ticketless Travel to book a ticket and then find out about your destination by browsing through the Cool City Hyperlinks.

URL http://www.iflyswa.com

Spa Source

Find a place to pamper yourself. Choose from spas around the world.

URL http://www.spafinders.com

Subway Navigator

Find maps for various subway systems around the world. A must-see for fans and users of urban railways.

URL http://metro.jussieu.fr:10001/bin/
cities/english

Travel Source

A huge travel guide with everything from airlines to yacht charters.

URL http://www.travelsource.com

Travelocity

Destinations and timetables from more than 700 airlines for the do-it-yourself traveler.

URL http://www.travelocity.com

TravelWeb

Find a room at any of thousands of hotels around the world and make a reservation online.

URL http://www.travelweb.com/index.html

TWA

Route maps, flight schedules and 50 years of trans-Atlantic flying history from Trans World Airlines.

URL http://www.twa.com

WebFlyer

Discover how to get more air miles for your money or just have fun reading the horoscopes.

URL http://www.insideflyer.com

TRIVIA

Alpha Sports Games

Play Pickmaster, WaCkY Ball or Beat The Analyst and you might win $10,000!

URL http://www.ctactics.com/alpha/alpha.html

Bullpen Ace

Put all that baseball knowledge to good use by stepping up to the mound and playing Bullpen Ace trivia! You could win cool baseball collectibles.

URL http://www.dtd.com/ace

Mondo Trivia

A new trivia question with new prizes to be won, every day!

URL http://www.new3.com/mondotrivia

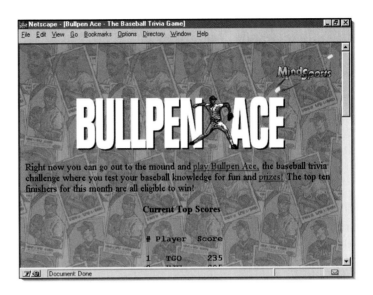

Music Trivia Contest

Think you know about music? Test your knowledge with Fred Bronson's grueling music trivia question and win a CD if you answer correctly.

URL http://www.billboard-online.com/trivia.html

Osiris Trivia Quiz

Multiple choice style trivia questions from a wide range of topics.

URL http://osiris.sund.ac.uk/online/quiz/quiztime.html

People Magazine's Movie Quiz

Different movie quiz questions each time you visit. The first letters of each answer make up the name of a movie star.

URL http://pathfinder.com/cgi-bin/people/moviequiz.cgi

T

TRIVIA *continued*

RealTIME Prizes Network

Register and get software to play for the chance to win up to a million dollars. There is also a T.V. trivia game offering more than $475 every week.

URL http://prizes.com/rtpn

Reno Brewing Company Quiz Game

Test your knowledge of beer and the beer industry while having a tall, cool one.

URL http://www.aztech-cs.com/renobrew/quiz_game.html

Riddler

Play games and win impressive prizes!

URL http://www.riddler.com

ROCK MALL Trivia Challenge

This site has many challenging trivia quizzes on subjects ranging from music to physics. If you are good, you can get on the top scores list!

URL http://www.rockmall.com/arcade.htm

Test your knowledge at our trivia sites.

Tangled Web—Twiddler Trivia

Ten new trivia questions of varying difficulty await you here each week. Answer correctly to move along the game board.

URL http://www.primenet.com/~doppler/twidpuzz.html

Trivuality

Answer questions or create one of your own and be both entertained and educated at the same time!

URL http://www.cyberclip.com/Triv

Two Minute Warning—The NFL Trivia Game

Pick a play and try this NFL trivia game to compete for monthly prizes.

URL http://www.dtd.com/tmw

WordsWorth Books Contest Page

Every week this site displays the first line or the last line of a novel. Figure out which book the line is from for a chance to win.

URL http://www.wordsworth.com/
www/present/contest

T.V. NETWORKS

A&E

Find information about *Biography* and other fine programs.

URL http://www.aetv.com

ABC

Upcoming broadcast specials and nightly listings are just some of the features ABC offers its visitors.

URL http://www.abctelevision.com

American Movie Classics Studios

"Play it again, Sam." This site offers information on this well-known cable network.

URL http://www.amctv.com

BBC

Check out what they watch on the telly in the U.K.

URL http://www.bbcnc.org.uk/tv/
index.html

Black Entertainment Television NetWorks

Television programming focusing on the African-American population.

URL http://www.betnetworks.com

Cartoon Network

Find out how to get the Cartoon Network on your T.V. today!

URL http://www.filmzone.com/
SpaceGhost/cartoonnet.html

CBC

Find out what's on at the Canadian Broadcasting Corporation.

URL http://www.cbc.ca/tv

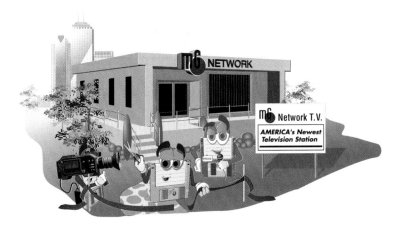

TU

CBS

Keep an eye on what's happening at CBS.

URL http://www.cbs.com

Christian Broadcasting Network

The site for one of the largest television ministries in the world.

URL http://www.cbn.org

CNBC Ticker Guide

This NBC-owned network focuses on business and financial information.

URL http://www.cnbc.com

CNN

The internationally recognized Cable News Network has a great Web site for news buffs.

URL http://cnn.com

Comedy Central

A flashy site to tickle your funny bone.

URL http://www.comcentral.com

CourtTV

Does this Web site have interesting information? You be the judge.

URL http://www.courttv.com

CyberSpice

The Spice Network has an Adult's Only site on the Web.

URL http://www.cyberspice.com

Discovery Channel

Both the U.S. and Canadian versions of this channel will help you explore the wonder of the world around you.

🇺🇸 **URL** http://www.discovery.com

🇨🇦 **URL** http://www.discovery.ca

E! Online

Entertainment news and gossip as well as movie and television reviews—all in one location.

URL http://www.eonline.com

Foxworld

Check out all your favorite shows and sports on Fox!

URL http://www.foxnetwork.com

fX

Find information about the people and the shows on the fX Network.

URL http://www.fxnetworks.com

Golf Channel

Learn what is coming up on the Golf Channel.

URL http://www.thegolfchannel.com

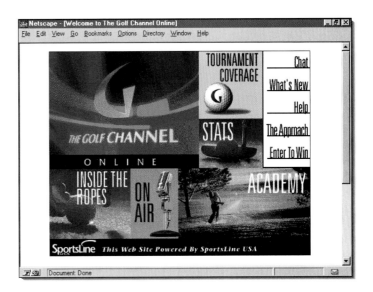

HBO

Entertainment news and interviews as well as the schedule for HBO's upcoming shows.

URL http://www.hbo.com

History Channel

Much more than just a programming schedule, this site also offers "This Day in History" and information on using The History Channel in the classroom.

URL http://www.historychannel.com

Home and Garden Television

Find out about this network's programs as well as home and garden events happening across the U.S.

URL http://www.hgtv.com

Lifetime Online

Tips on everything from health and exercise to romance and parenting are at this site for women.

URL http://www.lifetimetv.com

TU

T

MTV Online

The video generation joins the cyber-revolution.

URL http://www.mtv.com

MuchMusic

Canada's 24-hour music video station is on the Web with music news, concert listings and "much" more.

URL http://www.muchmusic.com/muchmusic/

NBC.COM

Find out what's hot in news, sports and entertainment at NBC.

URL http://www.nbc.com

Nick At Nite's T.V. Land Web Site

Video clips, photos, games and trivia on programs such as *The Addams Family*, *Green Acres* and more!

URL http://nick-at-nite.com

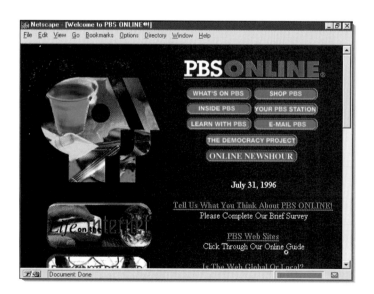

PBS

The Public Broadcasting Service offers programming that makes you think—and a Web site to match.

URL http://www.pbs.org

Playboy T.V.

If you're not old enough to watch this network, you're not old enough to visit the Web site.

URL http://www.playboy.com/
entertainment/playboy/pbtv/
index.html

QVC

All shopping, all the time.

URL http://www.qvc.com

Sci-Fi Channel: The Dominion

A great place to find out more about sci-fi programs and the genre in general.

URL http://www.scifi.com

Showtime Online

Find schedules, reviews and general information about this large cable network.

URL http://www.showtimeonline.com

Sony Pictures Entertainment

Sony produces many popular programs including the *Ricki Lake Show* and *Married...With Children*.

URL http://www.spe.sony.com/Pictures/tv

Travel Channel Online Network

Get away from it all. This site offers travel tips and expert advice as well as program information.

URL http://www.travelchannel.com

T.V. Food Network Online

Find new recipes every day and so much more at this cable channel's Web site.

URL http://www.foodtv.com

Find out what's on with these T.V. network sites.

Universal cHANnEL

Universal creates many of the cult programs on television, such as *Hercules* and *Dream On*.

URL http://www.mca.com/tv

VH1

Now that MTV shows many culture-oriented programs, VH1 has become the main network for music videos.

URL http://vh1.com

Viewer's Choice Interactive

Find out what's coming up on Pay-Per-View, from movies to sporting events.

URL http://www.ppv.com

Weather Channel

Weather reports from around the U.S. as well as a new piece of weather trivia each day.

URL http://www.weather.com

T

T.V. PROGRAMS

4616 Melrose Place

Weekly reports on the dysfunctional doings of the characters in this prime time soap.

URL http://melroseplace.com

Addicted to Sleazy, Cheesy Talk Shows

Speak your mind about talk shows.

URL http://www.morestuff.com/ talktv/a2talktv.htm

All My Children

A great spot to check out the latest happenings in Pine Valley.

URL http://www.amcpages.com

Babylon 5

Great resources for all those interested in the adventures at this exciting space station.

URL http://www.babylon5.com

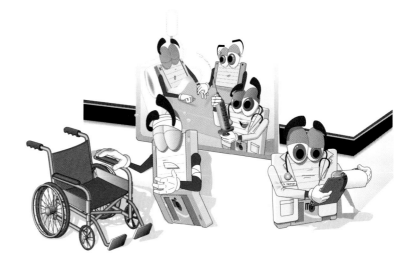

Baywatch

The most popular television program in the world. Need we say more?

URL http://baywatch.compuserve.com

CBS News: UTTMlink

Up to the Minute goes online to bring you many interesting news items as well as sounds, images and movies in an entertaining cyber-space environment.

URL http://uttm.com

CNET: The Computer Network

The site of this acclaimed computer news show lets you see a preview of next week's show or review the transcript from a previous episode.

URL http://www.cnet.com/Content/Tv

Coronation Street

This site has updates, pictures and other information of great interest to fans of this long-running British soap.

URL http://www.computan.on.ca/ ~grahame/cs.html

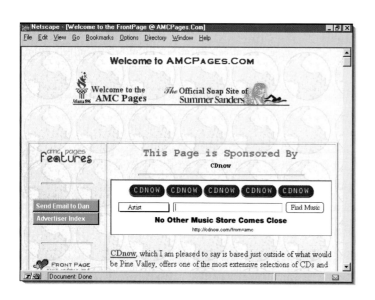

Daytime Talk Shows

Have you always wanted to be a guest on a daytime talk show? This site tells you how.

URL http://www.cs.indiana.edu/hyplan/
bodom/talk.html

Doctor Who

If you like Timelords and the TARDIS, you will enjoy this site.

URL http://aimservices.com/drwho

Dr. Quinn Medicine Woman

Fans of this frontier drama will find lots of pictures and facts to enjoy at this entertaining site.

URL http://www.DrQuinn.com

Due South

Check out the pictures and sound clips from this hit series.

URL http://www.duesouth.com

Frontline

A public affairs program from the Public Broadcasting Service.

URL http://www2.pbs.org/wgbh/pages/
frontline

General Hospital

Get your daily dose of GH gossip from this site.

URL http://purplenet.com/soaps/
GeneralHospital.html

Ghost Planet

Cartoon Network's official Web site for *Space Ghost Coast to Coast*, with lots of images, movies, sounds and more.

URL http://www.ghostplanet.com

Gilligan's Island

This site is packed with pictures and fun facts about one of North America's best-loved T.V. sitcoms.

URL http://www.lookup.com/Homepages/
58181/home.html

TU

National Talk Show Guest Registry

If you have a story you would like to share with the world by appearing on a talk show, these are the people to talk to!

URL http://ourworld.compuserve.com/homepages/ntsgr

Night Stand

A spoof of daytime talk shows such as *Oprah Winfrey* and *Jerry Springer*.

URL http://www.nightstand.com

One Life to Live

Chat with other fans, read the daily updates or vote in the Llanview Survey.

URL http://www.thegriffs.com/oltl

ReBoot

Venture into the land of Mainframe to learn about this animated show that is completely computer generated.

URL http://alliance.idirect.com/television.html

Sailor Moon

Lots of information and multimedia files on the popular *Sailor Moon* anime program.

URL http://www.dorsai.org/~mhsieh/paul9.htm

Saturday Night Live

Here you will find a collection of great skits, song lyrics and answers to your burning questions about SNL.

URL http://www.jt.org/snl/snl.html

Star Trek

The most popular television program on the Internet.

URL http://www.afn.org/~afn32406/startrek/main.html

URL http://www.starbase21.com/holodeck3

URL http://startrek.msn.com

Tales From The Crypt

Hear the Cryptkeeper guide you as you get all the behind-the-screams information on the new T.V. episodes and movies.

URL http://www.cryptnet.com

The New Red Green Show

The official site of *The New Red Green Show*.

URL http://www.redgreen.com

Tonight Show with Jay Leno

This site is updated every day with the latest jokes and scheduled guests.

URL http://www.nbctonightshow.com

Touched By An Angel

Find out more about the main characters or be inspired by The Quotable Angel.

URL http://www.angeltouch.com/webangel

Universal cHANnEL

This site is home to some of T.V.'s hottest shows, including *Law and Order*, *Partners* and *Sliders*.

URL http://www.mca.com/tv

X-Files

The truth is out there.

URL http://www.thex-files.com

Our T.V. program sites will entertain you for hours.

Young and the Restless

A fact-filled site with many pictures and even the theme song from the soap.

URL http://www.weicomp.com/php.cgi/yr/index.htm

Basic Linux

Linux is a free Unix operating system that runs on ordinary PCs. Stop by this site for a general introduction.

URL http://www.redhat.com

Help for the trn Newsreader

Threaded read news (trn) is a popular Unix tool for reading Internet newsgroups. This introduction will help you become familiar with newsgroups and trn's many commands.

URL http://www.isu.edu/departments/comcom/unix/trnhelp.html

Explore the power of the Unix operating system at these sites.

Houston Unix Users Group (HOUNIX)

HOUNIX is a pro-Unix group that aims to educate and promote the use of Unix.

URL http://cs1.cityscope.net/hounix

Introduction to Unix

This document explains Unix and compares it to DOS.

URL http://www.fsl.orst.edu/novell/fsdb/
mosaic/fsl/doc/unix/unixwork.htm

Quick Guide to Unix Commands

A help page for beginners to Unix that includes information on how to create, edit and move files.

URL http://mrcnext.cso.uiuc.edu/~kundert/
josh/docs/quickunix1.html

Unix Frequently Asked Questions

A good site for those who have advanced questions about the Unix operating system.

URL http://www.cis.ohio-state.edu/hypertext/
faq/usenet/unix-faq/faq/top.html

Unix Guru Universe

On your way to becoming a Unix guru? Check out this site to complete your training.

URL http://www.ugu.com

Unix Haters Handbook

Experiencing some problems with Unix? Take a break and read this humorous Unix sendup.

URL http://www.digital.de/people/jmh/
Unix_Haters

Unix is a Four Letter Word

The dozens of Unix commands featured at this site make it an excellent introduction to this operating system.

URL http://albrecht.ecn.purdue.edu/
~taylor/4ltrwrd/html/unixman.html

Unix Philosophy

Look over these concepts to get a general overview of the approach the Unix operating system takes towards computing.

URL http://playfair.stanford.edu/~ja/
unix.html

Unix Pine

Pine is a well-known Unix e-mail program. This thorough document will answer any questions you may have about it.

URL http://www.nih.gov/dcrt/helix/documents/pine/pine.html

Unix Review

Unix developers and administrators in the U.S. and Canada can apply for a free subscription to *Unix Review* magazine.

URL http://www.unixreview.com

vi Editor Tutorial

Helpful lessons on using vi, the default text editor for many Unix programs.

URL http://star.dwt.co.kr/~smlee/vi_1.html

Windows Emulator for Unix

Wine (WINdows Emulator) is a free software package that lets you run Windows applications on Unix-based computers. This is the official list of frequently asked questions about Wine.

URL http://www.asgardpro.com/dave/wine-faq.html

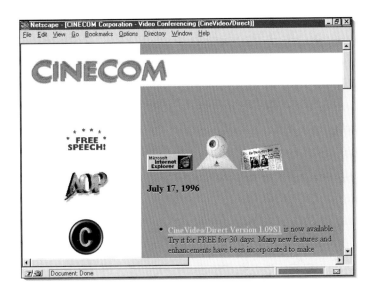

XFree86 Project

XFree86 is a free X Windows server designed for PCs running a Unix operating system.

URL http://www.xfree86.org

CINECOM

Experience videoconferencing live with CineVideo/Direct from CINECOM.

URL http://www.cinecom.com

CU-SeeMe

Turn your computer into a video phone with the help of this videoconferencing software package.

URL http://goliath.wpine.com/cu-seeme.html

Fish T.V. Video Clips

Cool QuickTime video clips from Fish T.V., including lava lamps, commercials and, yes, fish.

URL http://www.fishtv.com/videoclips.html

TU

VW

V

VIDEO *continued*

FreeVue Telecommunications Network

Copy free videoconferencing software onto your computer and join the FreeVue network to get listed in its directory.

URL http://www.freevue.com

FreeZone Video Clips

Grab clips from your favorite science fiction shows and films.

URL http://www.scifi.com/freezone/video.html

InterVU

A free MPEG video player for Netscape.

URL http://www.intervu.com

LiveNet San Diego BayCam

What does San Diego Bay look like right now? You can see live motion shots at this site.

URL http://www.live.net/sandiego

Movie Clips of Backflips & Renderings

The people who run this Web site apparently have some free time on their hands.

URL http://www.anders.com/clips2.html

NET TOOB

A highly rated multimedia player that handles MPEG, AVI, MOV, FLC and FLI video files.

URL http://www.duplexx.com

QuickTime

Everything about the QuickTime video format, including news releases and links to samples.

URL http://quicktime.apple.com

StreamWorks

Xing Technology brings live video with audio to the Web with its StreamWorks program for Windows, Macintosh and Unix.

URL http://www.xingtech.com

Video Clips from Sony

A huge collection of music video clips from Sony artists.

URL http://www.sony.com/Music/VideoStuff/
VideoClips/index.html

VRML (VIRTUAL REALITY MODELING LANGUAGE)

Corel's VRML Worlds

Use your VRML browser to walk around Corel Corporation's building or fly the Corel hot air balloon.

URL http://www.corel.com/freefunfantastic/
vrml/vrml.htm

Cybertown

Read about and tour Cybertown. This world of the future will connect you to many excellent sites on the Internet.

URL http://www.cybertown.com

HIT Lab VRML Repository

The Human Interface Technology Lab offers a gallery of virtual worlds to explore.

URL http://www.hitl.washington.edu/vrml

Interactive Origami in VRML

Wouldn't origami be easier to learn from a 3-D site than a 2-D book? Brush up on your artistic paper folding skills at this site.

URL http://www.neuro.sfc.keio.ac.jp/~aly/
polygon/vrml/ika

Live3D

Netscape brings you a VRML plug-in for your browser. Experience 3-D animation, sound, music and video on the Web.

URL http://home.netscape.com/comprod/
products/navigator/live3d/index.html

PointWorld

PointWorld is the first 3-D interactive Web search engine. Move through this town square to find what you are looking for.

URL http://www2.blacksun.com/pointworld

Sidhe and the Sword

An interactive VRML art piece, based on ancient Irish myth.

URL http://tcc.iz.net/sidhe

Terminal Reality

Ziff-Davis Interactive brings you its first VRML world, which looks something like an airport. Come and explore!

URL http://www.zdnet.com/zdi/vrml/airport.html

Unofficial Star Wars VRML Pages

You can check out models of various things from *Star Wars*, such as the Tie Fighter, X-Wing Fighter, C-3PO and R2-D2.

URL http://cbzoroms.uwsp.edu/vrml

Virtual Cities Repository

Cool links to 3-D models of real cities.

URL http://www.vir.com/~farid/ctrepos.htm

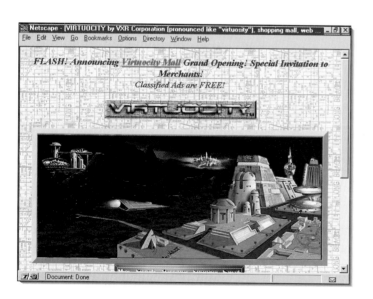

Virtual LEGO Objects in VRML

Create your own LEGO constructions online with the help of VRML.

URL http://www-lego.mit.edu/~lego

Virtual Universe

This is a VRML study of stars located within 50 light years of our sun.

URL http://bradley.bradley.edu/~dware/univ.html

Virtuocity

A large-scale VRML city with buildings, such as a shopping mall and virtual campus, that lead you to other Web sites.

URL http://www.virtuocity.com

V•Realm

Visit 3-D worlds with this plug-in VRML browser for Netscape 2.0 from Integrated Data Systems.

URL http://www.ids-net.com/ids/downldpi.html

VRML

This site features lots of fancy VRML interaction.

URL http://www.caligari.com:80/lvltwo/
vrml3.html

VRML Frequently Asked Questions

All you need to know about VRML. This site covers VRML basics, browsers, tools, cool sites and more.

URL http://vag.vrml.org/VRML_FAQ.html

VRML Repository

An excellent resource for anyone interested in VRML. This site has a bibliography, lists of software and many other neat things.

URL http://sdsc.edu/vrml

VRML Site of the Week

Virtus Corporation brings you an outstanding new VRML site every week, along with some pretty nifty runners-up.

URL http://www.virtus.com/vrmlsite.html

VRML with Audio

This site from Intel contains several VRML worlds that incorporate 3-D audio.

URL http://www.intel.com/ial/rsx/worlds

VRML Zoo of Mathematical 3-D Objects

Want to spin a dodecahedron? Check out this geometry center's VRML math objects.

URL http://www.geom.umn.edu/software/
weboogl/zoo

WEATHER

Australian Weather Forecasts

Explore the weather of Australia.

URL http://atmos.es.mq.edu.au/weather/
ausweather.html

Automated Weather Source Online

Here you can find real-time weather updates taken from various schools across the U.S.

URL http://aws.com

Current Weather Maps/Movies

Copy images and weather-related movies of Europe, Africa, Antarctica and North America.

URL http://rs560.cl.msu.edu/weather

Daily Planet

The University of Illinois brings you the weather and an impressive guide to meteorology.

URL http://wx3.atmos.uiuc.edu

Hurricane Watch

Don't get blown away! Check out this resource for the latest hurricane warnings and satellite images.

URL http://www.NetCreations.com/hurricane

Interactive Weather Browser

Click on a weather map to get the weather conditions for North American locations.

URL http://rs560.cl.msu.edu/weather/
interactive.html

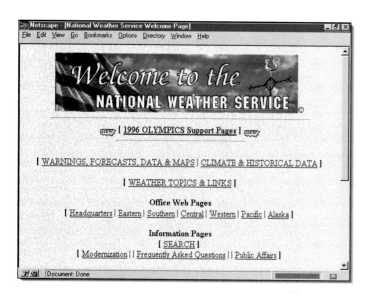

Live Access to Climate Data

An interactive program provides you with worldwide weather data such as temperature, wind speed and humidity.

URL http://ferret.wrc.noaa.gov/fbin/
climate_server

National Weather Service

Information about the National Weather Service along with current weather information.

URL http://www.nws.noaa.gov

Tropical Weather

Before you head for the tropics, check out the latest storm warnings at this site.

URL http://asp1.sbs.ohio-state.edu/
tropicaltext.html

Weather World

Look at a variety of satellite photographs and animation at this site.

URL http://www.atmos.uiuc.edu/wxworld/
html/satimg.html

WeatherNet: Weather Cams

Spy on the weather with current weather pictures taken from cameras mounted in a variety of locations all over the U.S.

URL http://cirrus.sprl.umich.edu/wxnet/wxcam.html

WEIRD SPORTS

Devil Sticks

These sticks are a challenging baton sport.

URL http://www.mts.net/~marchamb/devil.htm

Footbag WorldWide

The site for people who like to kick little bags of beans around.

URL http://www.footbag.org

Home Appliance Shooting

This event will not be part of the 1998 Olympics in Nagano, Japan.

URL http://www.csn.net/~dcbenton/has.html

Take the plunge into our weird sports sites.

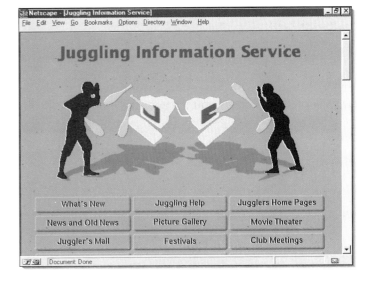

Juggling Information Service

Have you always wanted to learn how to juggle? If so, then check out the animated lessons at this site.

URL http://www.juggling.org

Korfball

One of the first mixed team sports, korfball is based on basketball.

URL http://www.earth.ox.ac.uk/~geoff

Road Luge

An extreme sport in which riders surf the concrete with no brakes.

URL http://www.tahoe.com/South.Tahoe/News/news.9.1.95/luge.rider.html

Skydive WWW

A guide to skydiving, including thrilling photos and videos.

URL http://www.skydivewww.com/mainmenu.html

WEIRD SPORTS *continued*

Ultimate Players Association
Learn about ultimate, the sport that is sweeping the nation.

URL http://www.upa.org/~upa

Unicycle Page
Riders of the one wheel unite.

URL http://www.unicycling.org

WHAT'S COOL

Awesome Sports Site of the Week
Your vote counts in deciding who will win the Awesome Sports Site of the Month.

URL http://www.awesomesports.com

Blazin' Bookmark
Visit maranGraphics and check out an exciting new site each week.

URL http://www.maran.com/surf.html

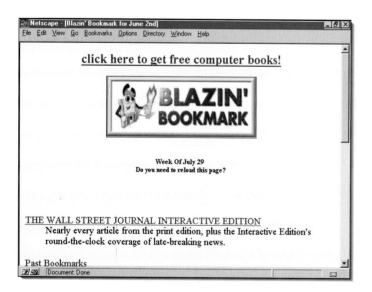

Take the fast track to the coolest sites on the Web.

Canuck Site of the Day
Check out these cool Canadian sites.

URL http://www.10q.com/canuck

Catch of the Day
They net 'em, you get 'em.

URL http://www.catch.com/cotd

Cool Science
OMNI presents a weekly list of top science sites.

URL http://www.omnimag.com/science/coolsite.html

Cool Site of the Day
InfiNet hosts the original source for cool links.

URL http://cool.infi.net

eyeSITE Awards
The coveted "Webby" Award for best site of the day, week, month and year.

URL http://www.eye.net/eyeSITE

HotWired's Surf du Jour

Hot new trends on the Web are explored.

URL http://www.hotwired.com/rensurf

Magic URL Mystery Trip

Take a random journey through hand-picked cool links on the Web.

URL http://www.netcreations.com/magicurl/index.html

Page du Jour

The Internet Learning Center brings you a descriptive list of interesting new sites each week.

URL http://www.ilcnet.com/dujour

Project Cool Sightings

Providing a vision of coolness on the Web every day.

URL http://www.projectcool.com/sightings

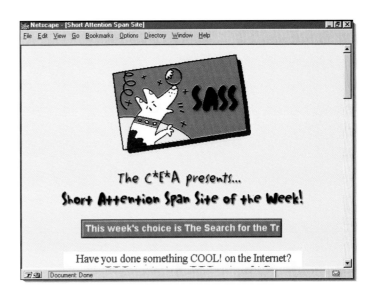

Scout Report

A weekly report of new Internet resources, aimed at researchers and educators.

URL http://rs.internic.net/scout/report

Short Attention Span Site of the Week

Keep yourself amused for minutes!

URL http://www.amused.com/sass.html

The Spider's Pick of the Day

A well-known daily pick server from a crazy spider.

URL http://gagme.wwa.com/~boba/pick.html

This Time It's Personal

A link to a new and happening personal Web site every day.

URL http://tabatha.hasc.com

355

W

WHAT'S COOL *continued*

Too Cool Awards

New dimensions of Web coolness are explored daily.

URL http://toocool.com/today.htm

Unusual or Deep Site of the Day

A trip down the unusual side of the Web.

URL http://adsint.bc.ca/deepsite

What's Cool from Netscape

A large list of interesting sites, updated frequently.

URL http://home.netscape.com/home/
whats-cool.html

What's Hot This Week?

America Online presents a weekly hotlist.

URL http://www.aol.com/hot/weekly.html

What's New with NCSA Mosaic

One of the longest-running sites on the Web, serving up a daily top five list.

URL http://gnn.com/gnn/wn/whats-new.html

Yahoo's Picks of the Week

The makers of the original Web index offer a weekly list of cool links.

URL http://www.yahoo.com/picks

WINDOWS & DOS

Adobe

Information about Adobe products along with a big library of plug-ins, patches and updates.

URL http://www.adobe.com

Bill Gates Personal Wealth Clock

Watch the dollars add up.

URL http://www.webho.com/WealthClock

CD-ROM Shop

More than 2,800 CD-ROMs in an online catalog, searchable by key word, category or publisher.

URL http://www.cdromshop.com

Claris

Check out the information about Claris' powerful business applications or get some templates, updates and trial software.

URL http://www.claris.com

Corel WordPerfect

The official site of the Corel WordPerfect suite of office applications has the latest company news, helpful articles and various Discussion Boards for software users.

URL http://www.wordperfect.com

Cyber Exchange

This company buys and sells software for PCs and Macs.

URL http://www.chattanooga.net/cyberx/ index.html

Egghead

An online hardware and software store where you can check out the monthly specials.

URL http://www.egghead.com

Galt Shareware Zone

A great collection of Windows programs you can try for free. Check out the screensavers, utilities and games.

URL http://www.galttech.com

History of DOS

Well, okay, this is a somewhat fictional history, but it's funny.

URL http://rodin.cs.uh.edu/~acm/jokes/ dosh.html

"I Hate Windoze" Page

A collection of anti-Microsoft humor, including "Is Windows a Virus?"

URL http://digital.net/~scp_os2/ihatewin/ ihatewin.html

357

Introduction to MS-DOS

Baffled by DOS? Learn about the mysteries of your autoexec.bat and config.sys.

URL http://www.cit.ac.nz/smac/os100

Jumbo Shareware

Cute elephants direct you to almost 60,000 programs. Choose from games, business applications, utilities and more.

URL http://www.jumbo.com

Jumbo's DOS Games

Quick access to tons of DOS games including sports, education and role playing.

URL http://jumbo.com/game/dos

Lynx Enhanced Pages

If you don't want to bother with graphics on the Web, then Lynx is for you. Find out why many people prefer this text-only browser.

URL http://www.nyu.edu/pages/wsn/subir/
lynx.html

Macromedia

The popular developer of multimedia programs such as Director and Shockwave for Director.

URL http://www-1.macromedia.com/
index_in.html

Microsoft

Get the latest company information, product news and samples from the creators of Windows and DOS.

URL http://www.microsoft.com

Microsoft Internet Explorer

Get the latest version of Microsoft's popular Web browser, along with some Web page creation tips.

URL http://www.microsoft.com/ie/msie.htm

Microsoft Windows FAQs

A collection of frequently asked questions about Windows.

URL http://www.metrics.com/WinFAQ/
index.html

MS-DOS Compression Programs

Get a wide variety of tools that make transferring programs and files much easier.

URL http://garbo.uwasa.fi/pc/arcers.html

MSN

Visit the home page of the Microsoft Network. Newcomers to the Web will enjoy the Internet tutorial offered here.

URL http://www.msn.com

PC Demos Explained

A thorough guide to the demo scene, including links to the best DOS demos.

URL http://www.cdrom.com/pub/demos/hornet/html/demos.html

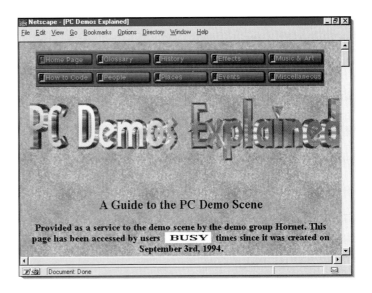

shareware.com

CNET offers 190,000 shareware and freeware demos, patches and upgrades along with tips on how to copy them.

URL http://www.shareware.com

Simtel.Net

An excellent collection of programs for DOS, Windows 3.x and Windows 95.

URL http://oak.oakland.edu/simtel.net

Software Source

More than 30,000 items from companies like Adobe, Lotus and Microsoft at special prices for students, teachers and schools.

URL http://iaswww.com/source.html

Sonic Foundry

Learn all about digital audio while checking out this company's digital audio editing products.

URL http://sfoundry.com

Stroud's Consummate Winsock Applications List

If you're cruising the Internet with Windows, you should check out the great range of Winsock software at this site.

URL http://www.servtech.com/public/rwilloug/cwsapps

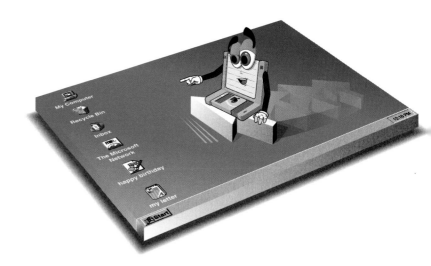

Toasted Berkeley Systems Online

This slick site from the makers of the After Dark screen saver collection offers the latest products along with freebies, customer support and more.

URL http://www.berksys.com/index.html

United CD-ROM

Search an online catalog of more than 5,000 multimedia titles.

URL http://www.unitedcdrom.com

Visual Basic Info Booth

Provides information about the programming language Visual Basic for Windows.

URL http://www.buffnet.net/~millard/vblinks.htm

Visual dBASE

Learn all about Borland's powerful database program, Visual dBASE.

URL http://www.borland.com/Product/DB/dBASE/
VisdBASE.html

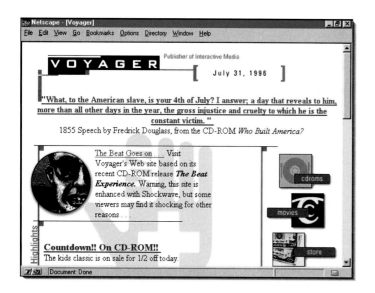

Voyager

Check out the special buys from these famous CD-ROM publishers.

URL http://www.voyagerco.com

WebCompass

This Windows application runs Web searches and sorts the results for you, so you can easily find what you need on the Web.

URL http://arachnid.qdeck.com/qdeck/
demosoft/webcompass_lite

Windows 95 Software Library

Microsoft's official collection of Windows 95 programs you can try out for free.

URL http://www.microsoft.com/windows/
software.htm

Windows 95.com

An excellent site with a huge amount of Windows 95 information, drivers and programs.

URL http://www.windows95.com

Windows Magazine

An online Windows publication with a computer buyer's guide, online shopping listings and other neat features.

URL http://www.winmag.com

Windows Shareware Archive

This searchable collection covers all kinds of software for all versions of Windows.

URL http://coyote.csusm.edu/cwis/winworld/winworld.html

Windows Sources

Ziff-Davis Publishing brings you this stylish Windows magazine.

URL http://www.zdnet.com/wsources

WINGate

This company creates software to enable communications between Windows and DOS applications.

URL http://www.wingate.com

Pull some great software out of our Windows and DOS sites.

WinSite Archive

A searchable collection of Windows software for almost anything you could want, from Web page design programs to an insult generator.

URL http://www.winsite.com

WinZip

The home page of the award-winning file compression program for Windows.

URL http://www.winzip.com

WordPerfect Magazine

The popular word processing program for Windows and DOS has its own magazine with articles, tips and guidelines for its use.

URL http://www.wpmag.com

World Software Library

A good selection of commercial software. Order online to get your software right off the site.

URL http://www.softwaremall.com

VW

WINDOWS & DOS *continued*

ZD Net Windows 95 Shareware Library

Ziff-Davis Publishing brings you this archive of applications, games, utilities and more.

URL http://www.zdnet.com/zdi/software/win95

WINTER SPORTS

1998 Winter Olympics

A listing of the events that will be taking place in the 1998 Olympics in Nagano, Japan.

URL http://phantom.ghost.linc.or.jp/Nagano/events.html

CyberSki

Skiing and snowboarding enthusiasts will find racing news and a gallery of photography.

URL http://www.iaccess.com.au/cyberski

EUROSKATING

News, pictures, interviews and more from the European ice skating scene.

URL http://w3.iprolink.ch/krupp/skating.htm

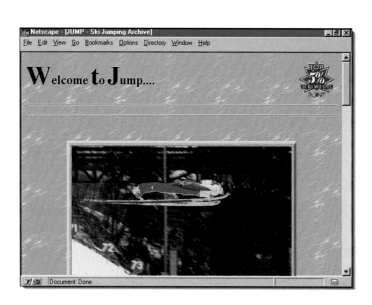

Ice Sculptures

An online gallery of ice sculptures created for the Winter Festival in Ottawa, Canada.

URL http://www.comnet.ca/~alain/alain/ice.htm

Ice Speed Skating

The speed skating home page features skating standings and events as well as links to ice skating sites around the world.

URL http://www.twi.tudelft.nl/~penninx/skate

Jump

Information on ski jumping, including World Cup news and a thrilling QuickTime movie.

URL http://www.cdnsport.ca/jump

Luge

An informative description of the winter downhill racing sport of luge.

URL http://www.lifetimetv.com/WoSport/SPORTS/LUGE/luge.htm

Skiing FAQ

Answers to frequently asked questions about skiing.

URL http://skiing.geo.ucalgary.ca/skiing/faq.html

Skiing Magazine

Look here for the latest trends in skiing gear, private online lessons and more.

URL http://www.skinet.com/skiing

Snow Cameras

Before you head for the slopes, browse through this extensive collection of Web sites offering photos of the snow conditions at various skiing resorts.

URL http://ski.websmith.ca/ski/cams.html

Winter Sports

The Winter Sports Foundation promotes the benefits of winter sports at this site.

URL http://www.wintersports.org

World Figure Skating Championships

Information from the championships, including news, stories and chat sessions.

URL http://www.southam.com/skating/skate.html

WOMEN'S STUDIES

A Celebration of Women Writers

Visit here for the books, biographies and pictures of some great women writers.

URL http://www.cs.cmu.edu/Web/People/mmbt/women/writers.html

Calendar of Women of Achievement and Herstory

Find out what women were born or made history on any given day of the year.

URL http://worcester.lm.com/women/history/woacal.html

Celebrating Women's Achievements: 21 Pioneers

Learn about Canadian women who made important contributions to society.

URL http://www.nlc-bnc.ca/digiproj/women/ewomen.htm

VW

Diotima: Women & Gender in the Ancient World

A site providing resources on gender issues of ancient Mediterranean times.

URL http://www.uky.edu/ArtsSciences/Classics/gender.html

Distinguished Women of Past and Present

The accomplishments and biographies of remarkable women.

URL http://www.netsrq.com/~dbois

ElectraPages

A listing of more than 7,000 women's organizations and businesses.

URL http://www.electrapages.com

Encyclopedia of Women's History

This resource was created by a Grade 5 class and has been growing with the support of teachers and students from around the world.

URL http://www.teleport.com/~megaines/women.html

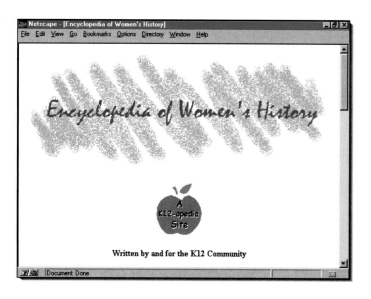

FEMINIST.COM

This site offers classifieds, articles and speeches and aims to empower women through awareness and activism.

URL http://www.feminist.com

Isis: OurStory

A collection of information on historically important black women, from a biography of physicist Shirley Ann Jackson to the story of a slave.

URL http://www.netdiva.com/ourstory.html

National Organization for Women (NOW)

Learn about the group that works to secure equality and fair treatment for all women.

URL http://www.now.org

National Women's History Project

The site for this nonprofit organization includes memorable quotations and a quiz to test your knowledge of women in history.

URL http://www.nwhp.org

Women Artists Archive

Images, biographies and statements on contemporary women artists along with a listing of female artists throughout the ages.

URL http://www.sonoma.edu/Library/special/waa

Women in Cinema: A Reference Guide

Bibliographies and guides to works on women in film.

URL http://poe.acc.virginia.edu/~pm9k/libsci/womFilm.html

WomenBiz

For women with their own businesses or those who want to start one.

URL http://www.frsa.com/womenbiz

Women's Health Interactive

Perform a Personal Action Plan, chat with other women or conduct an interactive assessment of your own health profile on the Women's Health Interactive™ Web site.

URL http://www.womens-health.com

Women's Health Resources

This site aims to organize, describe and evaluate the many different women's health resources on the Internet.

URL http://asa.ugl.lib.umich.edu/chdocs/womenhealth/intro.html

Women's Sports Page

Links to women's sports Web pages.

URL http://fiat.gslis.utexas.edu/~lewisa/womsprt.html

Women's Studies Resources

A great resource of information that includes biographies, film reviews, a picture gallery, government documents and job listings.

URL http://www.inform.umd.edu:8080/EdRes/Topic/WomensStudies

Women's Wire

An electronic magazine that deals with many issues of interest to women.

URL http://www.women.com

INDEX

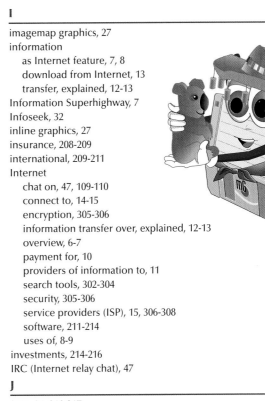

INDEX

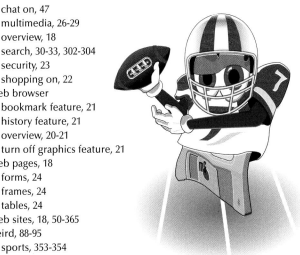